# ADVENTURES ON THE WESTERN FRONTIER

General John Gibbon

# Adventures on the Western Frontier

## Major General John Gibbon

*Edited by Alan and Maureen Gaff*

*Indiana
University
Press*

BLOOMINGTON AND INDIANAPOLIS

The paper used in this publication meets the minimum requirements of American National Standard for Information Sciences—Permanence of Paper for Printed Library Materials, ANSI Z39.48-1984.

MANUFACTURED IN THE UNITED STATES OF AMERICA

**Library of Congress Cataloging-in-Publication Data**

Gibbon, John, 1827–1896.
    Adventures on the western frontier / John Gibbon : edited by Alan and Maureen Gaff.
       p.   cm.
    Includes index.
    ISBN 0-253-32579-X
    1. Gibbon, John, 1827–1896.   2. Frontier and pioneer life—West
(U.S.)   3. West (U.S.)—History—1848–1950.   4. Indians of North
   America—Wars—1866–1895.   5. Generals—United States—Biography.
   6. United States. Army—Biography.   I. Gaff, Alan D.   II. Gaff,
   Maureen.   III. Title.
F594.G415A3   1994
978—dc20                              93-22935

1 2 3 4 5 99 98 97 96 95 94

# $\mathscr{C}$ontents

# Editors' Foreword

The name of John Gibbon is closely associated with two of America's best-known battles: Pickett's Charge and Custer's Last Stand. The climactic charge by the Confederates at Gettysburg on July 3, 1863, was directed at John Gibbon's division, which defended its position with unequaled determination. At the Little Bighorn, Gibbon's command arrived too late for the fighting, but just in time to rescue survivors from George Armstrong Custer's ill-fated regiment. These were but two highlights of a military career that spanned nearly fifty years, much of that time spent on the Western frontier.

*Personal Recollections of the Civil War,* an account of Gibbon's wartime experiences, was completed in 1885 and published in 1928, long after the author's death. The general also wrote reminiscences of his postwar career, but they were never published and only a few chapters have survived. The loss of Gibbon's chapters on his frontier service has left a sizable gap in the history of the United States Army. Gibbon was never a member of the inner circle of ranking officers in the army, refusing to engage in partisan politics (most of his peers proudly supported the Republican Party) and abhorring the popular notion that "the only good Indian is a dead Indian." He was well regarded by his contemporaries and had already demonstrated an ability to command, but his promotion to brigadier general did not come until the administration of Grover Cleveland. Gibbon was an outsider within the army, and thus his view of history would surely have counterbalanced the autobiographies of prominent generals such as George Crook, Nelson Miles, and Oliver O. Howard.

In addition to his book-length manuscripts, Gibbon also wrote numerous magazine articles on a wide variety of topics. Fortunately, these articles include several accounts of his experiences on the Western frontier. Among the stories are campaign narratives, scouting adventures in the wilds of Wyoming and Montana, and even a visit to Yellowstone National Park. While Gibbon's tales lack the insight that an autobiography might have included, they provide a fascinating glimpse of military life in the 1870s. As a counterpoint to these articles, we have included Gibbon's journal of his first trip across the plains in 1860, with all of its wide-eyed wonderment and naivete.

Throughout his postwar career, General Gibbon viewed the Indian with sympathy. He correctly observed that the Indian race would eventually be conquered by two forces: the military might of the army and the degrading influence of white settlers at the very outposts of civilization. Gibbon was one of only a handful of officers who keenly saw the Indian problem not just in military terms, but also as a sociological issue. Gibbon's candor on the Indian question certainly was a detriment to his career, but his conscience allowed him no other choice. Above all else, John Gibbon was a man of character who always had the courage of his convictions.

# A Biographical Sketch
## of General John Gibbon

On the night of August 9, 1877, Colonel John Gibbon
led a mixed command of soldiers and civilians against
Chief Joseph's band of the Nez Percé Indians. Stars were visible in the
darkened sky as the column advanced carefully across the rugged slopes
surrounding the Indian camp at Big Hole, Montana Territory. Colonel
Gibbon paused for a moment in a clearing and turned to his adjutant,
Lieutenant Charles A. Woodruff. Pointing to one particularly bright
star, Gibbon whispered, "Old Mars is smiling upon us to-night, that's a
favorable omen." Although Gibbon and Woodruff were both wounded
in the ensuing attack, "Old Mars" did indeed smile upon the colonel's
plan. But then Mars had always seemed to smile upon the military career
of General John Gibbon.

John Oliver Gibbon was born at ten o'clock in the morning on
April 20, 1827, near Holmesburg, Pennsylvania, now within the boundaries of the city of Philadelphia. He was the third son and the fourth of
seven children that blessed the marriage of Dr. John Heysham Gibbon
and Catherine (Lardner) Gibbon. Although the family name was originally "Gibbons," the doctor dropped the final "s" upon attaining his
majority, so that by the time Doctor Gibbon had married and graduated
from the University of Pennsylvania, the change was permanent. Catherine and the children followed Doctor Gibbon to Charlotte, North Carolina, where he had accepted an appointment as chief assayer at the
United States Mint. While living in Charlotte, young John Gibbon was
selected to be a cadet at the United States Military Academy, thus beginning a career in the United States Army that would last until his forced
retirement almost fifty years later.

Officially entering the Military Academy at West Point, New York,
on September 1, 1842, Cadet Gibbon was an average student who soon
proved deficient in the study of English grammar. Faced with the choice
of being dismissed or repeating a year, Gibbon chose the latter and

consequently did not graduate until July 1, 1847, ranking twentieth in a class of thirty-eight and receiving a commission as a brevet second lieutenant in the 3rd Artillery. Sent off to Mexico City and Toluca in the waning months of the Mexican War, the new officer missed the battles in which other West Point graduates won praise and fame. While graduates of the class of 1846—his original classmates—emerged with brevets to the ranks of first lieutenant, captain, and even major, John Gibbon's only promotion was to the permanent rank of second lieutenant in the 4th Artillery on September 13, 1847. However, the young lieutenant did learn an important lesson one night at a card table. As the story went, "He had joined with a few dollars, a horse, equipments, and pistols, and was urged to take a hand, 'just to make up a game.' The next morning, going on detached service, he was compelled to borrow a horse, saddle, bridle, spurs, pistols, and money for his expenses, but never again played cards for a stake" (Woodruff, p. 292).

After a brief assignment to Fort Monroe, Virginia, in 1848, Lieutenant Gibbon was transferred to Fort Brooke, Florida, where he spent several years with the force assigned to keep the Seminole Indians in check. While stationed at Fort Brooke, the lieutenant had the good fortune to serve with Captain John C. Casey (West Point, 1829), whose fair and considerate treatment of the Florida Indians made a lasting impression on the younger officer. Gibbon would later write of his mentor, "He *never deceived them;* never told one of them a lie; and never made a promise he did not fulfill, if within his power" (Gibbon, "Reading Signs," p. 397).

Promoted to first lieutenant on September 12, 1850, Gibbon joined Light Battery B of the 4th Artillery and spent the next two years on the Texas frontier, first at Ringgold Barracks and then with the garrison at Fort Brown. Following an extended leave of absence and a stint on court-martial duty, he was again ordered to Florida to assist in the removal of the remaining Seminoles.

On September 25, 1854, First Lieutenant John Gibbon began his duties as assistant instructor of artillery at the Military Academy, an indication of his demonstrated ability in that military art. The new instructor had also demonstrated his affection for Miss Frances North Moale, daughter of Samuel Moale of Baltimore, and the two were married October 16, 1855, the bride from a Roman Catholic family and the groom a member of no formal church, despite professing "a strong religious feeling" (Byrne and Weaver, p. 155). Returning to classes at West Point, Gibbon assumed the additional duties of post quartermaster on September 16, 1856, and performed dual assignments throughout that school year. He continued to act as quartermaster until August 31, 1859, with one brief absence to serve on a board testing the merits of new breech-loading rifles. Although his career as an instructor of artillery tactics ended on July 5, 1857, Gibbon reworked his class notes into a definitive artillery textbook that was widely used for several decades. Published by D. Van Nostrand in 1859, *The Artillerist's Manual* quickly went into a second edition and was adopted by the War Department, which purchased and issued hundreds of copies. The *New York Herald* had kind words in a notice of the publication, concluding, "The book may well be considered as a valuable and important addition to the military science of the country" (cited in Scott, p. 682).

On November 2, 1859, John Gibbon was promoted to captain and assigned to command Battery B, 4th Artillery, then stationed at Camp Floyd in Utah Territory as part of the peacekeeping force in the Mormon country. When the nation and the army were torn apart by the secession crisis and the surrender of Fort Sumter, Captain Gibbon was forced to decide between honoring his oath of allegiance to the United States or respecting the beliefs of his family in North Carolina. While at Fort Crittenden—the name of the post was changed after Secretary of War John B. Floyd resigned and joined the secessionists—Gibbon was accused by several fellow officers of disloyalty after he allowed the band to play "Dixie," a charge the captain vigorously refuted. Captain Gibbon was exonerated, owing in part to the support of his commanding officer, and he soon severed relations with the Gibbon family in Charlotte. Members of the Gibbon family were loyal Democrats and apparently owned a few slaves, so three of John's brothers chose to join the rebel army. More than three years later, one of his sisters made her way to the Federal lines, where she met John and was escorted north. John had sent a message to his younger brother to come along with her on the flag-of-truce boat, but the younger Gibbon responded with the curt message, "It would not be agreeable."

After John Gibbon decided to oppose the views of his family and to remain in the United States Army, the troops at Fort Crittenden were ordered to Fort Leavenworth, Kansas, some twelve hundred miles to the east. The march to Kansas was mostly uneventful, and the column arrived there on October 8, 1861. But Gibbon and his battery were ordered to continue on to St. Joseph, Missouri, where the men and guns were loaded on railroad cars and sent to the nation's capital. Upon arrival at Washington on October 29, Captain Gibbon was appointed chief of artillery for Brigadier General Irvin McDowell's division, a post he would hold until the following May. His responsibilities included not only training his own Battery B, its depleted ranks soon filled with volunteers from infantry regiments, but also instructing three volunteer batteries—the 1st New Hampshire Battery; Battery D, 1st Rhode Island Light Artillery; and Battery L, 1st New York Light Artillery. Captain Gibbon demonstrated "a natural talent for dealing with the volunteer soldier, whose possibilities, as well as limitations, he appreciated from the first" (*Dictionary of American Biography,* p. 237), and the four batteries soon won reputations for dependability unsurpassed in the Army of the Potomac.

Talented officers were desperately wanted to fill vacancies in the volunteer force, which had been recruited independently of the established Regular Army. To fill this need, qualified Regular officers were detached from their companies and assigned to command volunteers at a higher rank. Gibbon's initial success in organizing and training artillery volunteers led to a nomination as brigadier general of volunteers, a step which many other West Point graduates had already made. But Gibbon's confirmation was held up because he had no political friends in Washington. Finally, on May 2, 1862, after intercession on his behalf by some prominent New Yorkers, the artillery captain received a commission as brigadier general of United States Volunteers and was assigned to command an infantry brigade composed of four regiments—the 2nd, 6th, and 7th Wisconsin and the 19th Indiana. General Gibbon made an enviable name for himself and his brigade, subsequently called the Iron Brigade, in hard-fought battles at Brawner Farm on August 28, 1862, Bull Run on August 30, 1862, South Mountain on September 14, 1862, and Antietam on September 17, 1862. Although he left the Iron Brigade to command a division of the First Corps in November of 1862, the relationship between the general and his brigade remained strong for more than thirty years.

While commanding the Second Division of the First Corps at Fredericksburg on December 13, 1862, Gibbon was struck by a shell fragment which broke a bone in his hand and inflicted a painful wound in the wrist. After a period of convalescence, he returned to the army and was assigned to command the Second Division of the Second Corps, which he led at Chancellorsville and in the Gettysburg Campaign. During the fighting at Gettysburg, General Gibbon commanded the Second Corps when Winfield S. Hancock assumed other temporary duties, but he was with his division during the climax of the battle when "Pickett's Charge" was repulsed in his front. As he hurried reinforcements to relieve his threatened regiments, Gibbon was struck by a bullet in the left shoulder, which broke the scapula and inflicted a wound that would disable him for several months.

Lieutenant Frank A. Haskell, an aide on Gibbon's staff at Gettysburg, described the general as he appeared in July of 1863:

He is compactly made, neither spare nor corpulent, with ruddy complexion, chestnut brown hair, with a clean-shaved face, except his moustache, which is decidedly reddish in color, medium-sized, well-shaped head, sharp, moderately-jutting brows, deep-blue, calm eyes, sharp, slightly-aquiline nose, compressed mouth, full jaws and chin, with an air of calm firmness in his manner. (Byrne and Weaver, p. 134)

Haskell concluded his description with the statement, "He always looks well dressed." The lieutenant failed to mention a few of Gibbon's personal habits which he shared with many in the army—his fondness for pipe smoking, an appreciation of good whiskey, and his occasional use of "bad words."

After four months of convalescence, Gibbon returned to duty as commander of the Draft Depot at Cleveland on November 15, 1863, but within a week he was transferred to command the Draft Depot at Philadelphia, a post much closer to his wife and children, who were then living in Baltimore with the Moale family. The general resumed command of his division on March 21, 1864, and participated in the bloody campaign against Richmond, leading his men at the Wilderness, Spotsylvania, North Anna, Totopotomoy, Cold Harbor, and various operations around Petersburg. On June 7, 1864, John Gibbon was promoted to major general of United States Volunteers, a rank which would normally entitle him to command a corps, but despite a few weeks in command of the Eighteenth Corps, that honor did not come until January 15, 1865. On that day he was assigned to command the Twenty-fourth Corps in the Army of the James, and he led that unit in the final operations against the Petersburg defenses, including the pursuit of the Army of Northern Virginia to Appomattox Court House. At that place Gibbon was one of three commissioners selected by General Ulysses S. Grant to arrange details of the surrender of the Army of Northern Virginia. After the successful conclusion of the war, he commanded the District of Nottoway, Virginia, from August 18, 1865, until his muster out of the volunteer force on January 15, 1866.

In summing up John Gibbon's service during the Civil War, it is obvious that his steady advancement was due to merit rather than political influence, and for this reason his promotions often lagged behind those of well-connected officers of lesser ability. If he had managed to gain a few influential friends in 1861, there is little doubt that Gibbon would have been elevated to corps command much earlier, and perhaps even to army command before the end of the war. Although he had his detractors—one man referred to him as "A Dm squirt of a Brig Gen'l" (Beck, p. 139)—General John Gibbon had a solid reputation in the

Army of the Potomac. Colonel Theodore Lyman, an aide at army head-quarters, wrote two descriptions of the general that show how he was perceived during the campaign of 1864. In a letter describing affairs after the fighting in the Wilderness, Lyman wrote, "By the roadside was Gibbon, and a tower of strength he is, cool as a steel knife, always, and unmoved by anything and everything" (Lyman, p. 103). Colonel Lyman again noticed the general as he appeared on May 9, 1864, writing that "thither came steel-cold General Gibbon, the most American of Americans, with his sharp nose and up-and-down manner of telling the truth, no matter whom it hurts" (ibid., p. 107).

When he was mustered out of the volunteer service on January 15, 1866, General John Gibbon suddenly reverted to captain, the highest rank he had attained in the Regular Army. On January 30 Captain Gibbon began a seven-month assignment as a member of an artillery board which worked to restructure that arm of the service after the muster out of the volunteers. As a consequence of that reorganization, Gibbon was promoted to colonel of the 36th Infantry on July 28, 1866. When the list of brevet promotions in the Regular Army for Civil War service was announced in 1866, he found that he had received five—major, to date from September 17, 1862, for Antietam; lieutenant colonel, to date from December 13, 1862, for Fredericksburg; colonel, to date from July 4, 1863, for Gettysburg; brigadier general, to date from March 13, 1865, for Spotsylvania; and major general, to date from March 13, 1865, for Petersburg. (These brevets for his Civil War service were simply honorary and carried no additional pay, although officers were often addressed by their brevet rank.)

On December 1, 1866, Colonel Gibbon was ordered west to take command of the post at Fort Kearny, Nebraska, beginning a career in the West that would last until his retirement. He served at a number of posts during the remainder of his military service: Fort Kearny until May 1867; Fort Sanders, Dakota Territory, until December 1868; transferred to the Seventh Infantry on March 15, 1869; Camp Douglas, Utah, until 1870; Fort Shaw, Montana Territory, until 1872; superintendent of the recruiting service in New York City during 1873; Fort Shaw again (commanding the District of Montana and, briefly, the Department of Dakota) until 1879; Fort Snelling, Minnesota, until 1883; Fort Laramie, Wyoming Territory, in 1883; commander of the Department of the Platte in 1884; promoted to brigadier general, United States Army, on July 10, 1885; Vancouver Barracks, Washington Territory, as commander of the Department of the Columbia; and San Francisco, California, as commander of the Division of the Pacific until his forced retirement on April

20, 1891. In addition to his official duties at regimental, departmental, and divisional headquarters, Gibbon testified before congressional committees and army boards, addressed the graduating class at West Point on June 12, 1886, and even served as a member of the Board of Visitors of the United States Naval Academy.

John Gibbon's name was closely associated with two major Indian campaigns during his frontier service: the Sioux Campaign of 1876 and the Nez Percé Campaign of 1877. In the former, Gibbon commanded the Montana Column which rescued the survivors and buried the dead of Lieutenant Colonel George A. Custer's 7th Cavalry after the battle with Teton Sioux and Northern Cheyenne Indians on the Little Bighorn River. In the latter, although his force was outnumbered, Gibbon attacked Chief Joseph's band of Nez Percé at Big Hole, Montana Territory. The battle was actually a tactical defeat for Gibbon's small force, but the losses inflicted on the Nez Percé helped bring the campaign to a swift conclusion.

Throughout his post–Civil War career, John Gibbon devoted much of his spare time to writing. By 1885 he had completed a manuscript of his wartime experiences, although the volume, entitled *Personal Recollections of the Civil War,* was not published until 1928, and then only after some editing by his daughter, Frances Moale Gibbon. The book has since become accepted as a classic account of the war. The general also wrote more than two dozen articles for various magazines on a number of topics ranging from his Indian fights to women's rights. Only in his description of the wonders of the Yellowstone National Park did Gibbon seem at a loss for words to adequately describe the sights of the region. Those West Point instructors who had declared him deficient in grammar would have been proud of his literary legacy.

While John Gibbon would be remembered primarily for his military campaigns, Charles A. Woodruff recalled some of the traits displayed by John Gibbon the man:

> He loved nature, was fond of books, yet devoted to rod and gun, and encouraged every manly sport.
>
> Children always looked upon him as their personal friend, and for woman he had a respectful admiration, and was her earnest champion. A better husband and father I never knew. He was a model of faithful devotion, tender, thoughtful, and most considerate.
>
> He was of a very social disposition, loved to be in the midst of friends, old or young, and while he could keep up his end of the conversation with anecdote, reminiscence, or argument, was also a good listener. (Woodruff, p. 292)

Gibbon was portrayed as a man who "positively abhorred deceit" and whose motto could be summed up in three words—"Tell the truth."

Following his retirement in 1891, John Gibbon settled into the family home at 239 West Biddle Street in Baltimore. At 3:40 P.M. on February 6, 1896, a few months short of his seventieth birthday, the soldier who had survived Confederates and Indians finally succumbed to pneumonia. His remains were conveyed to Arlington Cemetery, where he was buried on February 10, near the old camps where he had drilled his batteries in 1861. Survivors of the Iron Brigade, the only brigade he had ever commanded, took up a collection for his monument. Although probably modest by some standards, it overlooks the capital of the country to which he had devoted his life.

## SOURCES CITED

*Appleton's Cyclopaedia of American Biography.* New York: D. Appleton and Co., 1881.

Beck, E. W. H. "Letters of a Civil War Surgeon." *Indiana Magazine of History* 27 (June 1931).

Byrne, Frank L., and Weaver, Andrew T. *Haskell of Gettysburg.* Kent, Ohio: Kent State University Press, 1989.

Cullum, George W. *Biographical Register of the Officers and Graduates of the Military Academy at West Point, N.Y.* New York: D. Van Nostrand, 1868.

*Dictionary of American Biography.* New York: Charles Scribner's Sons, 1943.

Gibbon, John. *Personal Recollections of the Civil War.* New York: G. P. Putnam's Sons, 1928.

Gibbon, John. Personnel File, Records of the Adjutant General Office, National Archives.

Gibbon, John. "Reading Signs." *Journal of the Military Service Institution of the United States* 5 (March 1884): 396–403.

Heitman, Francis B. *Historical Register and Dictionary of the United States Army.* Washington, D.C.: Government Printing Office, 1903.

Lavery, Dennis S. "John Gibbon and the Old Army: Portrait of an American Professional Soldier." Unpublished Ph.D. dissertation, Pennsylvania State University, 1974.

Lyman, Theodore. *Meade's Headquarters, 1863–1865.* Ed. George R. Agassiz. Boston: Atlantic Monthly Press, 1922.

Scott, H. L. *Military Dictionary.* New York: D. Van Nostrand, 1864.

Spillor, Roger J., ed. *Dictionary of American Military Biography.* Westport, Conn.: Greenwood Press, 1984.

Thrapp, Dan L. *Encyclopedia of Frontier Biography.* Glendale, Calif.: Arthur H. Clark Co., 1988.

Woodruff, Charles A. "In Memory of Major General John Gibbon, Commander-in-Chief." In *Personal Recollections of the War of the Rebellion,* vol. 2, pp. 290–301. New York: G. P. Putnam's Sons, 1897.

# Journal
# of the Plains Trip

*John Gibbon's fascination with the American West is obvious in his "Journal of the Plains Trip." Ordered to Camp Floyd, Utah, where he was to assume command of Battery B, 4th United States Artillery, Captain Gibbon and his family followed the old Oregon Trail across the plains. The young captain prepared for his trip by purchasing two books, Nicholas Biddle's* History of the Expedition under the Command of Captains Lewis and Clark *and Randolph B. Marcy's* The Prairie Traveler, *both of which are referred to in his journal.*

*From Fort Leavenworth to Camp Floyd, Gibbon chronicled his journey in a unique fashion. He would fill eight pages of lined paper with news, observations, and an occasional drawing, then send them alternately to the Gibbons in Charlotte, North Carolina, and to the Moales in Baltimore, Maryland, with instructions for the families to exchange the letters. These letters were later collected and bound into a slim notebook, although two portions were apparently lost—most of the trip from Fort Laramie to Fort Bridger, and the last stage of the journey from Bridger to Camp Floyd.*

*Gibbon's spelling and grammar are as written in 1860, with the exception of a few obvious mistakes which have been corrected. Confusion over references to his wife and daughter, both named Fannie, has been clarified by referring to the latter as "little Fannie," a term that Gibbon used himself several times.*

*The manuscript journal is now in the General John Gibbon Collection at The Historical Society of Pennsylvania in Philadelphia.*

## The Start June 6th.

We were all packed & got the wagon off by 9 and about 1 bidding all our kind friends goodbye we entered our ambulances & started on our long trip across the praries. Fannie & the babies with Mary & a driver lead off in the large ambulance & four mules, whilst Mrs. Morgan, child & nurse brought up the rear in the small ambulance, both being furnished with good drivers as far as our first camp. I followed on a pony and had proceeded about a mile when we crossed the ridge in rear of the fort & descended to the valley below along a steep hill. The first ambulance got to the bottom all safe & I was near the bottom, when turning around to see how Mrs. Morgan got on I was horrified to see the mules turning from the road at a rapid pace totally beyond the control of the driver. I galloped back just in time to reach the place as the team plunged into a deep ditch falling as they went & almost pulling the wagon on top of themselves. It partly turned over & was caught by a small tree the wheel on the opposite side remaining in the air. Both the men jumped out, one before the other after the wagon came to a standstill, the last springing to the window & taking out the baby laid it on the ground where he commenced squalling lustily. I sprang from my horse & helped Mrs. Morgan & the nurse out badly scared but unhurt. The mules were soon released by cutting a breast strap in two & scrambled out as if heartily ashamed of their part of the performance. A messenger to the garrison soon brought us help; the wagon was pulled out without injury & sadder but wiser we went on our way rejoicing & locked our wheels at every steep place thereafter, Mrs. Morgan dismounting but once. We had some beautiful views of a hilly & well cultivated country & met with no more accidents.

## First camp. (Prarie Travl. P. 266. C. Spring)

About 1/2 past 4 we came in sight of the tents & wagons camped on the side of a hill, convenient to a tolerably good supply of water, which we made beautifully clear by filtering with a simple little machine consisting of a tube attached to a piece of prepared carbon. I found the other ambulance all safe & Fannie wondering at my absence. Our tents were soon pitched beds made, faces washed & water boiling & we sat down at our camp table with good appetites to cold chicken, ham & excellent coffee & after it were as amiable & pleased a look[ing] set as the 5th Avenue ever saw. Sunset saw our mules brought in, our sentinels set although we are in a well settled country, our babies in bed & ourselves comfortable & visiting around among our neighbors we men pipes in mouth & correspondingly sociable considering it was the first night in camp we got every thing in tolerable order & Fannie spent her first night under canvass without experiencing any of the various ills which such a position is usually supposed to bring about.

On starting in the morning a wagon master at Fannie's solicitation took charge of her team, whilst I drove Mrs. Morgan down the first hill & then gave the reins to Sullivan, my driver & took a seat alongside Fannie's driver & after a few lessons from him in the art of driving four in hand, took charge myself and continued to drive all the rest of the day, very much to the satisfaction of every one, more especially myself as I was able to demonstrate my ability to drive four animals without the least difficulty. I expect now to drive all the way & have an idea should I ever have to leave the army to turn stage driver in some new country where locomotives are unknown. We enjoyed the drive today very much, passing thro' a thickly settled & well cultivated country where 5 or 6 years ago scarcely a vestige of civilization was to be met with & hardly any thing to be seen but herds of buffalo, deer & bands of wild Indians. Now the country is dotted all over with little shanties, which are seen as far as the eye can reach, from the top of one of the sloping hills which form the surface of the prarie scarcely a tree is to be seen except now & then along the bottoms of the valleys where bunches of timber & brushwood mark the positions of streams in wet weather, or of ponds of water in dry. We camped by 10 o'clock a.m. in a place only about 4 miles from Atcheson & during the evening received some visitors from the town. Capt. Dickerson again is stationed there & was to have come out to see us, but did not make his appearance. Soon after getting in camp I took my gun & Mack & started out in search of game, for altho. the partridges are all mated & it looks like a shame to shoot them, our necessity knows no law & we must have some fresh meat. I succeeded in pocketing 5 which furnished us a very good lunch for the next day. Water is very scarce & no more than enough for ourselves & the animals can be obtained & then pretty muddy, so that when during my hunt I came across a puddle deep down in the bed of what once was a stream beneath some willows I could not resist the inclination to strip off my shoes & stocking[s] & remove some of the dust which had been accumulating for the past two days. It was a luxury no one can duly appreciate until water becomes so scarce with him that he can soak his dusty feet in a mud puddle & sip at the same time the water which feels so refreshing to them. We had more water during the night than we bargained for, for we were waked up late by the roaring of the wind, the flashing of vivid lightning & the rolling of heavy thunder. For some time the rain came down in torrent[s] & the wind blew so hard that I was fearful the tent would not stand & got up & partly dressed so as to be ready in case every thing went by the board, as indeed one of the officers tents did during the storm. We weathered it all safely however & got off with nothing more than a bad scare.

Our starting hour is about 6 1/2 o'clock, 2 hours after reveillee, by which time most of the men & wagons are on the road. We trot along gaily passing the wagons until we reach the head of the column when we go along more slowly & usually reach camp about 11 or 12 after a march of some 15 or 18 miles. The country passed th[r]o' on friday & saturday was not quite so thickly settled as before & many of the farms in place of fences have a furrow run round them as a warning to outsiders not to intrude. One man had stuck up a sign where an old road had crossed his field with "FENCED in" printed with pen & ink the small letters at the end being rendered necessary by the board on which the sign was printed giving out before the information intended to be conveyed to strangers was completed. A little farther on a sign on a tall pole informed us that the road to

> # PIKE SPEAK
> # &
> # FT. CARNEY

turned sharp around to the right where some man had set up a grog shop & adopted this method of getting the travel to pass by his house. Altho' we cared nothing about Pike's Peak we concluded the other name must refer to Fort Kearny where we are bound & so turning to the right patronized the establishment as far as to water our mules at the well & buy a tin cup at the store. Friday night it rained most of the time but not hard & we had some difficulty in getting into the ambulances dry in the morning. The rain rendered the roads somewhat heavy, but as it was cool & there was no dust we came along in good time & reached about 12 a good camp with tolerable water about 6 miles beyond Walnut creek where we lie by to rest tomorrow.

Big Nemehaw, Tuesday 12th 7 1/2 a.m. We have just arrived & a mail station being close by I will write up & send this off. We had a rest, such as it was all day sunday. It rained & stormed heavily all the afternoon as well as all last night & the consequence is every thing is troubled with heavy damp, and we got off yesterday morning feeling very much as if we had laid out all night, but the sky cleared up before we had been long on the road & every thing improved & we arrived at a camp in the open prarie with no wood within half a mile & no good water nearer than a mile & a half, both had to be hawled to us. I managed to get some birds along the road today so that we had fresh meat for dinner & this with very good soup made of dessicated vegetables & fresh biscuit made by Mary made us a very good dinner & we got to bed early pretty well tired out with our days march & had a very good nights rest.

12th We made an earlier start than usual this morning & have just reach[ed] the city I suppose it would be called by the inhabitants of Seneca consisting of some dozen cabins & some thing which looks like a steam saw mill. Here we are promised ice which wonderfully improves bad water. Our friends at home may all rest satisfied we are getting along finely, enjoying good health & I am happy to say Fannie has quite improved in appetite. She ate this morning about sun rise a beef steak coffee & a small quantity of biscuit & says she is still quite well. She is just about getting on horse back to vary the trip a little & has so far outraged public opinion as to actually remove her hoop. I have no doubt in a few days that a pair of grouse or half a deer will be no where with her. We are now about 1/3 the way to Kearny, have beautiful weather which we hope will continue. The travelling is delightful & the roads the best natural ones I ever saw, hard & smooth & of any width we choose to make it. I intend to continue these jottings & shall send them alternately to Charlotte & Baltimore requesting that as soon as read they may be sent on. This goes to Baltimore, after reading it please send it to my mother [in] Charlotte No. Ca.

Fannie Jr. says she will tell Aunt Gussie when she sees her that Papa has named one of his lead mules after her & wants to know why I call the other Cam. I tell her it is after Capt. Van Vliet's little boy! He is very lazy & needs touching up now & then, when he becomes quite as fast as Gus. My wheel mules Bob & Nick are two steady old fellows who go along with their ears laid back in a very sober way & altogether this team is hard to beat.

## A Storm

## Camp on the Big Blue 13th June

After dispatching my journal from Seneca, we waited long enough to get a good supply of ice & fasten it on the ambulance when Fannie & I changed places with Lt. Dudley & Miss Heth, (sister to Capt. Heth 10th Infty who is going out to visit another brother at Fort Kearny) they taking their places in our ambulance & we riding their horses. It was very hot & we did not ride long, but after delighting the babies with a short ride took our places again & continued a very hot & tiresome march of 12 miles to camp. The men & animals suffered a good deal & a four months' old calf which I bought a few days ago with a very fine cow

died soon after our arrival in a very pretty camp on Clear creek, the first
running water we have seen, all the rest being stagnant pools with more
or less (generally more) vegetable matter intermixed. I fished for some
time in a deep pool, but meeting with no success stripped & had a very
refreshing bath. The troops are supplied with fresh beef by driving cattle
along with the train, several milk cows with calves being included so as
to furnish the officers with milk which is a great luxury. Our private
cows are driven along with this herd, so that we have but little trouble
with them. They killed the day before & we enjoyed a very good piece of
roast beef for the first time, since leaving Leavenworth. During the night
it threatened a storm, but we escaped without rain & with but little
wind, altho' this morning it had turned quite cool & very heavy clouds
were banking up in all directions, which grew darker & heavier as we
proceeded on our march. Vivid streaks of lightning seemed to divide the
clouds almost every instant, but so distant that we heard nothing more
than muttering thunder. At last after we had been several hours on the
road, the storm opened on us with great violence, the wind blew with
great force, the rain fell in torrents & the lightning flashed & thunder
roared around us in every direction in such a way as to make the bravest
feel any thing but comfortable & all others very uncomfortable. Altho'
the storm struck us on the side, the mules refused to travel along the
road & turning their backs on the storm stood perfectly still shivering
with fear & the cold, which was quite severe the wind being from the
north & threatening us with hail which fortunately was not added to our
misfortunes. At first when the thunder began to rattle around us & the
wind to rise Fannie showed a good deal of fear, but she soon got used to
it & went to work swabbing up the rain which in spite of a good cover
beat into the ambulance, using for the purpose a towel & poor little
Fannie's sun bonnet presented by Molly. As I sat in front driving the
idea of keeping dry was entirely out of the question, but thanks to a
good soldier overcoat, a good pair of boots, a pair of leggins & my
hunting coat thrown over my knees, I managed to keep tolerably comfortable. After a while we got under way again but had not proceeded far
before the wind suddenly shifted & the storm beat against us with
renewed violence from the opposite point of the compass. We, or rather
our mules, again turned our backs to the wind & anxiously awaited to
see what all this thunder lightning wind & rain was to result in. One
flash of lightning was so close that we all thought it was becoming
decidedly personal & one of the mules in the train is supposed to have
been knocked down by it. One team stampeded breaking their harness
all to pieces, but fortunately without doing further injury. All things
must have at least one end & storms are no exception to the rule so after

a while the thunder ceased, the wind went down the clouds drifted away in broken masses & we resumed our march th[r]o' black mud & the sloppy roads. The sun made several attempts to break th[r]o' its thick covering, but it was not until we had nearly reached our camping ground that it succeeded & as we drove up to our various positions he was shining out as brightly as if he had not a few hours before been obscured by one of the most severe, tho' not by any means, the most violent storms with which these praries are visited. Every thing was soon out & spread upon the grass to dry & the day is closing upon us one of the brightest we have had, so that but few feel any disposition to refer to our late ducking except by laughing over the different incidents. To reach our camping ground we had to ford the Big Blue, a fine bold running stream which it did our hearts good to look upon. We had to go down a very precipitate bank, where great care & half a dozen men holding on to a rope behind each carriage were necessary to prevent accidents, but we all got down safely & poor Mack was obliged to wade across & altho' it was not over his head, he did not seem to fancy the idea at first. Bee, Buford & myself tried fishing in the river, but returned to camp empty handed. Robertson afterwards caught a fine large cat-fish.

The first few days of a march are usually all confusion & it seems as if things would never get straight, but as the men become skilled in pitching tents & all hands get the hang of matters they become more systematized & every thing goes on like clock work. As we have now been out long enough to have gotten fully under way I may as well discribe the method of pitching camp for the edification of our friends at home. The ambulances being lighter than the wagons & travelling faster, the families reach camp in front of the baggage. As we are not yet in the Indian country, each officer with his family as he drives onto the ground, previously selected by the Quartermaster selects his own camping place & halts his ambulance on it. The mules are at once unhitched & either turned loose or picketed in the grass. The ladies & children remain in their seats until the tents are pitched, or if the weather is fine & they feel so inclined discend & walk about. As the wagons come in they are directed to the different positions convenient to the camping places, when they halt the drivers unhitch the mules & turn them loose with long ropes attached to their necks by means of which they are afterwards caught. They are then all taken charge of by two or three men, mounted, & driven to water & good grass, where they feed till near night when they are driven up, caught & fastened to the wagons or to picket pins for the night. As soon as the men reach camp, they are assigned their positions, and the mounted men, after unsaddling their horses & picketing them, are detailed in parties of 4 or 5 to pitch the officers tents, unload the wagons fetch wood & water, carry in the bedding &c. In this way an hour after the arrival in camp the ladies & children have a comfortable place to retreat to, to wash, dress & rest themselves. As we usually take a lunch about 9 or 10 o'clock there is no hurry about dinner which we usually take about 5. After the tents are pitched & every thing in order I take my gun & dog & jumping on a pony sally out to see the country & shoot for our table. As yet I have met with but indifferent success, as game is scarce & out of season, but hope to do better when we get farther on our route. We are now in fine working order & form our houses for a night & strike them down in the morning as we would say good night & good morning in an ordinary dwelling, all as a matter of course. We arrive at each new home with pleasure & leave it without regret. Fannie makes a first rate soldier & says she likes it very well so long as it does not rain. I think she is really beginning to enjoy it, as she has a most astonishing appetite for her & is in excellent health & as for the children they get along just as well & as happily as if in a settled home. Of course the life has its vexations & troubles, but what kind has not? & after a little while one easily becomes accustomed to them & looks upon them as a matter to be expected. Our party consists of about 150 recruits, half mounted. Col. Alexander is in command as far as Fort Laramie, after which Col. Cooke will have charge. The other officers are Capts Clarke 4th Arty, Bee & Gardner & Tidball 10th Infty, Buford 2d Drags, Gibbon 4th Arty, Lieuts. Tyler & Robertson 2d Drags, Villipigue & Jackson G. 2d Drags, Dudley & Murray 10th Infty, Beach & Miller 4th Arty, and Dr. I. H. Hull an employed citizen physician who knows Nannie. Our ladies are Mrs Alexander & Miss Howard her governess, Mrs Bee, Mrs Gardner, Mrs Robertson & Miss Heth, Mrs Gibbon & Mrs Morgan, altogether as pleasant a party as could be brought together. All the married ladies have children from one to 4 apiece. My 4 ordnance men I find very useful, as they remain altogether with us & have no duty to do in the way of sentries &c. I exchanged one of the St. Louis recruits for an old soldier of the Ord. Dept. at Leavenworth who was very desirous of going to Utah. He is a good driver & drives Mrs Morgan's ambulance, taking charge of my mules on arriving in camp. Another takes charge of Mrs Morgan's. The other two assist about the tents, tie up the bedding in the morning, pack the wagons &c.

14th. We had reveille later than usual this morning & did not leave camp until 7 as we only had 9 or 10 miles to go, on account of not being able to get water farther on. Fannie & I adopted a new plan in the ambulance today. She takes lessons in driving, sitting on the front seat with me whilst I read "Mable Vaughan" aloud. If any thing more romantic than this can be devised I should like to hear of it. As the road is excellent I have to take the reins but seldom & by the time we reach Camp Floyd I have no doubt she will be quite an adroit whip of a four in hand team. Every now & then I have to touch up one of the leaders with the whip, but as I generally shout out a name, at the same time they are beginning to learn their different cognomens, and "Gus" or "Cam" sung out in a loud voice is usually sufficient. By the way "Gus" has fallen a victim to her love of finery, for on leaving Leavenworth she put on a new collar which has rubbed her neck so badly that applications of cold water & ham fat became necessary & I hope soon she will again be presentable even as Fannie says in a short naked dress. [Little] Fannie has now all the names by heart & sings out to them as she kneels up on the seat behind me.

## Turkey or Rock creek 15th

We made a good march of about 17 miles & camped on a beautiful stream with plenty of wood & tolerable grass. We got very fine clear & cool drinking water from a spring a short distance from camp. Poor little Fannie has been quite sick today with a good deal of fever, but she has slept nearly all the afternoon since our arrival in camp & is now easier. At several of our camping places large numbers of wild gooseberries have been found & against positive orders she ate some of them raw & they effected her bowels giving considerable pain. "Jack," the little rascal, is in finer spirits than ever & is now lying in bed grinning at me as I write and resisting every entreaty to go to sleep. I found a string of Indian buttons near camp this evening & she is "playing visiting" by ringing them against the side of her cot for a front door bell. For the last two days we have been travelling on a short cut which was not quite as smooth as the old road which we were glad enough to strike again today, about 10 miles from camp. It is said we will reach Ft "Carney" tomorrow week.

## Camp on the Big Sandy, Sunday, 17th

We lie over here to rest today in a beautiful camp right in the forks of the Big Sandy & Little Blue the latter the largest stream in this part of the country & now swollen by the rains & rushing down like a millrace. We forded the Sandy & came across to a position directly on the banks of the Blue where we are convenient to both wood & water. I took advantage of the proximity of the latter to take an ellegant bath, both last night & this morning, which has effectually driven off the dust & lassitude resulting from yesterday's long hot march of 20 miles.

Little Fannie made us somewhat uneasy night before last by waking up quite wild & evidently out of her head. She did not sleep well at all during the night & of course we were awake a good deal. Mrs Morgan's baby too was threatened with croup, but plenty of Ipecac soon brought up his dinner & put him to sleep. This of course was any thing but a good prelude to our long march & on reaching camp at 11 I felt worse used up than I have since leaving Leavenworth. All hands are however much improved this morning & I have no doubt we shall all be ready for the start in the morning with renewed zest. [Little] Fannie is quite well again this morning & it is gratifying to find so many enquiries after her. She & Miss Kitty Heth have formed a great friendship for each other, and the latter has gained so much on our affections that there is nothing we like better than to have her take a seat in our ambulance, which is larger than any of the others & talk to us as we ride along. We got ice on our arrival yesterday & as we crossed the Sandy bought very good <u>rusks</u> from a woman living & cooking in a tent near the stream, at 50 cts. a dozen 30 cts. got us a dozen eggs & this morning whilst writing Lt. Dudley sent us over a fine soft shelled turtle all nicely cleaned with about a dozen eggs lying in the shell. Two of them were caught by the officers last night in the Sandy. They say we will be on turkey ground tomorrow and I think even an Englishman could "worry along" on soft shell turtle and Roast turkey. Of course nothing will be thought of today but stewed soft turtle with the accompaniments. The officers report plenty of turtle in the Sandy & a large party is made up to fish for them <u>today</u>. I am writing up this to take it over to the mail station close by, carrying my gun along in case I should see any thing to shoot. Fannie says she does not like this idea of stopping on sunday, as she can say her prayers in the ambulance, but can't wash clothes! There is but little difference however on the praries between sunday & any other day. Katie asked me today who I was writing to. I told her grandmother & asked her what I should say. She said "I want go" & hearing Fannie singing Gussin's Methodist hymn she said she wanted to go & hear old Mr Gussin's song there!

We enjoyed a good night's rest & slept till late this morning breakfasting at 9 o'clock, quite a fashionable hour for the praries. We are now about 105 miles from Kearny from which point my next sheets will probably be sent. It is said we may remain there several days to get supplies of provisions &c.

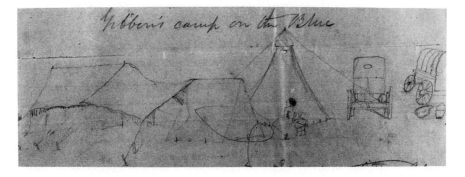

## 3d Camp on Little Blue June 19th, 1860

The above faithful and <u>lifelike</u> sketch was taken on the spot by our special artist sent out for the purpose (vide Frank Leslie's) It represents with <u>great accuracy</u> the position of our tents, ambulances &c, with a correct likeness of Mrs Gibbon in the foreground reposing after the labors of the day in the shade of Mrs Morgan's tent. At first sight it would appear as if she were seated upon a chair the greater part of which is seen behind her but this is an optical delusion, resulting from her hoops (now far below par) concealing the chair on which she is seated, the one seen in the picture being to the right & rear. The presence of mules, a milk cow, dog & children must be supplied by the immagination of the reader, as the want of time, proper materials & the necessary anatomical information, to say nothing of the want of space has prevented our special artist from including them in his sketch.

Yesterday & today we made marches of about 18 miles, passing through on the first the first real prarie we have seen. It was a dead level for several miles, and as far as the eye could reach on every side nothing was to be seen but a green plain in the midst of which marched our train. At the end of the march we again came in sight of the timber of the Little Blue on the bank of which we pitched our camp with plenty of wood, water & grass. Today our road lay along the bank of the river intersected with many gullies with steep precipitous banks down which our ambulances & wagons all passed in safety. We passed several houses & some cultivated fields in which the corn looked well advanced & healthy. We hear that 4 or 5 miles from our road plenty of buffalo are to be found, but as yet have seen none & it is even predicted will see none this side of Kearny. The emigration along this route is so large that all game is scared out of the country. Our camp tonight is again in a beautiful position on the Blue which is here still a fine rapid stream, much swollen by the rains, but evidently not near so high as it has been. A large ox team, belonging to the contractors, is now travelling along the road. Ten & twelves, in some cases fourteen oxen are harnessed to each wagon & we pass them every day on the road. The[y] usually start before us in the morning & camp beyond us in the evening, but their gait is much slower than ours and they are all day in making their marches. The animals however need but little attention & are simply turned loose to feed on the grass on the arrival in camp. Many of them look in very poor order & as if badly prepared for a march of 1200 miles.

I am officer of the day tonight & am trying to sit up till 12 o'clock in order to visit the sentinels as we are now desireous to have them well instructed in their responsible duties to be ready for the Indian country which we are now approaching. Fannie & the babies have long since gone to bed & muttering thunder in the west gives promise of a storm which I hope will not reach us before day, so that we may start on the march dry. For the first time the order is given for the officer of the day to stay with his guard in the rear during the march, so that I shall have to send my families ahead tomorrow & come on behind with the men.

## On the Platte 10 miles below Kearny

## Friday June 22d

We got no more of the storm than a brisk blow which cooled off the air, without doing any harm. I gave Sullivan the reins of my ambulance whilst Lt. Dudley volunteered to drive Mrs Morgan. It was very hot & dusty & as I was a good deal delayed picking up stragglers I did not reach camp until after one o'clk more than two hours after the command. One poor fellow who had been badly crippled by a fall from his horse some days before I gave up my pony to & footed it for the last 3 or 4 miles. It was pretty heavy work & the men suffered a good deal from the heat, dust & sandy road. I made them take off their shoes & stockings & bathe their feet which helped them along very much. At last after passing mile after mile without catching sight of the tents ahead I became very tired & mentally came to the conclusion that if I did not see them from the top of the next rise, mother, I would become desperate. As we rose the hill the tents appeared, but away across a plain 3/4 of a mile wide. This however we made out to cross & with my face feeling as if burnt to a crisp I found the camp beautifully pitched on the side of a hill within sight of the Blue & with a bright sparkling stream at its base, which furnished us with the best drinking water we have had since leaving Leavenworth & in which I had a splendid bath before I had been in camp many hours. The march today was the longest we have yet made 20 1/2 miles. Col. May passed camp in the stage on his way to attend a court at Leavenworth. He brought a couple of <u>New York Heralds</u> & the news of the death of Genl. Jesup & Col. Plympton. The Heralds gave us the only glimpse of civilization we have had for the past 2 weeks & were appreciated accordingly.

Yesterday I resumed the reins & drove all day but at the end of the march was obliged to declare myself beat & go to bed. A dose of blue mass & a seidlitz powder this morning bid fair to set all things straight again. We had no wood last night, but excellent cool water from a well close by our camp. Buffalo were reported within 4 or 5 miles of us in large herds & once when at a high point we thought we made out at a great distance with our glasses a large number of them on the top of a hill.

We had a cool pleasant day for marching today, passing th[r]o' pretty much the same kind of high rolling prarie as usual, but without seeing any timber or much water until we struck the valley of the Platte. The course of the river is marked out by large timber and as we rose the hills bounding the valley on the south a number of emigrant wagons were seen away off to the right winding their way along the road from St. Joseph's. As we turned off the road towards the river to encamp several dark objects were seen in the distance apparently approaching at speed. These turned out to be six buffalo pursued by Lt. Villipigue on a mule. He could not however induce his mule to close on the chase & soon gave it up. As the buffalo were running directly towards the column they soon had other horsemen after them, but they made their escape, altho' one was afterwards reported killed by one of the emigrants on the road. The chase was exciting & made me only the more anxious for my first experience in buffalo hunting. We are camped on a fine large branch of the Platte with any quantity of musquitoes near the bank, but comparatively few where our tents are & nothing but buffalo chips for fuel. Two nights ago I undertook to roast a beef head in the ground, but they did not use fire enough & the head had to be brought on to camp last night to finish cooking it & after our arrival today I opened it & found it very good. The skin is left on & tied around the neck so as to exclude the grit; the horns are knocked off & a hole large enough to contain it is dug near the camp fire. In this a fire [is] built until the earth gets well heated; the coals are then shovelled out & the head thrown in, covered with 3 or 4 inches of earth & the camp fire built over it & kept up all night. In the winter time & where there is plenty of wood the head is well done by morning, but as we have now warm weather & no great abundance of wood it took two nights to finish this one & as I was sick & unable to attend to it in person, I found the soldier had not burried it deep enough & had burnt off a part of the skin, allowing some dirt to get in. The meat is very soft & tender & the tongue like marrow. We are within 10 miles of Kearny, having marched today 22 miles. Lt. Berry 2d Drags rode into camp soon after our tents were pitched & is giving us all the news of the country. He called in just as we were going to dinner to invite us to take possession of his quarters on our arrival at Fort Kearny tomorrow. I accepted his offer on sight, as I have no doubt we shall find a house a very agreeable change & an advantageous one for 3 days, which will probably be the length of our visit.

From the appearance of the preceding page and of the beautiful sketch which I have made of our camp on the Blue, it may readily be imagined some other hand has been at work on my journal. I left it for a short time today unprotected, when Katie got hold of it & commenced placing her marks upon it. She had succeeded pretty well before Fannie discovered the mischief that was going on & arrested her desecrating hand.

## Fort Kearny June 24th Sunday

We reached here early yesterday morning, and very much against Fannie's inclination took possession of Mr. Berry's two rooms. She did not wish to break in upon the camp life & after we arrived I was somewhat sorry I had not followed her advice, on account of the trouble we gave Mr. Berry & because fixing up in a house was even more troublesome than in a tent. Before the night was over however we had great cause to congratulate ourselves we were under a roof, for about the middle of the night a heavy rain storm came up accompanied with wind & we were much more comfortable than if in a tent. The rain is a perfect godsend & will improve the roads & travelling very much. We found here four letters from Baltimore, but none from Charlotte, but as the mail comes in again on tuesday we hope to get letters then. We remain here until tuesday & then recommence our march for Laramie, taking the route laid down as the Lodge Pole route. (See map belonging to Stansbury's reconnoissance of Salt Lake) We find Fort Kearny an open square surrounded by mud & frame buildings standing out in the flat open prarie with no sort of artificial defences & people sleeping with doors which no inducement which can be offered is sufficient to close, much less to lock. From this may be inferred how little regard is paid to Indians in this part of the country. A band of Cheyennes who were on a war expedition against the Pawnees came in yesterday all dressed out with their lances & rifles & riding on horse back. We all went out to see them & it was amusing to see them lean forward & look at little Fannie who is now burnt almost the color of one of them. I suppose they were "speculating" as to what kind of a squaw she would make. She did not seem to take to them quite so readily & stood by holding my hand as if any thing but at her ease while Katie, who does not know what fear is walked boldly up by herself & stood staring at them with great apparent satisfaction & curiosity. Her arms & legs where uncovered look about the color of Fannie's natural complexion & with the varied shades on her body she looks, when undressed not unlike some species of zebra. They are both healthy and as good as possible <u>except</u> sometimes & of course children cannot be good always. I never did believe in <u>Model children</u>. I enclose some prarie flowers which can be forwarded with this to Charlotte.

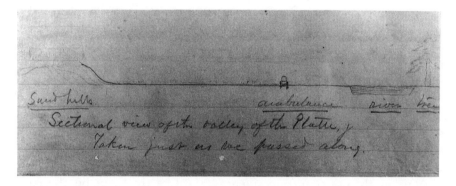

One naturally associates with a <u>fort</u> the idea of some prominent strategical point in a country, but Fort Kearny is an exception to this, for as far as its military position is concerned it may as well have been placed 100 miles above or below where it is. It is in the open prarie a few hundred yards from the south bank of the Platte, has no pretentions to a fortification & consists simply of an open square surrounded by the qrs, barracks, store-houses &c of the garrison. Most of these buildings are frame, altho' some of the mud huts originally erected when the post was established are still standing. Congress some time ago appropriated $60,000 for erecting suitable buildings at the post, but this sum was all expended in putting up one good substantial house for the Comdg. officer & the others still occupy the old buildings which are fast falling to decay. Besides a flag-staff in the center, the only other prominent military object consists of a dozen 24pd. Field Howitzers standing on one side of the square, mounted on carriages for <u>Flank casemate</u> defence! It is difficult to immagine how these fish out of water looking carriages could have wandered so far from their legitimate positions, unless our authorities in Washington have been as much misled by the term <u>fort</u>, as more ordinary mortals. Good water is obtained from wells & plenty of ice is stored up in winter time, but altogether I do not think it is exactly the place I would select as a summer residence. Possibly my estimate of the place was lowered from the fact that I here learned that my battery has been broken up by Col. Smith Comdg in Utah & sent off as dragoons after Indians 600 miles west of Camp Floyd. It is difficult to say what could have been the circumstances which would justify such a course by which the services of an indifferent Co. of dragoons is obtained in exchange for an almost total destruction of the only artillery within reach. It is thought that the Co. will be back & remounted by the time we reach Camp Floyd.

We left Fort Kearny on tuesday the 26th & have ever since been travelling along the valley of the Platte or Nebraska river. At the top of the preceding page is given a representation of the valley, the soil of which was, when we started, soft & spongy from the recent rains. Hence the embedded position given the ambulance wheels. The valley is a dead level, in the middle of which flows the river, now rapid & muddy as if from rains & nearly up to the top of its banks. In places the stream is very wide & intersperced with numerous islands generally covered with timber or tall brushwood. I amused myself as we rode along fancying the time when, from the crowded population in the east, this country will be thickly settled up this valley cut up into beautifully cultivated farms with fruit & ornamental trees in abundance & the sand hills on the left crowned with fine country residences, say like the print on the paper which forms such an adjunct to my sketch. That this time will come I have but little doubt. All the country wants is fuel & no doubt coal beds will be discovered after a while or in case they are not, rail-roads will be built communicating with the wooded districts, which are in some places not over 30 or 40 miles distant from this river.

The second day out from Kearny we met with a great loss in being obliged to sell our fine cow at a sacrifice. She was a very fine animal, cost 35 Dollars & I expected good service from her in Utah to say nothing of the road out. But she took sick after the loss of her calf & became so weak on wednesday as to be unable to travel. One of those numerous characters ever on the look out in a country like this for a bargain saw her, admired her & offered me 15 Dolls. for her. Had his offer been 5 instead of 15 I should have been obliged to accept it, as she could not travel & under the circumstances I rather think the fellow had some liberal ideas about him. As it was I lost our cow & 20 Dolls by the bargain, to say nothing of having our own fresh milk on the road. We get it now from the cows in the herd, but in very limited quantities.

June 30th. We have today camped on the bank of the river about 100 miles west of Kearny, at a point where the sand hills have assumed a more broken appearance & are nearer the water. At our camps for several nights past it was only necessary to walk thro' the high grass to raise miriads of musquitoes, which would buz about our ears, cover our clothes & attack with their sharp bite every exposed part of the face & hands. A brisk breeze has usually sprung up to drive them off, but last night they got into the tents in considerable number & tonight we think of looking to our bars for protection.

Fannie & I have both lately suffered a good deal from indigestion, and day before yesterday mine was brought to a climax by eating soup made of dessicated vegetables & bad water, obtained by mistake from a slough near the river & after marching on guard I was obliged to send for the Dr, get relieved & take to my bed. Today I am well again, tho' weak & expect to have no further trouble. As Fannie has already foresworn the dessicated vegetable which she declares made her sick once before I hope not to have to report her as badly off as I was. The children still continue well, tho' pretty cross at times, when they get hot & tired. Katie usually makes no trouble about getting up early, sitting up to be dressed with her eyes half open & a smile on her face, but [little] Fannie raises the biggest kind of a row & fight against it as long as she can & has even once or twice declared her intention of returning to Baltimore. I have recently adopted an expedient which reconciles them both a little more to the idea of getting up. The Lark, about sunrise utters a note which by a little stretch of the immagination is made to say "Get up Fannie wans" or "Get up Katie wates" according as one or the other is behind hand. As children's fancies are very easily excited these have both become interested & now when any difficulty occurs we have only to call their attention to the larks which are sure to be singing their morning songs.

We have seen but 8 or 10 buffalo since leaving Kearny altho' the valley is crossed by deep tracks worn by them as in times past they followed each other in single file from their grazing grounds to their watering places. These tracks are now overgrown with grass & remind one, like the grass grown streets of some deserted city, of the vast population which has passed along them. They are rather forceably brought to ones mind even when unseen by the bumping of the ambulance as its wheels go over them.

Sunday July 1st. We congratulate Foster on his promotion today & Gussie upon getting rid of the bob-tailed captain in the family, as well as upon the ascension to her military family of several Lieuts who today

Doff the Cadet and don the Brevet
And change the grey for the blue.

Last night for the first time we made use of a musquitoe bar, the insects being very troublesome & we piled the children into our bed the best way we could. Contrary to our usual custom we did not lay over today, but marched 20 miles chiefly at the solicitation of Col. Cooke who is anxious to get on & they say will push us much more rapidly after we leave Fort Laramie. We are encamped in a beautiful position on a fine stream of running water called Fremont's slough within sight of the Platte & half a mile from a camp of about 150 Sioux with women & children some of whom were in Genl. Harney's last battle. They are a wild looking set & soon overran our camp prepared to beg any thing or every thing but the Col. sent them off. Later in the day whilst I was off on a hunt they came into camp when Fannie & the children had a good look at them & little Fannie exchanged a piece of hard bread for a bird shot with an arrow by an ugly little urchin dressed in the minimum amount of rags usual among them. Both the children are now fast asleep. Katie after a hard struggle in her crib, playing, chattering & repeating every thing said in her presence. The drums & noise of the Indians "making medicine" in their camp are distinctly heard in the still air, whilst the splendid moon light night too fine to spend in bed is occupied by Fannie & I sitting on our bed writing up so as to be ready for the mail station at O'Fallon's Bluff 8 miles off.

We are now getting into a more broken and interesting country. The hills rise higher & steeper on both sides the river, we have been gradually rising all day & begin to appreciate the fact that we are getting well on our road to the Rocky Mountains & rising in the world. I shot a large long billed curlew whilst out this evening & saw 2 prarie chickens & a number of ducks which were however too wild for me to get a shot & I begin to appreciate the fact that we are approaching more of a game country. This feeling was increased by Mr. Dudley sending us some fine slices of veneson killed today by the Indians.

Although I stir[r]ed up thousands of musquitoes in my walk in the bottom near the river we are remarkable free from them in our tents which are pitched on the hills bordering the valley & they are kept off by a breeze blowing towards the river.

We meet every day numbers of trains coming in from Pike's Peak, mostly harnessed with oxen, the wagons filled with men who look as if they had had a hard time of it out in the gold diggins. They look ragged & dirty enough to have been away from water & their wives for the last six months. Now & then a woe begone woman is seen in the wagons & every body looks at us as we pass, as if glad to see a face just from the states.

We are all quite well again & with this fine weather are enjoying camp life under its most attractive phase.

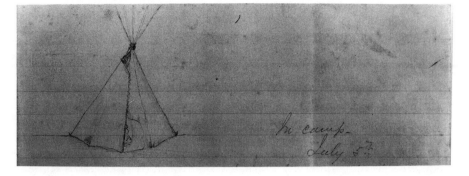

## In camp, July 5th.

On showing the above to Katie and asking her what it was she replied "that's a Dindian's tents" and as we have seen quite a number of them for the past few days & the children have noticed them particularly it may be inferred that "our artist" has been successful in his delineation of a Sioux lodge. It is formed of a number of poles placed slanting towards each other & tied together at the point where they cross. This skeleton is covered with buffalo skins sewed together, a hole being left at the top for ventilation & the escape of smoke & one at the bottom for the ingress & egress of the occupants. It is in fact the original of the Sibley tent now in use in the army & one of which Mrs Morgan is using on this march. After being in use for some time the buffalo skins become dirty & smoky & present any thing but an attractive appearance. The Sibley has but one (upright) pole with an iron tripod at the bottom within the legs of which a fire is built in cold weather, all the smoke going out at the top of the tent. I hear it much more highly spoken of as a winter than as a summer tent. There being but one thickness of canvass it is very hot in warm weather & not so comfortable as the old wall tent, which we have.

On the 2d we marched only 8 miles, and encamped at O'Fallon's Bluffs with the expictation of lying by all the next day, but our commander changed his mind & decided to go on, but the next day made only about 14 miles & we had the satisfaction of knowing that we had packed & unpacked twice when we ought to have done it but once in a distance of 22 miles. I tried very hard to get a duck for dinner, as there were a number about camp, but failed altho' I knocked one down. Lts. Dudley & Beach dined with us & we managed to make a very good meal off of broiled birds, veneson cooked in a chafing dish with quince jelly, a bottle of which I got from a store close by for $1.75, canned tomatoes, peach pies & a bottle of champagne obtained from the store for $3. This passes for our 4th of July dinner & was no doubt enjoyed quite as much as more sum[p]t[u]ous ones in the states.

As we left camp on the morning of the 3d I mailed two sheets of my journal to Ma & a letter from Fannie to Henry. On the march, an antelope having approached the train very near & been shot at I concluded to take a ride thro' the hills & see if I could not get a shot. I found the country high rolling prarie & during the ride of 6 or 7 miles to camp saw 8 antelope but altogether too wild to get a shot. They seem to appreciate the saying that "Eternal vigilance is the price of Liberty," for they are certainly not only eternally, but the most infernally vigilant animal I ever saw. I generally found them grazing in the valleys, and always rose the hills with the greatest caution, looking round in every direction to see if I could discover game. In every case except one they were too quick for me & were already when discovered bounding away up the opposite slope half a mile off. In the single case when my eye was the quickest I got down to crawl up, but when I rose an intervening hill found my antelope off at full speed, having been scared by a hunter crossing the valley a mile above. I saw 3 Jackass (or as Billy Wilson calls them <u>mule</u>) rabbits & got flying shots at two, but without effect. Supposing we were going to make a long march I got two or three miles beyond the camp the Sibley tents of which I saw from the top of a high hill where I went to "spy out the land."

Our 4th was spent like all other days on the march & in camp. No one noticed the difference except now & then as a returned Pike's Peaker passed he would pull out his pistol & fire away a salute of six shots on his own account, yelling out at the same time hurrah for the 4th of July. From what we saw it was evident that nothing but the high price & bad quality of the whisky on the road prevented the celebration from being just as enthusiastic as it doubtless is in many a place in the States. The heavens seem to have come out in honor of the day, for in the evening we had a most brilliant display of the northern lights. We are still travelling along the valley of the Platte, which late in the evening when the lights & shades are distinctly marked presents some fine views, more especially where the river spreading out to a great width is dotted over with numerous small green islands. The country however is becoming more sterile & parched up for the want of rain. Our camp today (5th) is in a particularly dusty & sterile place where ant nests & sand flys abound in disagreeable quantities. We have been carrying wood for the last few days there being none at these camps & but few buffalo chips, the cavalry had to be sent some distance away in order to get grass for the animals. Poor Mack met with a sad accident on the march today, which may yet terminate fatally. I foolishly allowed him to jump from the front seat where I always carry him, whilst the ambulance was in motion. He slipped & fell & both wheels went over his body. He suffers a good deal of pain at times & I am afraid may have received some internal injury.

## In camp Sunday 8th 1860.

A ten miles march from our camp on the morning of the 6th brought us to the crossing of the Platte, and I dare say the day will be remembered for a long time by many of the party. Being officer of the Day I drove the ambulance with the guard in the rear, and when we arrived at the river all the train was congregated there ready to cross. Some of the ambulances were just starting over & Col. Cooke at the head of the dragoons had just been pitched head foremost into the water from his horse stepping into a hole & floundering in the quick sand. The water was from 3 ins. to 3 ft deep & quite rapid. As we drove up to the bank an exciting view met our eyes. Obliquely across the stream were stretched out a long line of ambulances & wagons standing, walking or floundering in almost every direction whilst the teamsters & drivers were all shouting at the top of their voices to urge their frightened animals thro' the water. At the sides of the channels where the water was deepest the bottom rose in a steep slope against which the wheels would strike & the additional exertion made by the mules to draw the carriages up drove their feet deep into the quick sands & made them unruly, thinking they were going down. Some were going quietly along all right & nearly over, others, having got into bad bottom, were heading up stream trying to get firmer footing, whilst others were faced down stream, apparently because they could not face any other way. Bee's mules were both down & floundering in the water, whilst those belonging to both Gardner's ambulance & light wagon had fallen & been taken from their harness by the men in the water. After a while they all struggled over some helped out by men at the wheels, others with additional teams hitched to them. The cattle herd came up & was driven in & now came our turn after witnessing all this from the bank. With a warning to Fannie to keep quiet no matter what she might feel & an assurance that there was no real danger, the water being too shallow to drown in, I drove into the water with Sullivan beside me & Mack (now quite recovered from the effects of his accident) on the foot board at my feet. The bank was very steep & we came down into deep water with a jerk which almost flung me from the seat & brought the water over my feet. Mack not fancying his wet place sprang with a frightened bound over the partition into the carriage where he established himself on Fannie's cloak on the back seat. This, the shouting to & whipping of the mules & the rushing of the water stampeded [little] Fannie who began to scream, whilst Katie sat in Mary's lap her fingers in her mouth & looking as cool as can possibly be immagined. Fear that [little] Fannie's screams would disturb me & possibly injury my qualities as a coachman gave Fannie courage & she got across without showing any fear, altho' when on solid ground she acknowledged herself scared. As our mules gained the shallow water the front wheels struck the steep ledge & all the yelling at & flogging of the mules served only to paralize them with fear. They faltered, floundered, Bob stubbornly refused to pull at all as he found his feet sinking in the quicksand & we came to a dead stand-still, stalled in 3 ft. of water. Dr Hull on horse back & two or three men in the water came to our assistance & with long poles offered to lay them on the backs of Bob & Nick, Cam & Gus, with right good will. But I declined this & a short halt & a couple of men at the wheels got us out of the scrape, and altho' we had several other channels to pass thro' we got over without further trouble & found Mrs Morgan safe across with the Robertsons. After any quantity of shouting & flogging the teams all got across with the loss of two tongues broken in the river & we resumed the march glad to land safely on the north side of the South Platte. This takes us off the Pike's Peak trail & we meet no more trains of emigrants. The day was exceedingly hot & dusty & our march thro' a perfectly dry arid desert covered only with patches of thin parched up grass & little bunches of dwarf prickly pear was very tedious & only varied by our coming across a fine cool running stream of clear water (Lodge Pole creek) which appeared almost as much out of place as one of the oasis in Sahara. We found the command incamped on this beautiful stream, whose banks are scarcely fringed with a thin growth of willow & so far have but little grass along them, the dry sandy soil having more effect on vegetation than the stream, large as it is, can exert. The grass in camp was so light & dry that several fires occured, one very near burning up Lt. Dudley's tent. A violent norther came up during the night which kept us awake for some time by the flapping of the canvass & got me out of the tent at one time to look after the pins & changed the atmosphere in the morning to an exceedingly cold & disagreeable one. The wind continued to blow a gale in our faces all day, in the midst of which we met Lt. Swaine, wife & two little children, one 7 weeks old, coming in from Utah with an ambulance, one wagon & three or four discharged soldiers. He brought a letter to Mrs Morgan, left Camp Floyd on the 13th June & brings us news of importance. We camped again on Lodge Pole creek still with no wood, but grass a little better. I put the tents directly on the bank & whilst pitching them shot a couple of ducks quietly floating down stream, probably, poor things to join their little ones or visit their nest. Necessity is a hard master & our friends at home would have smiled as I did to hear Fannie tell me as I took aim to wait & get them together so as to kill both! Hearing there were fish in the stream I took my rod & after several hours very good sport brought back 39 very fair pan fish & broiled duck for dinner with fresh fish for breakfast did a great deal to relieve our consciences of any qualms they might have had for the poor fowls' posterity, or the young ones paternal loss.

Instead of marching 2 1/2 miles further yesterday and lying over to rest today, we were made to break up camp again this morning & repitch our tents after marching certainly not over that distance, this to prepare for what is called a "Journada" of 25 miles, or a day's march without water, which we are to make to cross from this Lodge Pole creek to the old road along the north Platte. We took this Lodge Pole creek route, which was originally surveyed by Frank Bryan, for the purpose of avoiding a piece of sandy road and a very steep descent into Ash Hollow near where Genl. Harney had his fight with the Indians. It is shorter than the other route, but is almost devoid of wood & grass, although the water is excellent & plentiful. I caught today a bucket full of fine fish, Sunday as it was, but they did not go down any the less readily for that when they made their appearance on our table fried in corn meal in Mary's best style. These, one of the ducks shot yesterday and a prarie hen just thro' hatching out her brood formed a very good dinner for our Sunday dinner. Company (Lt. Dudley)

## July 9th. Camp at Muddy Spring

### (So called on account of the clear water!)

As we had a long march before us today reveillee was sounded at 2 1/2 a.m. but, thro' the mistake of one of our neighbors' cooks who heard Capt. Clarke calling to his to make their fires, we were waked up in a hurry at 2, with the information that reveillee had sounded some time before. Some few fires were lighted, but the men did not appear to be stirring, and altho' I began to suspect we were up under a false alarm, we were dressed and had eaten our breakfast of fried fish & coffee before the bugle sounded, much to our own disgust & the amusement of our neighbors, with the exception of Capt. Gardner, whose cook had waked them as well as us. I found them all sitting in their ambulance, waiting, like darkies in a cotton field, for daylight. However we consoled ourselves with the reflection that we would be ready in time & half an hour or so loss of sleep was no great matter after all. The children both went sound to sleep in the ambulance & we got off before sunrise. The road lies over a high rolling

prarie such as we have several times passed over before, but the soil is dry
& sterile, altho' from the traces of buffalo, it has once been a great grazing
country. The trails all pass in the direction of the route & were doubtless
the guides to the laying out of the road. I made Sullivan drive & took a
nap inside to make up for lost time. I was waked up about an hour
afterwards by the cry of "antelope" & on looking out found a fine large one
very quietly loping past not very far off. I jumped out and gave him a
passing shot with my pistol at 3 or 400 yards which he did not seem to
mind at all, but stood staring at me as if feeling perfectly secure from my
popgun. As if to close the door after the escape of the steed I loaded my
gun with buckshot & mounted the pony for the rest of the way into camp,
thro' a very broken rocky country from the highest points of which most
beautiful views were obtained bounded in the far distance by the pur-
pleish blue hills with broken irregular tops which bordered the north side
of the North Platte. Away off to the north, lifting its head far above the
intervening hills arose the "Court House Rock," or as I would call it
Capitol Rock as it resembles more the dome of the capitol in Washington
than any thing else. It rises alone from the valley to a great height &
seems to be formed of successive layers of stone, which have been worn
away by the frost & rains of ages to its present shape.

Our camp is on a bluff, overlooking a small cool spring & stream,
large enough to supply abundance of water for the whole command, but
which disappears within a few hundred yards in the dry & sandy soil.
The road being good & the day fine we made the 25 miles without
difficulty & are now within sight of the Platte & only a few miles from
the old road. We write up for the down mail which we meet tomorrow.
Rumors have reached us of some trouble from the Sioux (whom we
passed on the 1st) resulting from Col. Alexander's incivility in ordering
them out of camp. They are reported as leveeing a tax on emigrant trains
& if any reports of this reach the states our friends may know we are far
beyond the place.

Chimney Rock (near view)

# July 11th

Yesterday we made what is called a "cut off" to save 3 or 4 miles, but altho' the distance was some shorter the road was new & almost entirely unbroken & the wear & tear on the mules & travellers in carriages was much greater than it would have been from the additional distance. We crossed a fine bold stream (Laurence's fork) with the water nearly as cold as ice-water and passed close by the Court House Rock which does not look, on nearer view, any more like a Court House than does chimney Rock like a chimney. We struck the old road several miles from our camp & it was so good that it made us regret all the more having taken the "cut off." In this country when a man establishes a ranche & wants the road to pass by it to get the trade &c. he forms a "cut off" and electioneers among travellers to take it. It is supposed this cut off was formed in this way & with no other object. We camped directly on the bank of the river & four or 5 miles below Chimney rock which we passed on the march this morning at a distance of about 2 miles, altho' it did not look more than a few hundred yards, the distance is so deceptive on level ground. We camped in low ground near the river, and had cause to regret it afterwards. Two miles before reaching camp passed a number of Indian lodges & I saw among their horses a beautiful little cream colored pony which I should have been very glad to purchase for Fannie but the owner asked too much, $80.

Towards night a heavy black cloud appeared in the north, and the animals gave unmistakeable signs of a coming storm, by prancing around their picket pins &c. As the cloud approached us and shut out the high bluffs we heard a roaring sound like a heavy surf & soon after hail stones the size of pigeons eggs comenced to fall & looking up the river we saw the water dashed into foam by thick showers of hail & we were soon surrounded by a falling mass of ice, which pelted the poor animals & every body exposed to it most unmercifully.

The ground was soon thickly covered with this mass of white ice & cool water was the first thing thought of, but more important matters soon claimed our attention. The wind rose & the hail turned to heavy rain which beat thro' the side of the tent & soon flooded the low ground on which it stood. Mrs Morgan came into our tent for the sake of company, and all six of us, babies & all perched ourselves on our bed to protect ourselves from the water which became 3 inches deep on the floor, flooding every thing. A deep ditch dug around the tent by one of the men soon filled & did not better the matter & we just had to stand or rather sit with our feet perched up & take it. As soon as there was a lull I went out & found Mary crying in her tent as she saw the different moveable articles floated out of her door, with an idea that the river was rising & going to carry her away. She was perfectly soaked thro' & had been calling for help which the raging of the storm prevented any one from hearing. Mrs Morgan went to her own tent which was on rather higher ground & took Mary to sleep with her, whilst the seats in my ambulance were put down & Fannie & the children transferred to it for the night with blankets & pillows. Scarcely were these arrangements made when the storm recommenced with redoubled violence, accompanied with very heavy thunder & lightning, but fortunately with but little wind. Satisfied that Fannie & the children were tolerably dry for the night I turned in in the tent, and when the thunder began to be more distant fell asleep & slept soundly till daylight to wake up & find poor Mack who could not find a dry spot for the sole of his foot, lying beside me his dirty wet hide not improving the looks of the sheets, as he forgot to wash himself before retiring! Half our animals had stampeded & 16 horses & several mules were missing from camp two of mine being included among the latter. The mules were soon found, but when we left camp at a late hour the horses were still absent and the dragoons were left behind in camp to recover them. The sun came out bright & cheerful & altho' suffering from the dampness & loss of sleep our spirits rose as we trotted along the sandy road much improved by the heavy rain. We passed directly thro' Scott's Bluffs to the left of that portion of them which I have sketched. Some parts of the passage through were very broken & at one place the road was so steep & rough that the ladies & children got out & walked down. As we reached the top of the ridge a beautiful view opened before us, the valley spreading itself out as far as the eye could reach, bounded by high broken ridges which looked for all the world like the ruins of some ancient cities as seen in the Old World. We marched about 15 or 18 miles & camped in the river bottom again but this time in not quite such low ground. "A scalded dog fears cold water!" The day was very warm & soon after our arrival in camp the sun had all our clothes, beds &c dry again. Heavy clouds threatened us again in the evening, but we only got a slight sprinkling of rain. For the want of more noble game I have commenced shooting the black birds which accompany our cattle herd in great numbers & find them exceedingly fat & very good eating.

13th. We had a long sandy march thro' the hills, but made rather a late start as the Dragoons not having come up we got no assistance in striking our tents & packing our wagons. Camped near a fine clear stream in the river bottom and were a good deal worried by the musquitoes until the evening when it became cooler & they let us alone. Mr Fitzhugh the sutler at Fort Laramie passed our camp this evening having in charge the remains of poor Solomon (who was ordered to West Point in my place) & those of Lt. Potts who died in Utah. He reports us 24 miles from the Post & as I am officer of the day & have to stay with the rear guard it is probable we will have a tedious time of it.

## Fort Laramie Sunday 15th July

We reached here about 2 P.M. yesterday after a very hard march, a good deal of the road being either muddy, sandy hilly or rough. The first view of the post is rather pleasant seated as it is on the left bank of the Laramie River a fine clear rapid stream & as we approached on the road being half hidden by the green trees growing in the bottom. But a nearer view was not so favorable, the garrison itself being almost entirely destitute of trees & placed on a gravelly knoll without the least show of grass. I found the men encamped about 1/2 a mile below the fort & the detached officer[s] 1/4 mile above & we had not been many minutes in camp before Lou Marshall made his appearance & offered his services. We accepted them in the form of some wood, tent pins & a very fine leg of mutton, which proved a very agreeable change from the regular beef diet. I rec'd. here a letter from Jennie & ma & one from Henry, the former dated the 15th June & the latter the 21st & forwarded from Kearny, where it was directed, on the 7th July, also a package of papers of the 25th forwarded in the same way. This makes the 3d package of papers rec'd since leaving Fort Leavenworth, so Henry can judge whether we recd. all he sends or not. If we don't it is hardly worth while to forward any more unless they contain something special, as I do not think the newspaper mail is very well attended to in this part of the country.

Marshall had us all up to dine with him today and a very nice dinner we had. The babies were also invited but we concluded it was best to leave them in camp until later in the day & then let them come up to parade. All the ladies of the command except Mrs Alexander were there & we sat down to two round tables covered with <u>clothes</u> in the most luxourius style, and many were the fears expressed that such dainties as oyster soup, roast chicken, boiled mutton and iced champagne would spoil us for the march, but we all seemed to think we could stand spoiling once or twice on the road. We remained in the garrison until evening parade enlivened by the double quick (<u>Popper</u> goes the weasel) from the 10th Infty. band, which is stationed here.

Col. Cooke and the Dragoons arrived today, and we hear we will not resume the march before wednesday which will enable us to shoe horses, mules &c and to get another mail from the states, a matter of no small importance.

The vacinity of this post is crowded with Indian Lodges, and the children are edified constantly with the sight of the little half naked savages who wander about staring at every thing they can find to look at or swimming like so many duck[s] diving & splashing about in the river near our tent, whilst the half civilized squaws walk about, some in blankets others in bright calico dresses, and one was even seen with a hoop skirt on! Many of them too go about with large cotton umbrellas, tho' it is difficult to immagine how any exposure to the sun could injure their complexions.

<u>July 16th</u>. We do not leave here till day after tomorrow, in consequence of not being able to get all the horses shod before. The mail arrives from the west tomorrow & I close this to go by it. I have had the good fortune to secure a fine large cooking stove from Capt. Bee, who finding one in his quarters here does not want the one he brought with him. This will be of great benefit to us in Utah where they sell for 150 Dollars apiece. We all walked up to parade this evening and then took tea or rather coffee with Marshall enjoying his waffles amazingly.

## Camp on La Bontee creek

## Saturday July 21st

We left Laramie about 3 1/2 P M on wednesday the 18th marching only about 8 miles, and have since been passing thro' one of the grandest, at the same time, one of the most desolate [countries] perhaps ever seen. Our road lay over a high and in some places very rough & broken country, running generally within a few miles of the Platte. On the left, behind a succession of rounded hills, composed of masses of rock covered with coarse gravel & a thin soil with just enough grass growing to "swear by" & make the earth look like a moss covered rock, rises a range of sharp pointed mountains the most prominent of which is Laramie Peak which we first saw two days before reaching Fort Laramie and which is still in sight, very hard to get round as we have found after a week's travel. On the right are the Black Hills, a range of very rough, rugged hills covered to their summits with a growth of cedar the dark color of which gives the name to the range. Occasionally the Platte has worn its way thro' these hills, and seems to have picked out the highest part as if to demonstrate the power of water. At some of these points the rock rises perpendicularly from the water's edge, and is sometimes of a deep red color from the presence of iron or sand stone, looking as if the rock had been blasted out to allow the Platte to pass on the way to the sea. We had a very heavy rain yesterday afternoon & all last night, which made the road, altho' on very high ground, very heavy & tiresome for the mules. Robertson came very near meeting with a very severe accident similar to Mrs Morgan's just after leaving Leavenworth. From some derangement in the harness his mules turned off the road coming down a steep hill & ran into a gully, just in time to stop the ambulance from running into a deep chasm which looked awfully just in front of the mules heads, <u>after</u> we had extricated the carriages and animals from their position. Poor Mrs Robertson was sound asleep & was awakened only by her husband calling to her to get out & of course was a good deal scared.

<u>Sunday 22d</u>. We were threatened with rain this morning but it blew over and instead of lying over we made the march to La Prelle (The Rush) creek over pretty much the same kind of country altho' the road was somewhat better. This rough travel is telling on Mrs Morgan's ambulance which today gave way by the breaking of the curved piece of wood connecting the tongue with the axletree, and Mrs Morgan was transferred to Col. Cooke['s] ambulance leaving the driver to make the best of his way into camp, where the Qr. Mr's blacksmith went to work to repair it. I had a very interesting ride over the hills in search of game, had some very fine views and rejoined the ambulance with a fine Jackass rabbit, to find that as usual in my absence they had had another accident. The last sunday we spent on Lodge Pole creek I went on a hunt & the mules becoming refractory Fannie got scared & made her exit by the window with no more serious damage. Today, just before I rejoined, whilst the driver was locking the wheel to go down a very steep hill & Lt. Beach holding the reins, "Bob" became unruly & slipt his bridle, whilst Gus & Cam took it into their heads to turn around & look into the ambulance window, where Fannie not liking the idea of their visit nor the proximity of a steep bank at the side of the road, gave Mary hasty orders to beat a retreat with the children who were hurriedly deposited on the ground with a few slight scratches & all got out in

safety, after which the mules, having no further cause to make a distur-
bance became quiet. [Little] Fannie remarked as I retook the reins "now
the mules won't make any more trouble cause Papa's got em." We
camped on a fine fast running stream where wood was plenty, but the
grass very poor. I asked Col. Cooke to dinner to help us eat the Jackass
rabbit & whilst out in search of something more with my gun came
across an old crow making a most tremendous fuss as I approached,
caused, as I soon discovered, by her newly fledged brood, which were
hopping about on the ground. As I looked on an idea suddenly struck
me. "These birds are young and tender. I have heard, I think that young
crows are good to eat." I captured three, with the feelings of a murderer
cut their throats & went to work picking them. Knowing how much
prejudice has to do with peoples taste and desiring to have an unbiased
opinion (as in the case of the alligator in Florida) in regard to the
edibility of crows I wished to remove all indications of their species
before presenting them at home. But I soon got tired of the job & after
picking one decided to run the chances. With an air of triumph I presented them to Fannie saying they were a kind of large black bird which
grew in this country (So they were!) Fortunately for me her ornithologi-
cal knowledge was not extensive enough to enable her to detect me &
with great delight she turned them over to Mary as a welcome addition
to our dinner, submitting that we should now scarcely want the rabbit. I
told her however she had better have that served also, and as I did not
feel at liberty to play such a trick on Col. Cooke let him into the secret.
They came on, in order, were declared by all hands as rather insipid & it
required all the countenance I had to answer the close questions with
which I was assailed. "I declare" says Mrs Morgan "I do believe they are
crows or something of that kind" at which Fannie expressed the greatest
indignation. As soon as dinner was over I informed them they had made
a dinner of young crows! which I pronounced with considerable stret[c]h
of conscience as good as squabs. No ill effects followed, but I don't think
any of us feel any inclination to repeat the experiment except in the most
extreme necessity. Col. Cooke stuck industriously to the rabbit.

## Camp near Deer creek 23d.

Fannie sat up till near 12 o'clock last night writing to Nannie as we
expected to meet a stage today, but in coming out of camp the wrong
road was taken, which altho' shorter than the mail route was a good deal
more hilly. We passed the mail station at Deer creek about a mile back
but no body being there who spoke English & the office being closed we
could not mail our letters. Dr Hull says he is going to ride back to mail

some in the morning & I am writing up this to send by him. Deer creek is a fine clear stream, but we neglected to fill our canteens as we passed & camping on the river found the water very muddy & decidedly the worst water we have yet had, too muddy as Fannie says to wash in. Nothing is more remarkable in this desolate arid country than the number of fine springs & clear streams of water thro' it. We have been passing them constantly ever since leaving Laramie, and it is one of the greatest luxuries we have. Sometimes the water bubbles up strong & so cold that it makes the fingers ache to hold them in it, and in a few yards it disappears entirely in the dry parched soil. We now get plenty of fine wood all cut & dry to hand, and this is another of our luxuries. We are all in fine health with most astonishing appetites and Fannie has been told over & over again that she has improved in appearance more than any lady on the march. She sleeps sound at night, hears reveillee before I do in the morning and sees the sun rise oftener than she ever did in her life. As he makes his appearance above the hills we sit down to breakfast & we begin to crave something more than coffee, with which we contented ourselves when we first started from Leavenworth. Just before reaching camp today we met a party of emigrants from Illinois who had gotten disgusted on their road to California & concluded to turn back. One of the men looking into our ambulance called out "How de do Kitty." I thought the fellow was getting familiar with Mary on short acquaintance, but found out afterwards that he had seen & talked with <u>Katie</u> at Fort Laramie & was thus renewing his acquaintance! Capt. Gardner talked to them & told them it was a shame to have so little spirit, and they actually turned back again & are now camped with us on their road to the Pacific. The grass was so poor they were afraid they would never be able to get some fine American horses they had across & only needed a little encouragement & the sight of some one who knew something of the road to decide them to continue. They had received glowing descriptions of the quantity of buffalo & other game on the road & are not a little disgusted to find none and that travelling on the plains is not a prolonged picnic.

After getting into camp I took a long hot walk over the hills in search of game, but returned after walking 4 or 5 miles without anything having had a shot at a Jackass rabbit and Mack having run himself nearly to death after two of them. It is almost impossible to keep him from chasing them. They jump out of a bunch of grass & go loping off slowly for all the world like the little donkeys we used to see around Vera Cruz. Poor Mack thinks he can pick them up at once, but finds after a hot run of a mile that he is getting farther & farther from the rabbit which can run if it chooses like a race horse, but seldom exerts itself much unless pushed or badly scared.

We feel now that every day's journey of 20 miles is sensibly diminishing our long trip & Mrs Gardner, who stops at Fort Bridger, begins to feel very much like getting home, altho' she is still some 300 miles from it. Quite a large Mormon train is on the other side of the river on its way out, and I hope yet to see something of them before we get to Bridger. The days are now very hot, but we have but little dust and the nights are cool and pleasant and ellegant for sleeping.

## Fort Bridger Aug. 9th 1860

I had only a few moments whilst Lt. Hill remained in our camp on Black's Fork to add a postscript to so much of my record as I had written up announcing our arrival to within two days march of this place.

On the 4th we passed over the same miserable barren country from the Little Sandy to the Big Sandy where we found things in camp worse even than we have yet had them. Grass exists only in little patches on the banks of the stream, now muddy & the bluffs are so high & steep that it is impossible to get wagons down. So that our tents were pitched in real sand beds with here & there a sage bush or little bunch of sparse grass to relieve the monotony. This bunch grass as it is called, altho' very poor to the eye is very good & nutritious for the mules who eat it eagerly. This is the part of the route through which Col. Cooke made his terrible march in the fall of 1857 to join Genl. Johnston, during which he lost nearly half his animals by cold & starvation, and had many of his men badly frozen. He pointed out to us the place where his mules ate up the wagon tongues. It is truly as he says "a lifeless treeless, pathless desert," is bad enough in all conscience in summer & must be terrible indeed for a march in the winter. We saw as we came along the remains of one of Genl. Johnston's trains burnt by the Mormons, and the sight brought up in my mind all the absent features of this miserably conducted question. A circle of black ashes one half on each side the road still remains to show where the train was parked or "coralled" as it is called, for the night and was devoted to the flames by these rascals, pardoned before they would even admit they had ever done any thing wrong.

Now & then a wheel tire, or other piece of iron is seen, but most of these have been scattered or carried off. We had a heavy rain this afternoon which laid the dust.

5th. The same lifeless desert as ever, but we met with a change on our arrival at Green River, a very fine large cold clear stream winding between beautiful green banks fringed with cotton wood and willow. A steep hill where all the ladies & babies got out, and a pretty deep ford which we crossed without accident brought us to the other side where we encamped on hard green sod with plenty of wood a perfect contrast to yesterday's. We found here two stores competing with each other, where we bought eggs packed in Salt from Salt Lake city at 40 cts a dozen & tolerable butter from the same place for that amount a pound. Lt. Dudley in the midst of a heavy shower caught some very good fish in the river & dined with us today, as the consciencious caterer of his mess refused to have any thing cooked on <u>sunday</u>. I go on the principle that one may as well be hung for a sheep as a lamb, and if we buy eggs, butter and <u>potatoes</u>, as we did today, there is no reason why we should not enjoy them decently cooked, <u>provided</u> always that we are correspondingly <u>thankful</u> for the luxury. Within a few hundred yards of our camp are the remains of two other trains burnt by the Mormons, the black circle of ashes and broken bottles, probably from the hospital stores, being all that now point out the spot, the old iron having all been carried off, probably by those living near.

<u>6th</u>. As we left camp this morning we drove out of our way to look at these remains, which had the effect of putting me in a passion again. We crossed over to Black's Fork today and keeping up it reached a mail station at the mouth of Ham's Fork where we witnessed for the first time the practical operation of Mormonism. In a miserable hovel covered with filth & dirt of every kind appeared two ugly dirty Irish women both the wives of one man who was absent! They kept pies for sale, but we felt no disposition to become customers under the circumstances, and passed on up to our camp on the west side of Ham's Fork after crossing it near another settlement, half Mormon half Indian, and it was from here I despatched my last leave to Ma by Mr. Hill. I went out with my rod and captured a fine string of fish, not brook trout however tho' I hope before long to get hold of some of these.

<u>7th</u>. "Bob" who has occasionally given us some trouble at starting, by refusing to stand still till we were ready behaved worse than usual this morning, and we were very late in getting off. As however I was officer of the day this made but little difference, but his misbehavior and attempts to jump on the pole makes me fear for its stability, as Sullivan broke it badly yesterday by careless driving down a hill. This is the scene of Col. Alexander's celebrated march & counter march before the arrival of Genl. Johnston to take command of the Utah Army and on his return from up Ham's Fork he camped in the position we left this morning. Fortunately for us we made a short march of only about 15 miles, and after crossing Black's Fork twice encamped in a very pretty position on its bank. Robertson and I went fishing & to be sure not to be caught in the lurch I took my gun along & it was very well I did, for when we

returned to camp after an hour or two's absence, he had a string of small fish, and I was loaded down with two fine young geese and six sage hens, decidedly the best luck I have yet had in hunting, and we begin to think we are at last about to reach the Happy Hunting ground of which we have heard so much. Capt. Gardner and his family drove on into Bridger, and are now no doubt happy at having reached their journey's end. On going over to camp to march off guard I was astonished to find that Dr. Taylor, Lt. Armistead and <u>Shunk</u> had arrived from Bridger, coming out to meet us. Of course all was astir, and I soon seized on Shunk to go over & see Fannie and <u>Booney</u>, as he calls [little] Fannie. We were all delighted to see him, found him the same funny fellow as of old, and are only too sorry that he is ordered out of Utah, as we shall miss his gay company very much at Camp Floyd. He takes breakfast with us in the morning & rides in our ambulance to Bridger where his men are encamped.

<u>8th</u>. Shunk took breakfast with us & getting off in good time we drove rapidly over an excellent road passing every thing on it until I spied a flock of sage hens when we came to a halt & I started in pursuit. I killed one & by the time I got into the ambulance again Morgan & the Infantry had passed us. But we accomplished the distance (16 miles) in good time and were blessed with a very pleasant sight on our arrival. Fort Bridger is beautifully situated in the green valley of Black's Fork which here divides itself into three or four branches and comes tumbling down over its pebley bed clear & cold direct from the snowy peaks of the Rocky Mountains in sight. The white washed walls of the low one story cottages which form the quarters gleamed beautifully thro' the trees as we rode into garrison, and our admiration was not lessened on finding the parade ground a beautiful green sod with a couple of streams of fine cold water winding their way thro' it. These are crossed in various directions by rustic bridges and Col. Cooke remarks that it is a singular coincidence that Fort <u>Bridger</u> should have so many <u>bridges</u>. Altogether it is the prettiest place we have yet seen, and the only one we should care about remaining at. The quarters are not all finished & we found Capt. & Mrs. Gardner head over heels in a half finished shell of a house, waiting till their own was finished. I made their old nigger cook laugh when exclaiming at the magnificence of their splendid mansion. We camped in by far the most delightful spot we have seen since leaving Leavenworth. In a sea of grass a short distance above the Fort & on the bank of a stream which cannot be surpassed by any in clearness & coolness we pitched our tents. The opposite side of the stream is covered with a thick growth of willows which completely shut out the view in that direction. This is the position occupied by Genl. Johnston & his army during the

winter of 1857. Hearing that <u>trout</u> were to be caught in the stream I was not long in camp before my pole & flies were out, and on a fishing excursion. It was some time before I met with any success, but at length I <u>felt something pull</u>, and pulling in return I soon succeeded in landing a fine trout 12 or 14 inches long on the bank & was quite elated to find him beautifully speckled from head to tail. I caught 4 very good sized ones, and had just enough of the sport to give me a relish for it. The sutler, Judge Carter asked us up to take dinner with him, and after our camp life and fare we enjoyed very much a white table cloth, fricasseed chicken, <u>new</u> potatoes, turnips & ice cream.

We found here Mrs. Moale['s] letter to Fannie of the 10th June, Henry's of the 2d July & Ma's of the 24th of June to me together with a Herald forwarded by Henry, all forwarded from Laramie which point they reached too late for us. We were pleasantly lulled to sleep at night by the splashing of the stream behind our tent and it sounded so pleasantly the next morning when I woke up that I rushed out about 7 o'clock & jumped into a hole of nearly ice cold water not 20 feet from the tent, and returned to dress much benefitted thereby.

9th. Dr. Taylor, the fisherman of the garrison, went fishing with me today, and after an absence of several hours we returned with a very pretty mess of 33 fine trout, all of which he insisted upon leaving with us, so that we had enough to share with Capt. Clarke & Robertson & all hands pronounced them most excellent. No fishing is fishing except trout fishing & I think Nick would appreciate highly a clear stream like this with plenty of vigorous bites. I am glad to hear that every stream between this one & Camp Floyd is well stocked with these delicious fish. All are busy shoeing mules, repairing wagons &c. for the last stage of the route, and our ambulance tongue was thoroughly repaired with the rest. These repairs &c will detain us until saturday morning when we take up our line of march for the next and last stopping place <u>Camp</u> Floyd.

10th. The sun was not far above the horizon before I was again in the big cool hole behind our tent with Robertson to follow my example which after trial he pronounced a good one. The weather is delightfully cool & pleasant, whilst our letters & papers are filled with the oppressive heat in the east. Another trip with my rod got us a mess of fish for dinner, which was further added to by a loin of mutton, a present from Lt. Armistead. We leave at 9 in the morning all well & in good spirits for the <u>Muddy</u> 12 miles distant.

# An Autumn in the Rocky Mountains
# Searching for Lewis and Clark's Pass

*In the years following the Civil War, the 7th United States Infantry scouted and mapped an area larger than New England, often with Colonel John Gibbon commanding scouting parties in the field. When he prepared for active campaigning, Gibbon packed, in addition to his military equipment, three essential items: a fly rod, a shotgun, and a pocket edition of the history of the Lewis and Clark Expedition. Gibbon's fascination with the deeds of those famous pathfinders is evident in "An Autumn in the Rocky Mountains Searching for Lewis and Clark's Pass." Having an opportunity to explore a remote section of the Rocky Mountains in the summer of 1870, Gibbon and his party apparently rediscovered the pass that Captains Meriwether Lewis and William Clark had used in July of 1807 on their return from the Pacific Ocean. This pass through the mountains was then unknown to the few settlers who lived on its eastern edge.*

*In October of the following year, Gibbon confirmed the location of Lewis and Clark's Pass by exploring the western slope and comparing the countryside to their published account. Despite this success, Gibbon's identification of Lewis and Clark's "Prairie of the Knobs" was erroneous, an admission he made after discovering the actual location of that geographical oddity during the Nez Percé Campaign of 1877. The colonel also visited Hot Spring Mound near Deer Lodge, Montana, participated in a black grouse hunt, and viewed the puzzling geological formations on the eastern and western slopes of the Rocky Mountains.*

*"An Autumn in the Rocky Mountains Searching for Lewis and Clark's Pass"* appeared in the American Catholic Quarterly Review 4 *(January 1879): 81–100.*

In the summer of 1870 I started with two companies of cavalry to post them at Cadotte's Pass in the Rocky Mountains, with a view to prevent certain Indians supposed to be hostile from making use of the pass as a thoroughfare to reach the settlements on the western side of the mountains. On first arriving at Fort Shaw, we were told that Cadotte's Pass was directly behind a conical peak called the "Haystack," plainly visible from the post, and standing directly up Sun River. As this stream was the one down which Captain Lewis and his party travelled in 1807 when on his return from the Pacific coast, I anticipated a good deal of interest in tracing out his route and comparing his description of the country with its appearance at the present day. Hence I carried along a pocket edition of Lewis and Clark's expedition, little thinking, however, of what importance it was to prove to me. Captain Lewis must have passed the present site of Fort Shaw on the 10th of July, 1807. On the 22d of the same month, sixty-three years afterwards, we left that point and followed his track back towards the mountains. Although the appearance of the country must have looked about the same, under what different circumstances were the two trips made! Then, this region was a perfectly unknown wilderness, actually swarming with game, for Captain Lewis's journal says:

"We saw a great number of deer, goats, and wolves, and some barking squirrels (prairie dogs), and for the first time caught a distant prospect of two buffaloes. Captain Lewis here shot a large wolf, remarkable for being almost white"; and "about this time the wind, which had before blown on our backs and put the elks on their guard, shifted round, and we shot three of them and a brown bear"; and on the 10th "they (a portion of his party) had been pursued as they came along by a very large bear, on which they were afraid to fire, lest their horses, being unaccustomed to the report of a gun, might take fright and throw them."

On our trip we had no such sport in prospect, and pursued our way up the river, seeing nothing more formidable than a few timid antelopes, one of which I wounded at long range, and captured after a sharp chase. We camped after a twenty-eight mile march on Captain Lewis's Shishequaw Creek, now called the Elk or South Fork of Sun River, with settlers' cabins scattered all along it. We had with us an officer who in the early spring had been conducted by one of the guides of the country to what he called Cadotte's Pass, but I could obtain no information whatever in regard to Lewis and Clark's Pass, nor indeed did anybody seem to know that there was such a pass in existence. To find this was therefore the first object of our search. Accordingly, the next morning, the main command was started across the country in the direction of what was supposed to be Cadotte's Pass, whilst with a few men I started along the foot-hills to try and discover any trail leading into the mountains. Passing close under the steep rocky sides of the "Haystack" (the only name we then knew for it), we pursued our way to the southward over rolling, grassy hills and through beautiful little timbered bottoms, in which we several times caught sight of white-tailed deer skulking, until we reached an opening in the mountains, out of which came quite a large stream, and up which led a plainly marked trail. This was at once declared by Lieutenant S. to be the Cadotte's Pass to which he had been conducted in the spring; but our guide declared it was not Cadotte's Pass, and we at once proceeded to explore it. The guide was equally positive from the first that we were not on a *lodge-pole* trail, and after we had gone six miles into the mountains, it was patent to all that we were not in any "pass" at all, for the trail became fainter and fainter, and soon after became so overgrown with trees and obstructed with rocks as to render any further progress with horses impracticable. We therefore retraced our steps, and on coming out of the mountains found the main command waiting for us, and we went into camp for the night. Lieutenant S. was positive this was the point he had been brought to for the mouth of Cadotte's Pass, and after searching about amongst the brushwood along the bank of the stream we found the location of the camp they had made, with bits of paper and empty fruit cans lying about. The guide was sent out late in the afternoon to look for any well-marked trail leading towards the mountains, and came back to say he had discovered one, very old, but evidently made by lodge-poles. A lodge-pole trail differs from a simple horse or game trail by the fact that the dragging poles make parallel tracks, which in some places are almost as regular as wagon-wheel ruts.

The next morning we made an early start, and directing the main command to march in a certain direction, I started across the hills to strike the trail discovered by the guide the day before. Within a mile or two, we came to a plain well-worn trail of several ruts running directly south and about parallel to the mountains. Taking from my pocket the copy of Lewis and Clark, I read:

"July 8th. At three miles from our camp we reached a stream issuing from the mountains to the southwest; . . . we called it Dearborn's River. Half a mile further we observed from a height the Shishequaw Mountain, a high insulated eminence of a conical form, standing several miles in advance of the eastern range of the Rocky Mountains, and then about eight miles from us, and immediately on our road, which was in a northwest direction."

Turning back on this trail, I rode to the top of a high ridge, and there before me, standing out in plain view and bearing in a northwest direction, was "Haystack" Butte, the Shishequaw Mountain of Lewis and Clark, and we were in all probability upon the very trail used by Captain

Lewis's party sixty-odd years ago. The question would be definitely settled if in following this trail half a mile back in the other direction we should come to the Dearborn River. Directing the main column how to march so as to strike the river lower down where our wagons could get across, I took a few men and followed back on the trail. We had gone about a mile when we came to a stream answering in every way to the description given of the Dearborn by Captain Lewis, and now the only thing to be decided was as to the pass by which he crossed the main divide of the Rocky Mountains. Following the trail still to the south, we found it after a time turn to the westward and enter the mountains. Our guide was very positive that this was not the trail leading into Cadotte's Pass, and now, with the spirit of exploration strong upon us, we pushed ahead, determined to decide for ourselves where it did lead to. It was very evidently a lodge-pole trail, for as we drew closer to the mountains and entered the timber, the marks of the lodge-poles upon the trees standing close to the trail were plainly to be seen. The trail, however, had been for a long time in disuse, and as the timber got thicker, we found in several places the way obstructed by fallen trees. The ground rose more and more rapidly as we advanced, and after issuing from the dense timber and climbing a very steep hill, we at length stood upon the highest point of the ridge, and had a magnificent view of the surrounding country. Turning to Captain Lewis's journal again, I read under date of July 7th:

"After travelling seven miles we reached the foot of a ridge, which we ascended in a direction north 45° east, through a low gap of easy ascent from the westward, and on descending it, were delighted at discovering that this was the dividing ridge between the waters of the Columbia and those of the Missouri. From this gap Fort Mountain is about twenty miles, in a northeastern direction."

Taking out my compass, I placed it in position, and then looking to the northeast, there stood Fort Mountain (now called Crown Butte, three miles from Fort Shaw), looming up above all the surrounding country, and forming the landmark which Captain Lewis made use of to mark out the pass by which future explorers could determine the point at which he crossed the Rocky Mountains. The distance, however, from the top of the pass to Fort Mountain is nearer fifty miles than twenty. There could be no question now; we had been following Lewis's trail, and were standing in the very gap where he stood sixty-three years ago, "delighted at discovering" himself once more on the eastern slope of the continent. Not satisfied at reaching the top, we rode on a short distance further and looked down on the other side over that "easy ascent from the westward" to which he refers. We had started in the morning with no idea of travelling so far from camp, but had pushed on, mile after mile, carried away by the desire to solve the interesting problem, and now, late in the afternoon, found ourselves on the very top of the Rocky Mountains, tired and hungry, with horses worn out with the long trip and hard climbing. These we unsaddled and turned loose for an hour, to satisfy as best they could their cravings of hunger on the sparse grass which grew on the mountains, whilst a few mouthfuls of raw bacon, which some of the old soldiers carried in their saddle-pouches, tended to allay our cravings. The "gap" described by Captain Lewis as a "low" one was so only in reference to its surroundings, for although high peaks rose on both sides of it north and south, the gap was high enough to give a very extended view of over a hundred miles to the eastward. At certain seasons, too, it was evidently high enough to be a very breezy place, for the stunted pines which grew there were all lying bent to the eastward very close to the ground, forced to grow that way apparently by the strong western winds which sweep over the mountains.

We had now discovered the existence of a second pass through the mountains not known to the people of the country, for our guide was positive that this was not the one known as Cadotte's Pass, and our next object was to find where that was. From Lewis and Clark's report we know of the existence of another, called by the Indians on the western slope, "The Road to the Buffaloes," the trail through which separated from the trail to Lewis and Clark's Pass, near a place named by Captain Lewis "The Prairie of the Knobs," and the inference was that the trail issued from the mountains to the eastward not very far from the one we were now on. As we came down from the pass therefore, we kept a lookout for any break in the mountains, but our guide could discover no landmarks by which he could locate the pass. After leaving the mountains we had a long ride over a rough country in search of our camp, which we expected to find on the Dearborn River, but when we reached the steep rocky banks of that stream it was nowhere in sight, and, as the sun was rapidly sinking behind the western mountains, we began to contemplate the possibility of having to make a supperless bivouac when we discovered a man on a distant hill, and travelling towards him soon came in view of the camp nestling in the deep valley alongside the bright stream. Soon after we reached it our guide discovered a large plain trail crossing the river just below, and this being followed towards the mountains the next day was found to lead into what was declared by him to be the "Cadotte" Pass, named after some modern explorer who "discovered" the pass, and gave it a new name, long after it had been discovered and named by somebody else, a very common thing by the way in this Western country, one of the most notorious cases of which is the modern so-called "discovery" of the now celebrated "South Pass."

As the pass we had "discovered" was without doubt the one used by Captain Lewis and named after the two greatest explorers of the age, it became a matter of some interest to decide whether the modern Cadotte Pass was or was not the other pass spoken of by Lewis, and called from information derived from the Indians, "The Road to the Buffaloes." To do this, explorations would have to be commenced from the western slope, and the country there compared with the description of it given by Captain Lewis.

Accordingly on the 1st of October, 1871, a party of six set out from the town of Helena, and having been kept up all night before by a fire which threatened to destroy the town, reached the Hot Springs, three miles distant, with appetites to do justice to a good breakfast, rendered all the more enticing by a bath in the delicious waters of the springs.

These Helena Hot Springs are destined to a great celebrity at some future day. The waters are strongly medicinal, and hot enough when first issuing from the earth to boil an egg, and for bathing purposes have to be first tempered by cold water, which is pumped up from a well close by. You can have a bath of almost any temperature you please, but from 90° to 95° is usually found warm enough, and I know of no greater luxury than a bath in these waters, whether taken in hot or cold weather. The water had been analyzed and found to be essentially the same as that of the Hot Springs of Arkansas. Its use is found to be especially beneficial in rheumatic and neuralgic cases, and some astonishing cures have been effected in these complaints. The water hot from the spring is drunk as well as applied externally, and the patient issues from his bath in a delicious glow and gentle perspiration, which I have never experienced from any other water. When taken after great fatigue the effect is to restore the energies in a most remarkable manner. Similar springs are very common throughout this whole region of country, and it seems as if nature had kindly placed close at hand a remedy for the diseases with which she afflicts her children in this climate. The poor miner, toiling night and day in the cold mountain streams frequently falls a victim to painful rheumatism, and comes to these springs as to a nursing mother, to leave, after a few weeks' bathing, free from his pains and aches.

Lewis and Clark mention several of these warm springs as existing west of the mountains, and say:

"The principal spring, which the Indians have formed into a bath by stopping the run with stones and pebbles, is of about the same temperature as the warmest bath used at the Hot Springs in Virginia. Captain Lewis could with difficulty remain in it nineteen minutes, and was then affected with a profuse perspiration. The two other springs are much hotter, their temperature being equal to that of the warmest of the Hot Springs in Virginia. Our men, as well as the Indians, amused themselves with going into the bath; the latter, according to the universal custom among them, first entering the hot bath, where they remained as long as they could bear the heat, then plunging into the creek, which was now of an icy coldness, and repeating this operation several times, but always ending with the hot bath."

Another group of such springs, which we shall see in the course of this ramble, is situated a short distance from Deer Lodge. Still another is near Camp Baker, forty or fifty miles east of Helena; a very hot one on the Yellowstone east of Fort Ellis, whilst the National Park is full of them, and all of them possess medicinal properties to a greater or lesser degree, besides being of immense benefit to persons afflicted with nothing more serious than dirt.

Thus fortified by our visit to the Hot Springs, we commenced to climb the main divide of the Rocky Mountains, over a winding well-graded road, and were soon amongst the clouds and timber of the summit, from which we dipped down on to waters running to the westward, and as the sun was rapidly approaching the snow-capped peaks in the west, we caught sight, far down in the valley below us, of the pretty little town of Deer Lodge. It appeared to be only a mile or two away, but, accustomed as we are to the deceptive distances in this high, rarefied atmosphere, we are not surprised when darkness overtakes us before we draw up at Sam Scott's Hotel.

Our host is a character. He "knows how to keep a hotel," as we readily acknowledge when he seats us at a table supplied with most excellent coffee, *real* cream, elegant tender elk steaks, and all the et ceteras which go to make up a good substantial meal. A good comfortable bed ended the day, and the next morning we were to witness our first wonders in the *"Hot Spring Mound"* of Deer Lodge valley.

This valley runs nearly due north and south, is amply supplied with water, which is (and can be more extensively) used in irrigating its rich bottom lands, which produce the finest grasses and grains. It is surrounded by mountains in the gulches of which rich deposits of gold are found.

The Great Northern Pacific Railroad must go through or across this valley somewhere. Just exactly *where* is at present the all-important question, which is of almost vital importance to every ranche man in it. A party of railroad engineers are encamped at present in the outskirts of the town, busy on work which is to help decide the matter.

A ride of twenty miles up the valley (south) behind Sam Scott's fast team, through a level country dotted with farmhouses, grain and grass fields, brought us to the Hot Spring Hotel, and a view of the Hot Spring Mound.

Out in the open prairie, which stretches for miles westward till it meets the foot-hills of a range of mountains wooded to their summits, and now partially covered with snow, stands a mound of what is now solid stone, some twenty or thirty feet high, and four or five times that in diameter at the base. Up the side of this we climb, and standing upon its comparatively level top, look around us. In the centre is a nearly circular spring, several feet in diameter, filled nearly to the top with water just warm enough to permit holding the hand in it for a few moments. Around this are several smaller openings, also filled with warm water, as I find to my cost. For, in attempting to play a trick upon one of the party, by pushing him into the larger hole, I stumble into one of the smaller ones and get the worst of the bargain.

We examine this mound with curiosity. It is partially covered with grass and weeds, but in places the solid stone is exposed, and is found to consist of a friable mass of yellowish substance, not unlike petrified wood in texture, and presenting every appearance of having been deposited in ages past from the water as it overflowed at the top and trickled down the sides. In this view of the matter we are confirmed by observing on the plain below what is now taking place.

Apparently this mound has worked its way up to a point beyond which it can go no further, and as the pressure from below forces the heated waters to an outlet, fissures have been formed around the base of the mound where the waters bubble up, in some places so hot that the hand cannot be held for a moment in it. This water, as it rises and overflows, deposits its sediment on the rim of each basin, and smaller mounds are rising around each spring.[1] But careful how you step, for the sediment has not yet become hard like that in the principal mound, and unless you keep upon the solid turf formed by the grass, or the boards which have been carefully laid for visitors, you are liable to sink through the soft yellowish soil with the uncomfortably warm water beneath.

A strong smell of sulphur impregnates the cloud of steam which arises from these warm springs, the waters from which are conducted into a tank, and thence in pipes to the bathing-house close by.

All round the mound the low quaking ground, gradually falling away, in some places wet and miry, in others only damp, is covered with

---

[1]The similarity between the formation of this mound and the one in the National Park known as the Cap of Liberty, will be remarked.

a thick, tall growth of coarse sedgy grass, through which a path leads to the mound.

We lingered a long time about this curious freak of nature, testing the heat of the various springs, and were shown one in the very midst of all the warm ones, where the water was found cool enough for palatable drinking water. Looking at the various smaller mounds, from a few inches to two or three feet high, I could not help speculating as to the vast period it had probably taken to form and solidify the principal mound, judging from the slow process now going forward in the smaller one. We were shown a spot in the soft yielding ground where some man, mounted on horseback and stimulated probably by that daring spirit of inquiry which "*strong waters*" sometimes give, came very near being engulfed, horse and all, in the treacherous soil beneath. Walking back from the mound and along a path made through the tall coarse grass which surrounded its base, we picked up specimens of grass covered with delicate crystals of the yellowish earth, and reminding one in everything but their color, of the appearance of the foliage on the morning after a sharp frost.

A few yards from the mound stands the hotel, a modest two-story frame building, with a neat, well-carpeted parlor, dining room, and clean comfortable beds upstairs, which we were invited to inspect. Close by are the bathing rooms, nicely and comfortably carpeted, and fitted up with all the articles necessary for a splendid bath in hot sulphur-water, right straight from the bowels of the earth. Here you can bathe in, drink and smell sulphur-water to your heart's content, and if not disposed to be exclusive in your enjoyment (a thing not looked upon with much toleration in this Western country), you can go a few steps farther and enjoy a *dip* in the public bathing-tank, large enough to enable you to exercise yourself at swimming, provided it is not too full of swimmers. The water even here, so far from where it issues from the earth, is so warm that at the first plunge one is reminded forcibly of what must be the sensation of the poor lobster when man "goes for him" as an article of diet.

Sam drove me home slowly, whilst the rest went at a more rapid pace, for Sam is an inveterate sportsman. I had my gun, and there were ponds he said along the road where ducks were in the habit of resorting about sundown. We found them where he said; three were brought down, and then, after a good deal of hard work with long poles abstracted from a farmer's fence close by, were brought out of the deep miry slough into which they had fallen, and we drove into Deer Lodge long after dark, and too late to keep an appointment we had made to sup in camp with a hospitable engineering party, but not too late to enjoy some of the good cheer set out on a long table in the open air, and afterwards the merry song and witty story around the bright camp-fire, which carried us back to many a similar scene in times not very long passed, when not quite so much boisterous noise was allowed "after taps."

I thought I had seen a wonderful thing in the Hot Spring Mound, and so I did, but the next day was destined to show me a still more wonderful one. I had heard of a Warm Spring Creek, which had a pretty fall, where all sorts of "*petrifactions*" were to be found, and near which any quantity of elk, bear, and especially black grouse were waiting at all times to be shot. I did not care so much for the petrifactions. I have shot elk, though never a bear, and as "Mac" of our party says, have never *lost* one, but black grouse is my weakness, and I would travel a good way to find a flock.

The black, blue, dusky, or mountain grouse (for by all of these names it is known), is the most beautiful bird of the country, and moreover, is the most delicious for eating. It is larger than the Eastern pheasant, or partridge, its plumage of a deep slate-blue color, and its flesh as white and delicate as that of a spring chicken, whilst its body is as round and plump as an apple. It frequents only the highest mountain regions, where it lives amongst the pines, and is therefore very little known by sportsmen or others, and seldom seen unless sought for in its haunts. There, if found on the ground and disturbed, it flies at once to the trees, and sitting perfectly motionless, is difficult to distinguish from the bark and foliage of its roosting-place. Gregarious, like most of its kind, when you find one you are apt to find many, and unused as it is to the sound of a gun, the flock will sit still as if asleep on the trees, whilst you shoot down one after another from the boughs above your head.

The morning of the 3d of October was bright and beautiful, and an early hour found me driving down the fine valley of the Deer Lodge, with Sam as my guide, towards the Warm Spring Creek. Others of the party, preferring their beds, did not rise so early, but were to join us later in the day. Ten miles brought us to the mouth of the Little Blackfoot, where locating our camp, we crossed some rolling hills and reached Mr. P.'s ranche on the Warm Spring Creek. Here, mounting our horses, we rode up a pretty little valley along a fine bold stream, which came tumbling down from the mountains seen ahead, covered to their tops with dense pine timber.

Two miles brought us to the falls, but as on first sight they did not appear to be anything very remarkable, we pushed on above them, rifles in hand ready for the elk or bear, which we expected to make their appearance every moment.

The bottom of the valley was filled with a dense growth of elder, choke-cherry, and service ("Sarvice") berry, which were broken and twisted in every direction by the bears in search of the fruit. But not a berry was to be seen, and the bears having evidently exhausted the supply, had gone to other scenes for food and we saw none, nor did we see any elk. We had now reached as far as we could go with our horses, and had begun to despair of seeing anything to shoot, when with a loud "whir," a flock of grouse rose before the dogs, and took refuge in the trees which covered the steep mountain-sides above us.

Our rifles were at once exchanged for shotguns, and climbing the steep and rocky ground, we soon were all peering as anxiously amongst the limbs above us, as were the train of teamsters on the oak and pine clad hills of Cerro Gordo when, during the Mexican war, they happened to see the celebrated Herr Alexander stop in his buggy, and, as if unmindful of their presence, pick half a dozen fine oranges from the boughs of an *oak* tree above his head.

But we were more successful in our search for grouse than were the teamsters after oranges, and soon the silent woods re-echoed with the sound of our guns, and bird after bird fell to the ground, the stupid things sitting there all the time to be shot, as if they had no possible interest in the turmoil going on beneath them.

You may call it murder if you will, and so in sportsman's phrase it was, but we were in the condition of the boy who, being in chase of a badger, was asked if he thought he could catch it. His reply was, "Stranger, I am obleeged to catch him; *we are out of meat.*"

We were *out of meat,* but that night our larder was reinforced by nineteen fine, fat, plump grouse.

As the day was drawing to a close we started down the valley again, and reaching the falls, curiosity prompted me to stop and examine them, and richly was I repaid for the delay. I find it difficult to describe the remarkable freak of nature which was presented to us.

Imagine a narrow valley overgrown with tall grass and brushwood, and shut in by high hills, covered from foot to peak with dense pine timber. Suddenly the bottom of this valley rises 30 or 40 feet above itself, the dividing line being a precipice of that height extending all across. This precipice is, however, abrupt only in one place, the centre, where the descent of the main body of water has worn a passage for itself, and at the same time excavated a great cave. On each side of this cave, and extending back to the sides of the valley, the ascent from the lower to the upper level appears to be by successive steps or terraces, all, however, so overgrown with tall grass and brushwood, as to nearly hide the formation at a short distance.

On nearer approach the ground appeared to be quite marshy, and full of water. Stepping, as I thought, upon a soft mossy prominence, I was surprised to find my foot upon a solid rock, though covered with moss and grass, with water trickling through. Another step and then another, and I found myself standing upon a narrow ledge of solid rock, nearly circular in shape, and forming the rim of a basin filled with bright clear water, which trickled over the edge, here and there, where there were depressions. Picking my way carefully along this narrow rim, scarcely wider than the sole of my boot, and in danger every moment of either stepping off into the water to my left, or of falling off into another basin to my right, but on a lower level. I reached a point where the rim of my basin ended in a perpendicular wall, from eighteen inches to two feet high. Here on a higher level commenced the rim of another basin, upon which stepping, I continued my walk, meeting basin after basin, and rising step by step until I had nearly reached the top. The basins are of all sizes, nearly semicircular in form, most of them filled with water, which was constantly filling the lower ones, through depressions in the rims of those above, and all filled with grass, weeds, water plants, and bushes, soil enough having accumulated in the bottoms of the basin to support, with the plentiful supply of water, the vegetation.

Picking my way partly down the steps again and passing around to the right, I found the terraces there came to an end, and a beautiful green grotto opened itself to my view. The main body of water, after breaking its way through the upright wall and forming the cascade, had, from the accumulation of debris in front, been forced back towards the wall, into the face of which it had worn so as to form a great cave, the top edge of which, at the upper level of the valley, projected far to the front, and was covered with a rank growth of bushes, grass, flowers, and vines of different kinds, the last hanging down over the edge, and the whole surface covered with a layer of deep-green moss. A portion of the water, distributing itself over the level space above, had found its way to the edge of the cave, percolated through the grass, mosses and vines, and from every pendant leaf, twig, and tendril, trickled a tiny stream, the whole forming as beautiful, wild, and natural a cascade as I ever saw.

Passing across the face of the cave and to the other side of the valley, I found the same terraced formation there, many of the basins, however, being dry, the water having ceased to flow into them, probably where the main body broke its way through the wall.

This remarkable formation was so regular, beautiful, and novel, that the question at once arose, how was it brought about? In looking for the so-called petrifactions amongst the masses of rock thrown down by the main waterfall, we found branches of trees, twigs, and leaves encased in a hard covering of rock, in some places as smooth and hard as flint. These then were probably the nuclei on which the substance in the water (probably carbonate of lime) had originally formed, and a beaver dam, formed of twigs and bushes, might possibly have, in the first instance, furnished the basis of the stone one, the upper side being filled in to a level by the washings from the mountains.

But how were the basins formed? They were evidently not washed *out* from the rock, for in that case the rims would have been irregular and broken, instead of being, as we found them, perfectly level and comparatively smooth. The horizontal edge could have been formed only from water in a state of rest. Hence, our conclusion was, that a rill of water, falling against some projection, stick, or nucleus of some kind, commenced to deposit there its sediment. This continued until the formation reached such a height that a little pool of water was formed behind, and then the still water would naturally deposit its solid matter more readily on the edge, where it was slowly forming over the obstruction it had itself raised, and this went on, little by little, until it finally shut itself in its little basin, and then running over at separate points, it went on building up basin after basin, until the whole structure was formed as we found it.[1]

We gazed long and admiringly at the beautiful scene, which we named "The Terrace Falls," and my fingers fairly itched to go to work, clear away the dead tangled brushwood and rank weeds, which here and there obstruct the view, plant beautiful flowers, water-plants, lilies, etc., stock each bright little basin with gold and silver fishes, and present the whole to Central Park, as a natural aquarium from the Rocky Mountains. What a picture it would make there for admiring thousands to gaze at! But here it is born to lush unseen, except by the few adventurous hunters who make their way to this retired spot. But even here we found that some enterprising Yankee had found his way, and speculating, doubtless, what a resort it would be at some future day when this country is filled up with the population it is destined some time to have, had stuck in the forks of a bush by the trail a piece of dirty paper, with this written upon it:

"Tak notis that I have this day settled on this *clame,* which I intend to improve and occupy accordin to law made and provided.
JAMES BROWN
September 17th, 1871."

---

[1]This formation is almost identical with that at the Mammoth Hot Spring, in the National Park, which I had not at this time seen.

That *clame,* in this Western country, with the addition of four logs laid crosswise on the ground to indicate the foundation of a ranche, stands good until some other more enterprising man comes along, tears down the "notis," puts up a ranche on the foundation logs and makes it his "home."

The water at the falls is at a pleasant tepid temperature, though a mile above, it is cool and pleasant to the taste, the warmth below being due to a hot spring which flows into it, and probably furnishes the materials out of which the walls of the basins are made. Below the falls the water grows gradually cooler, and as we rode back we could see good-sized trout darting in and out of the thick grass which grew upon the bottom.

Upon reaching Mr. P.'s ranche, Mrs. P., with true Western hospitality, insisted upon our sitting down to a good dinner she had prepared for us, and whilst we did justice to it she was induced by Sam to give us an account of an adventure she had had with a bear not long before, near the site of Terrace Falls.

It appears that she and her husband, who is a noted hunter in these parts and fond of collecting the young of wild animals, had gone up the creek in search of game. They encountered a bear and her young cub. The old one ran off, and Mr. P. soon succeeded in lassoing the youngster. Then, giving the end of the lasso to his wife, who was on horseback, he went with his rifle in search of the old one. The latter, attracted by the cries of her captured cub, hastened to its relief, escaped the hunter, but reached his wife and prepared to assert her maternal rights. But the impromptu nurse held her ground and the lasso, calling loudly for help, and as Mr. P. rushed back with his rifle, the bear, a large grizzly, beat a hasty retreat into the brush. Knowing how savage these animals are when their young is attacked, we could not restrain our admiration at the valor of the woman, and asked, "How near did the bear come to you?" "About the length of this room" (twenty feet) was the reply. "How did you keep her off?" "I just said '*Sic, sic,*' when she raised up on her hind legs, and she didn't come any nearer, and then my husband came and she ran away."

Fancy, if you can, such a scene in the midst of the wild Rocky Mountains. A woman on horseback holding a struggling cub by a rope, while its furious mother, indignant at such treatment of her child, and rushing frantically to its rescue, is paralyzed by—what? The utterance by a woman of the first syllable of the proud boast of the mother of States as emblazoned on her escutcheon. This method of arresting a grizzly seemed to possess so many advantages over that pursued by Marcy's naval officer in the early days of California, that we determined to try it the first tight place we got into with one, if for nothing else than to settle the question whether or not the sex of the defendant had anything to do with the matter.

It was long after dark before we reached our camp, where we found the rest of the party snugly ensconced and waiting dinner for us. They listened with interest to our enthusiastic description of the Terraced Falls, and in a grand council afterwards it was decided to "lay over" the next day and pay a second visit to them.

The next morning, early, found us on horseback, and striking across the country in a bee-line for the falls. We went over them again with increased delight, whilst the new visitors joined us in exclamations of wonder and astonishment at the singular formation.

As the hunters of the party were induced to make this second visit as much by the hope of game as by a desire of another view of the falls, they continued their trip up the stream, and just where they found the birds the day before, came across another flock of blue grouse. Bang, bang, went the guns and down came the beautiful birds in quick succession.

The mountain-side was exceedingly steep, and climbing difficult and exhausting in the rarefied atmosphere. Whilst leaning against a tree, panting for breath and almost decided to go no higher, I happened to raise my eyes to the branches above, and there only a few feet from me sat a fine large grouse apparently unconscious of my presence. He soon dropped at my feet and further examination disclosed the presence of another, another, and another, until the trees seemed literally filled with them. I loaded and fired as quickly as a breechloader permits, and soon had half a dozen or more fluttering at my feet or rolling down the steep mountain-side.

The birds seemed to be sitting as if half asleep, and if so, were probably resting from some migratory flight and dreaming of other flights and fields of pasture. They appeared to be but little disturbed by the, to them, unusual sound of a gun, and it was some time before the survivors seemed to awaken to the fact that the locality was dangerous, and flew off to more peaceful parts.

By this time, however, I had bagged eleven, which, strung upon the back of one of the horses, gave him the appearance of a non-descript animal, half horse, half bird. "Daniel Boone," one of our party, coming up announced that he also had eleven. Now Daniel is an ambitious hunter, and nothing delights him so much as beating his fellow huntsmen in the number of his game, especially when any of them happen to stand higher than he does on Uncle Sam's register. It is the only way he has of revenging himself on their higher rank. If he can beat a captain he smiles. Beating a major or lieutenant colonel is sure to result in a succession of broad grins, with now and then a hearty laugh. But to beat a colonel is his highest ambition, and the announcement of his victory is sure to be followed by a series of yells worthy of wild Indians in their hour of triumph and glory. Knowing his weakness we set a little trap for him, into which he fell with charming simplicity.

During the rest of the hunt we separated, and it so happened that an orderly, who carried a bag containing all of Daniel's birds, accompanied me. After this I got but a single bird, which I placed in *his* bag and said nothing. He also had killed another.

On reaching camp we all assembled to witness the counting of the game. Daniel's bag was opened first, and one by one he counted out his birds until he came to the twelfth, when, seeing there was still another, he jumped to his feet and commenced uttering his yells of triumph. In vain I protested there was some mistake. He would listen to nothing, and we could hear nothing but his wild and victorious yells. At length, when he had nearly exhausted himself, I called for the man who had *his* bag.

Daniel interrupted himself in the midst of a yell as I asked the question,

"Smith, did not I kill a bird upon the side of the mountain?"

"Yes, sir."

"What did you do with it?"

And Daniel's face fell to twice its length, and he muttered to himself "sold" when the answer came,

"I put it in *Mr. Boone's* bag."

As the whole party had been summoned to witness Daniel's discomfiture, it was a long time before he heard the last of the joke, and frequent references were made, during the trip, to his ambition as a sportsman and his skill with the gun.

Our camp is near the site of one of the winter cantonments of Mullan's wagon-road party, exploring a road from Fort Benton, on the Missouri River, to Walla Walla, on the Columbia, and our route the next day led up the Little Blackfoot on that road to Blackfoot City, where, instead of crossing through Mullan's Pass, we turned northward, and crossing a very rough rocky country, covered in every direction with masses of timber, struck Captain Lewis's route near Lincoln Gulch, on the Big Blackfoot, undoubtedly the stream referred to by Captain Lewis as the one called by the Indians the Cokalahishkit, or the "River of the Road to the Buffaloes." After a visit to the somewhat dilapidated mining camp of Lincoln Gulch, we followed up this stream and encamped, in a dismal drizzling rain, just where the stream came out of the mountains.

Beyond this we could not take our wheels into the mountains, and during the evening prepared to continue the trip with pack-mules, sending our vehicles around by the road, to cross the mountains and meet us at the Dearborn River on the other side.

The morning of the 8th of October opened upon us in a sufficiently discouraging way. The ground was covered with a heavy fall of snow, and it was still coming down in a way which bid fair to make our trip across the summit a disagreeable one, even if it did not put an end to it altogether. But it was no time for hesitation, for if the storm should prove a severe one we might be detained here a week, snowed in in the mountains. Preparations were therefore at once made for our departure, and in the midst of the heavily falling snow we bade good-by to our wagons, and with horses and pack-mules started up the trail towards the mountains. Being now on the route of Captain Lewis, every foot of the way is of especial interest, and the journal is consulted at every step. We look around us in the "Prairie of the Knobs," so named by him "from the multitudes of knobs irregularly scattered through this country," but look in vain for the quantities of game which he reports as existing there. "We saw," he says, "goats, deer, great numbers of the burrowing squirrels, some curlew, bee-martins, woodpeckers, plover, robins, doves, ravens, hawks, ducks, a variety of sparrows, and yesterday (July 5th) observed swans on Werner's Creek." Now we see none of these, and perhaps no fact speaks more plainly of the advance made in the settlement of the country, than that a region which sixty-five years ago was teeming with game of all kinds is now a solitary wilderness. Not a living thing except ourselves is to be seen, and as we move along through the white waste, we brush from the heavily loaded limbs overhanging the long-unused trail the masses of snow which have accumulated there. There is very little wind, but the silently falling snow is very wet, and as it grows colder we begin to feel wet, chilly, and disagreeable, and finally halt to build a fire, around which we all gather for warmth. When we resume the march, however, and commence to climb the long steep hill which leads to the summit, having previously left Lewis's trail and kept to the right on that of "The Road to the Buffaloes," we begin to feel the wind, which was sweeping as usual fiercely over the tops of the mountains. When at length we reached the summit, it was to find the trail totally obliterated by the deep snow, which was piled up in drifts by the heavy winds. We were in the midst of a howling storm, on the top of the Rocky Mountains, with no guide who knew anything of the features of the country, and no way to get out of it but by following a trail we could not see, except here and there where the snow was blown off of it. Our horses would not face the fierce gale and blinding clouds of snow, and we hunted for some time before discovering where the trail led down the mountain. When we at length found it, however, the marks upon the trees aided us in following it in spite of the snow, and being now protected by both the timber and the mountains from the storm we made very good progress, until we formed our bivouac high up on the eastern slope, with the design of having a hunt in the morning. Our camp was but a sorry one in the midst of the wet snow, and we had no shelter but a wagon-sheet pitched as a tent; but we put it up in a little grove of timber, and a roaring fire soon gave us all the comfort we could reasonably expect under the circumstances, and we slept the sleep of tired travellers. The next morning the storm had considerably abated, and with our rifles we started out early in search of game. But we soon became aware that the hunting days of Lewis and Clark were past, for after climbing over miles of the rough mountain spurs without seeing so much as a single deer, we returned to camp, packed up and resumed our trip eastward down the mountains. Our guide, as we issued from the foot-hills, announced that this was the modern Cadotte's Pass, and as we got farther away from the mountains, the landmarks around the entrance of Lewis and Clark's Pass, explored in the preceding summer, were distinctly recognized at about three miles to the north of us; so that we had demonstrated not only the existence of *two* passes close together, but that they were the two described by Lewis, and named by him "Lewis and Clark's Pass," and "The Road to the Buffaloes." We had a rough tedious ride after leaving the mountains, and it was long after dark before we reached a ranche, on the banks of the Dearborn River, where our vehicles were to meet us. Our pack-mules got separated from us in the darkness, and we were very glad to accept the hospitality of the ranche-man, eat his food and sleep on the floor in front of his blazing fire. The next morning our packs rejoined us, our wagons and buggies made their appearance, and jumping into the latter we in a few hours drove rapidly over the thirty miles which separated us from Fort Shaw.

Passing from one side of the Rocky Mountains to the other, nothing strikes the traveller more forcibly than the contrast between the scenery on the two sides. On the east, after you leave the mountains, there is a total absence of timber, except close alongside the few streams which water the country, and the high rolling prairie lands commence to assume those features characteristic of the "prairie country" west of the Missouri River. From the top of the *divide,* the country looks anything but like a prairie, for it is *broken up* and *washed out* into an infinite variety of hills and dales, bluffs and bottom lands, and these appear to spread out before you as you advance, into an almost endless succession. But as you overlook the country and notice the prominent points in it, you will observe that whilst some of these have evidently been projected *up* from the general surface, like "Bird Tail Rock" and the adjacent peaks, others bear such a relation to each other, that there can be no doubt they have been left standing after all the rest of the country has been *washed out.* Cast your eye along the tops of the prominent peaks in front of you, and observe how nearly the formation and general level agree with each other, and if, in your *mind's eye,* you can manage to shut out the intervening valleys, you cannot fail to trace the general outline of that vast slope, which, before the deluge of water came to wash out its valleys, stretched eastward from the mountains like the great glacis of a fort. When you descend into this region too, you will note in detail the action of the water which in times past has swept over this country with a force which only the hardest and most enduring of rocks could resist. Standing upon the parade ground at Fort Shaw, situated in one of these washed-out valleys, you can trace in profile on the opposite side of the river the long slope, extending from the snow mountains in the west, and gradually declining out of sight to the eastward, whilst if you examine the ground under your feet, where it is exposed on the bank of the river, you will find that, low down, it is composed of large rounded boulders, which become smaller and smaller as you approach the surface, until near the surface you find nothing but pebbles and gravel surrounded by loose soil. Now, if you turn your eyes to the southward, you will notice a line of rugged bluffs, which mark the continuation of the long slope on the other side of the river, and turning still farther to the south, the top of Crown Butte (Lewis and Clark's Fort Mountain), is seen to continue the marking of the general surface in that direction. Ascend these bluffs anywhere, and when you reach the top you will see that the general surface of all is the same, and that the heights are merely the remnants of a former level left standing. The work of demolition is still going on, but now very slowly, for the steep ledge of hard granite near the top, is succeeded by a long slope of disintegrated rock extending to the valley below. This is yearly increased, but the rains of spring and frosts of winter work more gradually than the heavy deluges of water, which in former times swept torrent-like across the face of the country.

Turning now to the western slope, we find an entirely different state of affairs existing. There, instead of the total absence of timber, as on the eastern slope, the whole broken surface of the country is covered with a dense growth of timber, mostly pine. This probably is accounted for by the fact that the western winds, laden with moisture from the Pacific Ocean, are deprived of most of it as they pass over the high mountain ranges intervening, and after crossing the main divide, they sweep over the slope to the eastward as the dry winds so characteristic of this region. Trees will grow on the eastern slope, if only they are supplied with the requisite moisture, as has already been satisfactorily demonstrated. This is the case not only with trees, but with all sorts of grasses, all the small grains, and most of the common vegetables, and the so-called "bench lands" of the territory are destined to play an important part hereafter in agricultural products. Indian corn does not grow well, the nights are too cold, and in only a few favored localities will it mature. But the product of small grains is astonishingly large, and the flour produced from the wheat grown here makes the sweetest bread I ever tasted, although not so white as that made with Eastern flour. Vegetables, more especially roots, grow to a remarkable size, and even in soil strongly impregnated with alkali, the finest specimens of beets, turnips, carrots, etc., are produced.

These "bench lands" form a distinguishing feature of the landscape in this country, especially in the mountain valleys, where several of them are frequently found rising one above the other, forming well-marked terraces. I have often speculated as to the manner in which they were originally formed, and was much interested lately in an account of a lecture delivered by Professor Tyndall descriptive of the so-called "parallel roads of Glen Roy," in Scotland, the description of which agrees perfectly with that of the "bench lands" of this region, except that the former are much narrower, varying from one to twenty yards. They are described as "three perfectly horizontal and parallel roads, directly opposite on each side, those on one side corresponding exactly in elevation to those on the other." It is somewhat remarkable that their perfectly horizontal position should not at once have suggested water in a state of rest as the cause of their origin, but with the characteristic tendency of the popular mind to assign *any but a natural cause* for such formations, they were at first supposed "to have been made for the heroes whose deeds have been sung by Ossian," and then that "they were designed for the chase, and were made after the spots were cleared in lines from wood, in order to tempt the animals in the open paths after they were roused, in order that they might come within reach of the bowmen, who might conceal themselves in the woods above and below!" The next supposition was that they were made for irrigating purposes, but any one who reflects upon the nature of water to seek its own level, and that irrigating ditches must have a certain inclination, would find this supposition incompatible with the horizontal position of the "roads." It remained for science, in the person of Dr. MacCulloch, to suggest that these "roads" were the borders of ancient lakes, whose waters were in some way held for a long time at the several levels, to enable the washings from the surrounding hills to form the level benches in the edges of the still water. The facts in the case were afterwards brought forward by Sir Thomas Dick Lander, whose explanation could not yet be accepted for the want of a demonstration regarding the barriers necessary to hold the waters at those levels, the action of ancient glaciers not then being understood, and it remained for the great Agassiz, who had studied glacier action in his native Switzerland, to discover the marks of such action in Great Britain, and to pronounce, after a visit to Glen Roy, that the barriers which had obstructed the glens were glaciers. This ascription of glacier action attracted the attention of Professor Tyndall, who made a visit to the Glen, in 1867, and was so perfectly satisfied with the evidences of the action of ice and water, that he says: "The theory which ascribes the parallel roads to lakes dammed by barriers of ice has, in my opinion, an amount of probability on its side which amounts to a practical demonstration of its truth."

There can, I think, be no question that the "bench lands" of this region are the result of similar action, and it only remains for science to demonstrate the existence of the remains of glaciers, some traces of which have already been observed at the outlets of the valleys, to render the demonstration perfectly conclusive.

# Rambles in the Rocky Mountains and The Wonders of the Yellowstone

*The next selection is John Gibbon's account of his trip to Yellowstone National Park in August of 1872, five months after the region was preserved for the American people by an act of Congress. The following May, while serving as head of the army's recruiting service in New York City, Colonel Gibbon presented an address, entitled "The Wonders of the Yellowstone," to the American Geographical Society of New York. In April of 1876, while the colonel was in the midst of the Sioux Campaign of that year, his article "Rambles in the Rocky Mountains" appeared in the* American Catholic Quarterly Review. *The article, which was concluded in the July issue, offered far more detail of the journey than did his address to the Geographical Society, although the latter did include a few additional anecdotes of interest. In order to provide a single narrative without duplication, a few items from his address have been edited into the body of the* Quarterly Review *article.*

*Gibbon's party followed the standard circuit through the park, admiring in turn each of the natural wonders, several of which left the colonel groping for words to describe their beauty. While trout were plentiful in the Yellowstone Lake and the various rivers and grouse were abundant, Gibbon did express regret that a single deer was the only big game encountered. This circumstance he attributed to the season, although the real reason may have been that the animal population had already been decimated by overzealous hunters. The Yellowstone region had been dubbed "Wonderland" by those who had seen its beauties, but the area was still a wilderness in 1872, as the colonel's party discovered when it ran short of supplies. The Gibbon River, which flows through Yellowstone Park, and Gibbon Falls were named for Colonel John Gibbon.*

*"The Wonders of the Yellowstone" appeared in* Journal of the American Geographical Society of New York *5 (May 1873): 112–137. "Rambles in the Rocky Mountains" appeared in* American Catholic Quarterly Review *1 (April 1876): 312–336 and (July 1876): 455–475.*

*N*early three-quarters of a century ago Captains Lewis and Clark of the United States Army made their remarkable explorations through the Rocky Mountains, and published an account which, to schoolboys of their day, vied in interest with Robinson Crusoe, at the same time that it possessed the charm of being fact instead of fiction.

These bold explorers, passing through an immense tract of country where no white man had ever been before, encountered, on their way up the Missouri River, the Great Falls. Making a portage around these of about twenty miles, they continued their way up the main stream in a southerly direction for over a hundred miles, when they came to what is still called "The Three Forks."

The branch coming from the west was named the *Jefferson*. It being a little the largest of the three, and bearing more nearly in the direction the explorers desired to travel in order to cross the main divide of the continent, they followed it to near its source in the main range of the Rocky Mountains, where the stream was so small that one of the party placed himself with a foot on each side, and "thanked God he had lived to see the day when he could bestride the great Missouri."

The middle fork was named the *Madison*, and flows directly north from its source away off in the snowy range to the south. The original explorers little dreamed of the wonders to be found around its head-waters, where is situated the Great Geyser Basin of the West. Had any rumors of the magnificent spouting geysers to be seen there reached them, Captain Clark on his return trip would probably have proceeded up the Madison instead of choosing the third of the three forks for his exploration.

The third or eastern fork was called the *Gallatin*, and takes its rise to the south and east in ranges of high mountains not forming a part of the continental divide. Up this fork Captain Clark, in the summer of 1804, when returning from the mouth of the Columbia, took his way, and, after passing through one of the most magnificent valleys of the whole West, reached its head near the present site of the military post of Fort Ellis. The post guards several passes leading to the eastward through the range of mountains, which separates the waters of the Gallatin from those of the Yellowstone. Through one of these passes, under the guidance of a friendly Indian squaw, Captain Clark reached the Yellowstone; and constructing boats from the timber on its banks, he proceeded down the river to its mouth, unwittingly turning his back upon the great wonders of the Yellowstone, some account of which I propose to give.

On a warm pleasant morning in July, 1872, a party of nine persons on horseback wound its way out of Fort Ellis and over the rolling hills behind towards a deep cañon, through which dashes one of the bright forks of the East Gallatin. Preceding the party were three or four pack-mules loaded down with bedding and buffalo robes, hard tack and bacon, pots, kettles, and pans for the trip. One of these mules was strongly suspected of having served for a long time in the army, for he had not gone far from the post before he began to play "old soldier," and very quietly laid down in the road, refusing to rise until a part of his load was removed and placed upon the back of one of his stronger or more willing companions, furnishing thus another evidence of the truth of Darwinian theory that the lower animals are governed by the same feelings and principles as the more recent and, in some cases, the nobler development.

Through a wild deep gorge up into the rolling hills beyond, the party pursues its way, stopping now and then to adjust a pack, to allow the animals to nibble the fresh green grass which lines the road, or to drink from the clear ice-cold streams through which the wily trout is seen to dart at every step.

Bright green slopes dotted with flowers rise in succession before us. At length we reach the last one; the waters run the other way, and before us lies the broad beautiful valley of the Yellowstone, partially hidden by intervening hills, and bounded on the east by mountain peaks towering to the skies, floating clouds about their tops, and great snow-drifts extending far down the gorges in their sides.

We follow down a beautiful little valley, leave it where it turns towards the Yellowstone, and, rising a gentle slope to our right, reach the top of a commanding ridge, from which we have an unobstructed view of the Yellowstone River and its valley. It stretches far up to the mountains on our right, and away off to our left enters the gorge of what is called the first or lower cañon. Opposite to us the land rises in successive terraces or "benches," showing where, in long ages past, existed the shores of a great inland lake, which, fed by the streams above, remained at the level of these "benches," until the river, thundering through the gorge below, wore for itself a lower passage-way. Then the waters, draining out, lowered the level of the lake, which there remained until another break in the cañon below took place; the rains and snows of season after season in the meantime bringing down from the mountains around the disintegrated rock and vegetable matter to form in the edges of the lake these level benches; and so on until the cañon was worn down to the bottom of the lake, when the river cut out a channel for itself at the lowest level, and left these benches to tell us how they were formed.

On these level benches great herds of cattle are feeding on the luxurious "bunch" grass which covers them. Here they can live and fatten all the year round, save only in those exceptional winters when snow falls to a great depth and lies for a long time on the ground. The sight of these cattle reminds us of civilization; we take a good look at them; for it is about the last of such signs we shall see for some time to come.

We reach the bank of the Yellowstone just as the sun is sinking behind the high mountain peaks in our rear, forming long bands of bright sunlight and dark shadows across the valley. Our bivouac is formed beneath a wide-spreading cottonwood, and whilst the mules are being unpacked our rods are brought out, and, before the cook is ready for them, we have wriggling upon the grass around our camp-fire, enough fine brook trout to supply the whole party with a hearty supper.

No one but a man who has ridden for twenty-five or thirty miles through a new and interesting country, can appreciate the appetites with which those trout, fresh from the cold waters of the Yellowstone, were enjoyed, nor the sound sleep which followed our feast.

We slept as tops are proverbially said to sleep, breathing the pure air of heaven, with no canopy but the star-bedecked sky; and opened our eyes to greet the smiling sun as he came up over the tops of the mountains the next morning. Remember this was the last day of July, we were in sight of perpetual snow, the night was cool, we were covered with blankets and buffalo robes, and you who were sweltering in the heat of the East, may be able to fancy how we did sleep.

Our route the next day led us directly up the valley of the Yellowstone, growing narrower and more narrow as we approached the place where the river leaves the mountains. At times the trail, a well-marked wagon-road, led directly along the bank of the river, still unusually high for this season of the year; its peculiar light-green waters being tinged with mud. Now and then the stream was divided by wooded islands; and in places where from the formation of eddies the water had a chance to settle and become comparatively clear, great trout could be seen lying lazily in the water with heads up stream, or dashing suddenly to the surface to capture some imprudent fly, which, unmindful of the many sharp eyes on the watch for him, would venture too near the surface. In other places our route would lead us across the flat prairie bottom far back from the river-bank, where occasionally would lie a great tree-trunk, devoid of limbs and rubbed smooth, showing how at times during the spring freshets, the water extended back so as to cover all but the highest points.

We passed several ranches with little patches of cultivated gardens flourishing with potatoes, onions, tomatoes, and other vegetables, and at one of them two or three little tow-headed children appeared on the door-step, to look with open-eyed wonder at the unusual sight of a party of white men.

Suddenly a fence appears, and enclosed by it a wide field of luxuriant grain. We cross the irrigating ditches leading from the hills, and from which this field obtains its moisture, and approach a house nestling in a beautiful little nook in the hills, surrounded by a grove of trees, and with a clear stream alongside. This is Boettler's ranche, with one exception the most advanced of the settlements in the valley. Here is kept a post-office; and letters and papers are mixed up with milk pans, cups, and butter dishes. For Boettler's is a dairy ranche, and one portion of it is literally filled with pans full of rich cream-covered milk, from which we are invited to drink with true Western hospitality. The noisy brook as it tumbles down from the hills has been led into a trough, and rendered still more noisy by being made to turn a wheel attached, with Yankee ingenuity, to a churn, where butter for the Bozeman market, some forty miles away, is made. It costs nothing to keep the cows, which roam at will over the broad rich bottom land or crop the sweet bunch grass on the foot-hills.

We turned our backs upon Boettler's thrifty homelike ranche, and continued up the river towards the second cañon. The mountains now come down close to the river-bank, and in one place we have to cross a steep spur along which the trail, still a wagon-road, runs, with the great river roaring as it rushes along, far below and almost under our feet.

Away off to the south, on the other side of the river, "Emigrant Peak" thrusts its top up into the clear atmosphere, its sides covered here and there with perpetual snow, which glistens in the warm sun, and makes one feel cooler by looking at it. These patches are formed of perpetual snow, because before this warm August sun will have reduced them to water, another layer will be deposited on their smooth, shining surfaces, and long before any falls in the deep gorge at the base of the peak upon the miners who pursue there the search for gold.

We pursue our way up the river—here swiftly flowing past, there quietly winding its way along—its smooth, clear surface broken only occasionally by the leap of a great golden-yellow trout, springing at some imprudent fly whose fluttering wings carry him too close to the glassy surface, beneath which thousands of bright and eager eyes are watching for just such fellows as he.

We are now approaching the second cañon of the Yellowstone, and after crossing two deep rapid mountain torrents, turn to the left, and leaving the wagon-tracks, which terminate here, follow a narrow trail into the mountains. At the very mouth of the gorge stands a great rock, a hundred feet high or more, and as we pass along at its foot, its face towards the cañon is seen to be worn as smooth almost as glass, with here and there deep furrows. This is a relic of the far-distant past, standing here like some old sentinel of the guards, to speak with his seams and scars of the battles he has passed through. As it cannot, like the old soldier, shoulder a crutch and tell how fields were won, we shall have to do it instead, and fancy the time when this immense gorge in front of us was filled to the top perhaps with a mass of ice, rock, sand, and rubbish slowly pushing its way down to the sea. This great glacier encounters here in its path the solid obstacle. Against it the mass crushes and grinds; other masses come behind, driving the forward portions ahead, and trying to open a way to the sea. Bravely the old sentinel stands his ground, whilst high up upon his front the rocky, icy mass is piled, and goes grinding, crushing across his face towards the narrow gorge at his side, down which it finally makes its way, flanking the obstacle, but leaving upon its face ample records of the struggle to tell to future ages the battles of the past.

Passing the "old sentinel" our way becomes more and more contracted; shut in by high hills on the right, by immense mountain peaks on the left, with the river dashing along at their feet. Right before us rises a steep wall of rock, seemingly barring our further progress; but wild animals have been here before us, and tame ones too; for far up along the steep hill somebody has evidently been trying to cut a road. We pick our way carefully among the rocks and along the narrow path, dismounting here and there where the route is steeper or more difficult than usual.

At length we reach the top, and gaze with silent wonder at the grand view before us. Still towering above our heads the hills on our right are covered with timber, whilst on the left the far higher, rugged, rocky peaks are devoid of all foliage except a few scraggly pines, their rough, rugged sides seamed here and there with long smooth slopes of disintegrated rock, down which an enterprising schoolboy might "coast" in winter-time for a thousand feet or more; though how he would get to the top to commence his operations is his business, not ours. Directly before us lies a peaceful little green valley crossed by sparkling streams, beyond which rises another wall of rocks, narrowing the valley until there is just room enough left for the rider to make its way. On the left, and almost beneath our feet, rushes the river, here of a bright sea-green color, there churned into a milk-white foam, where the channel is still further contracted by great masses of rock which have toppled from the crags above. Beyond, far up through the gorge, the country widens out into a green valley covered with trees, through which the Yellowstone is quietly flowing preparatory to its mad rush through the gorge below, whilst still further beyond, as far as the eye can reach, mountains rise above mountains to the skies.

From this enchanting spot we wind our way down into a pretty little cove in the midst of the cañon, where pure streams of clear, cold water, flowing across from springs at the foot of the wall, fall into the river. Beyond this, we encounter another rough, rocky point, extending down to the very shore of the river. Crossing this, we enter the narrowest part of the gorge, picking our way along the narrow path, between overhanging masses of rocks, sometimes crowded so close together as barely to allow room for the passage of a horse, much less a horseman. Many an exclamation of pain is uttered as shins come in contact with the sharp rocks, and one is tempted to echo the wish of the discontented individual who made the remark, that if *he* had had originally the making of man, he should have put the calf of the leg in front, where it would at least have been of some use. Here the slightest misstep would send one hurling into the raging caldron below.

After making the passage in safety, we halt to wait for the packs, eat a lunch, fish, and shoot young grouse, which are just now reaching a proper size. The packs get through for a wonder without being rubbed off more than once, and we push ahead again over dry arid hills to our camp by the side of a mountain torrent, by whose music we are lulled to sleep after a hearty supper on immense trout caught in the deep quiet pools.

The country is now becoming more broken and rougher than before. Dark, black, volcanic hills rise up in all directions around us, throwing up here and there a peak higher than the rest, in the gorges near the tops of which banks of snow appear, and from these come the ice-cold streams which cross our path at intervals. The disintegrating sides of some of these hills present a curious appearance, looking for all the world as if some great factory had been for ages dumping down on the slopes all their refuse coal and scoria. Some of the hills again present in places bright-red streaks suggestive of iron or cinnabar, and one of these is so strongly marked that it has been named "The Cinnabar Mountain." If it deserved its name it would prove a mine of wealth, and would ere this have been covered with "claims," but no valuable metal, I believe, has up to this time been discovered in the vicinity.

Our route to-day leads us along the foot of "Cinnabar Mountain"; when we reach its southern face the formation of the mountain is seen, and in one place presents a curious spectacle. Volcanic action has thrown up the layers of rocks until the strata stand almost vertical, outcropping towards the sky. In some places the outcropped edges have become disintegrated, and form slopes extending from the top of the mountain in curves to the bottom. This is especially marked in one place, where the disintegrated material of a deep-red color sweeps in a graceful curve for hundreds of feet down the side of the mountain. Of course, the softest material is disintegrating first and fastest. Where the rock is very hard the weather seems to have but little effect upon it. Hence results a remarkable formation, to which the name of "The Devil's Slide" has been given. Two great ledges of hard rock have been thrown up until they stand vertically across the length of the mountain. These ledges, some six or eight feet across, are distant from each other some three or four hundred feet. Between the two the softer material has been entirely washed out to a depth, in places, of some hundred feet, leaving these great bare walls standing like the ways of some immense shipyard. The immensity of the work done impresses one with the magnitude of the watery power which performed it, and the long period which must have elapsed since the forces ceased to act, is shown by the great trees now growing in the amphitheatre between the walls, and the still larger ones which lie decaying on the ground.

We turned our backs upon "The Devil's Slide," casting many a glance behind, supposing we were taking a last look, and little thinking that in a day or two some of us should see it again.

Our route now leads us over ranges of desolate barren hills till we strike the valley of Gardner's River, up which we turn to the right, following a plainly marked trail along its bank. But desolate as is the country in appearance, it contains a wonder, the life of which I doubt can be seen anywhere else upon the earth's surface. Other countries have their wonders—their earthquakes; their volcanoes, extinct and active; their hot springs; and their geysers. America alone, so far as I have heard, has her "frozen cascades"—falling waters turned literally to solid stone.

Six or eight miles from its mouth, Gardner's River is divided into three branches—the eastern, middle, and western; and to the north of the western fork occurs the wonder which in coming time will attract the visitors of the world. A valley some four miles long, and varying from two hundred yards to a mile and a half in breadth, is filled with a formation unique in itself, and, I suspect, without parallel in the world, unless possibly in New Zealand.

After travelling some five or six miles the trail grows suddenly fainter, and soon disappears entirely in the grass. The appearance of the country, several streams of warm water, which our horses refuse to drink, and the hollow sound given out by our horses' feet, assure us that the object of our search, the Hot Springs, cannot be far distant. All eyes are turned upon the ground searching for the trail. Someone looks up, and an exclamation of surprise arrests the attention of the whole party. Looking over to our right a great snow-white hill is seen looming up like an immense snowbank, surrounded by timbered mountains. We turn towards it and cross several smoking streams, where the yielding and hollow-sounding rocks under our horses' feet produce the disagreeable impression that it is barely possible we might break through and be swallowed up in some great caldron, or disappear we hardly knew where; but the smoking water suggests that the place might be uncomfortably warm.

As we proceed, however, we gain confidence and finally reach solid ground in a belt of tall timber, through which passes a trail with fresh horse-tracks upon it. This we follow, gradually rising until we reach an open and perfectly level plateau upon which, here and there, a great tree is growing, and bright-colored flowers are occasionally seen. To our left and in front of us high hills, covered with trees and grass, rise up from the plateau.

The dusty trail and some horses in a grove near by assure us we are nearing the end of our day's journey. Turning a point of the hill to our left, a magnificent but novel view bursts upon us. The valley, shut in by high hills, is, where we stand, only about two hundred yards across. It widens out farther up to as much as a mile and a half. As far as we can see, the whole valley above us is filled with a pure white marble-like structure, arranged in terraces, one of which stands some fifty or sixty feet in height, and is the snow-white hill we first noticed.

Directly before us stands a column sixty or seventy feet high, which from its form has been named "The Cap of Liberty." At its foot, and extending some distance beyond, is a structure which looks as if the giants of old had been laying a foundation of the purest white marble for some great edifice. The perfectly horizontal tiers rise one above the other like successive layers of masonry, and at a little distance each successive layer looks as if composed of stone on which the chisel of the sculptor has engraved the most exquisite forms. We stop and look in wonder, dismount, and walk through a substance which reminds one of walking on loose flour. Approaching a place where the substance is a little damp, we take up handfuls of it, and find it just like plaster of Paris, and moulding in the hand like putty.

A closer inspection shows that in the horizontal lines, which at a distance resembled layers of masonry, are the rims of basins formed by the deposition of material held in solution by the water. These basins are of all sizes, generally of semicircular form, and rise to a height determined by the level to which the water rises in each. If, from any cause, more water runs in, the deposition takes place most rapidly on the edge, where the water is stillest, building up the edge and keeping it always just above the surface of the water at all points, and hence always perfectly level. Where the water runs out of this basin another one is formed, and so on indefinitely. Any one can start a new basin to forming by breaking an opening in one of the old ones.

The formation, although solid enough to bear our weight, yields to the foot, and as we move about we destroy thousands of beautiful forms, which probably have been years in forming. At first a feeling of regret is experienced at the idea of such destruction, but this is soon removed by the reflection that thousands of new ones are forming every day, and in every direction, wherever the water runs. These basins rise, step by step, from the general level of the plateau to a height of six or eight feet, where a large oval basin of boiling hot water is found, the source of all the basins below. We are warned by the heated air and seeing the centre of the pool boiling up eighteen or twenty inches high, not to test the heat of the water with an imprudent hand.

But whilst we are waiting, looking at and admiring all these wonders, our poor animals are nearly eaten up by the great buck-flies, which swarm around them like bees. Teeth, tail, and feet are kept constantly at work, to beat them off; and now we begin to understand why it is that the drove of horses we have just passed are, on a warm day like this, crowded so closely together, trying each one to get in the centre of the herd, and rubbing against each other to drive away the innumerable pests.

In a pretty little valley close by, thickly shaded with trees, and with a stream of snow-water tumbling down through it, several rude cabins appear. Near these are a number of tents pitched, and farther back shelters of a ruder kind, pieces of canvas stretched over a ridge-pole, with perhaps one end closed by a blanket. These are all for the shelter of the invalids who come out to this modern Saratoga of the wilderness in search of that health which the use of these waters is said in the most marvellous manner to bring.

Men, women, children, and dogs rush out to greet the newcomers; and a shade of disappointment may be seen to pass over the faces of some when all of us leap lightly from our saddles, and none, in the last stages of disease, need to be helped off; so natural is it for "misery to love company."

We locate our bivouac higher up in this pretty little vale; and saddles, bridles, and packs are hastily stripped from our suffering animals, with the hope that by rolling or running they may gain some relief from the swarms of flies. We are soon assured by the oldest inhabitants of the place that there was absolutely no escape for the poor creatures, as they were tormented all day long by a constant succession of flies, and that animals sometimes *"stampeded"* under the infliction, and sought places lower down the river, where the flies were not so bad. To guard against losing our horses, it was proposed to picket them out, but we were assured this was certain death, as no picketed animal could defend himself against the swarms of flies, and we soon, by ocular proof, became satisfied of that fact and let our animals run loose. The poor creatures, maddened by their pests, which would settle like a swarm of bees on their withers as the safest spot, ran off to the hills, and we felt secure in the fact that they were tired by their day's journey, and probably would not go far.

The buck-flies did not trouble us so much as they did the horses; but swarms of mosquitoes, bred probably by the ponds of warm water, surrounded us, and we were glad after a lunch to move about and explore the vicinity of our novel position.

Our first visit was to the neighborhood of the "Cap of Liberty." This singular column we found on inquiry to be hollow. In ages past this open space was filled with the hot water of the springs from above, which, running over at the top, deposited the substance it held in solution, and built up the column now standing. In the course of time the water found an outlet at some lower level, and left the column standing to tell its own story as to how it was formed. The storms and frosts of many a winter have beaten against it, and decreased somewhat its dimensions, without much, if any, lessening its height. Not far off stands another column of smaller size, and, standing between the two, the rush of subterranean waters could be plainly heard. On the plateau, between the two columns, several bath-houses have been erected, and troughs from the main spring conduct the water into the bathing-tubs. We saw the first primitive bathing-tub which had been used. It consisted simply of a hole dug in the soft yielding material large enough for bathing, and into this the water, hot from the spring, was led by a trough hollowed out of the surface of the ground. Over the hole is pitched a tent, and this constitutes the bathing establishment.

Other more pretentious structures have since been erected, and these are now occupied by wooden bathing-tubs, to which the water is conducted in wooden troughs. Three or four of these bathing-houses are scattered over the plateau, and each one is supposed to possess some special health-giving qualities. Should you require parboiling for the rheumatism, take No. 1; if a less degree of heat will suit your disease, and you do not care to lose all your cuticle, take No. 2. Not being possessed of any chronic disease, and it being a warm afternoon, I chose for my ablutions the coolest bath to be found. A stream of what is called cool water was turned on, and I prepared for the bath with a feeling of satisfaction at the coming luxury. The feeling was, however, short-lived, and at the first plunge I thought I was so too, and uttered what must have sounded to outsiders like a dying warwhoop, for the water was almost scalding hot, and the sensation experienced somewhat akin to what may be imagined that of a lobster when being prepared for the table. What the *hot* baths would be I did not care to test, but for the benefit of future visitors I would suggest they go prepared with bathing dresses made of asbestos or some other heat-defying material. As I languidly sauntered back to camp I took a better look at the boiling caldron which supplies all this heated water. Thinking over my recent experience I could not help fancying what a splendid institution this would be for one of those hotels where all the provisions, beef, pork, mutton, wild turkey, tame turkey, venison, ducks, and potatoes taste as if boiled together in the same pot. On the edge of the pool, where the water is more shallow and cooler than elsewhere, a thin film of porcelain-like structure forms, looking like a thin layer of ice. As if in keeping with my idea regarding cookery, several pots, kettles, pans, and bottles were standing in this shallow part, imbedded through the sheet of ice. Had the water been cold it would naturally be supposed these vessels contained milk and other substances placed there to cool. As it was, we were informed they were filled with the yeast settlings of the visiting housekeepers, put there to rise.

Later in the afternoon, when it became cooler, we all sallied out on an exploring expedition to see wonders which we were informed were awaiting us higher up the valley. Taking a steep, well-worn path, we mounted to the plateau immediately behind that on which stands the "Cap of Liberty."

This plateau is evidently an old one, for the pure white of recent formation is replaced by a dull-brown, the surface is much disintegrated and worked down into a soil. Here and there large pine trees are growing, and patches of grass and flowers are scattered about. Now and then we pass a vent with hot steam hissing forth, and occasionally a hole is met with from which the gurgling sound of subterranean waters issues.

Right before us is the grandest spectacle of all. On the far side of the plateau rises the wall of the next one. Tiers of beautiful pure white basins rise one above the other to the height of sixty or seventy feet—the basins of all possible shapes and sizes. Most of these are filled with water in all states of temperature except cold. Some are cool enough to bear the insertion of the hand; others are still and covered with the thin ice-like film already referred to; whilst others are in an active state of ebullition, showing an underground connection with the hot springs above. In one spot the hill of basins juts out with bold prominence and steep sides, at the top of which a bold stream of smoking water comes tumbling over. In places where the flow of water was greatest it was observed that instead of forming basins, the materials were deposited in the form of a cascade; and as the deposition appears to be uniform when the water, from finding some other outlet, ceases to flow, it leaves what may be described as an exact white *plaster cast of rippling water*; and so perfect is the imitation that in a photograph of the scene the eye is unable to decide which is running water and which solid stone. Hence the name "Frozen Cascade." The general effect may be described by imagining a thousand small-sized Niagaras, placed alongside and above and beyond each other, suddenly turned by a magic wand into solid white marble.

As we pass along the foot of this bold point we reach a spot where the water has broken out anew, within a comparatively recent period, and with its deposit overwhelmed a grove of trees growing upon some more ancient formation. The dead and decaying limbs stick out above the surface of the still forming deposit to tell how they were over-whelmed.

Picking our way through this grove, and tramping through the shallow spread of water which is warm to the feet, we turn towards the hill and commence to climb up its steep face, using the edges of dried or partially dried up basins as stepping stones, and crushing under our feet at every movement the beautiful crystal-like structure. At every few steps we pause to enjoy the ever-changing and always novel view presented to us. Each new view appears more charming than the last, as it brings in sight more water, nearly every basin in this portion of the "cascade" being not only full but running over.

At length we reach the top, and stand at the same time upon the highest point of the terraced slope and on the edge of the corresponding plateau, the witnesses of a scene which it is thought few white men have ever enjoyed. The eye cannot take in with satisfaction at the same moment all the beauties presented, and, after gazing for a moment in silent wonder at the magnificent spectacle, I turn from the more beautiful part, as though desiring to leave that for the last, and picking my way along the very edge of the plateau, halt at a point where the whole hill is brought under the eye, and each successive white marble basin filled with bright blue water. The edges beautifully curved and scolloped stand out in relief, one beneath the other, down to the bottom of the hill; and then with a gentler slope the basins disappear in the grove of dead and dying trees at its foot. Such a sight amply compensates one for many a weary mile of travel, and yet it is not the finest we are to see. Turning around and stepping a few paces back from the edge of the plateau, we find ourselves standing upon the rim of an immense boiling

GETTING A SPECIMEN
Gibbon's party discovered that souvenirs from
Yellowstone's hot springs could be obtained only
by using a hammer on the formations. *Scribner's
Monthly Magazine*, May 1871.

TRAVELING IN THE YELLOWSTONE COUNTRY
In 1872 the Yellowstone National Park was a
virgin wilderness where fallen timber often
made passage virtually impossible. *Scribner's
Monthly Magazine*, February 1872.

caldron, some twenty feet across, or rather a series of caldrons, for there are several of them, divided by walls built up by themselves, through apertures in which the water flows off from one to the other.

The pool nearest to us is of a bright sky-blue color, and on the edge where it is still we look down into its clear depths to an unknown distance. We approach the edge with a cautious awe, for a false step or a weak spot in the rock would send one to certain death. Step by step we approach and peer over into the depths below. One naturally starts back in affright; for the rock, growing thinner and thinner as it approaches the edge of the water, projects over as it rises, and the water is so very clear and pure that we seem to be standing suspended in mid-air. Closer examination shows the rock perfectly solid and firm; and now, becoming bolder we proceed to a more minute inspection.

The projecting edge rests just at the surface of the water. The water apparently has reached its freezing-point, and is covered with a thin film of ice-like formation. You can write your name in the thin, brittle structure with your finger; but you will find the water beneath still warm. The formation looks like the most delicate film of porcelain, and is probably the same material of which the basins are formed. It is formed of beautifully undulating curves, and these are tipped with a series of pure porcelain-like pieces shaped like finger-nails. These are as hard as flint, as sharp on the outer edge as a knife, and so firmly attached to the rocky edge as to require a sharp blow with a hammer to detach them. This peculiar scolloped edge extends all around the pools.

Near by us is one of the partition-walls, through a break in which, highly colored with rich red and brown, the water flows into the neighboring pool, changing its blue tint into a rich brown or saffron. The color is not constant, but varies as the waters intermingle, so as to give almost every conceivable tint, and the variations are still further increased by the waters mingling with those of a third pool deeply tinged with yellow from the sulphur held in solution by the water which supplies that pool.

Now imagine all these pools boiling and bubbling in the centre, sending their little tiny waves surging to the edge, splashing up under the porcelain-scolloped edges, a white mist rising from the whole, the play of all these colors in a bright sunlight, and some faint conception may be formed of the sight.

Words are weak in any attempt to describe the picture, and the photograph makes no record of the colors, to which even the skillful painter's brush fails to do full justice. A most admirable picture of the scene I have attempted to describe has been painted by Moran, and was some time ago on exhibition at Shay's, on Broadway, New York. The same artist painted the view of the Great Falls of the Yellowstone, which was put up at the head of the Senate stairway in the Capitol. These falls we shall visit as we prolong our rambles in the Rocky Mountains.

We linger in admiration around these beautiful pools, noting the splendid play of the colors, and finding new beauties at every step. Apparently there is no living thing in the water, but where it runs off from the pools to dash itself into the basins beyond, there is deposited at the bottom of the channels a sort of vegetable substance, as fine and soft as silk, which clings to the rock, and waves back and forth in the rippling water like long feathery plumes. On these long plumes the water deposits a part of its coloring matter, and the effect as they sweep gracefully from side to side in the running water, flashing up their rainbow hues, is indescribably beautiful. All the way down the slope these colors can be traced, growing fainter and fainter as they near the bottom.

I am afraid if some of our lady friends could catch sight of these waving plumes they would get out of conceit with those which they now wear, for the former are far more handsome. Nature is always more beautiful and perfect in her works than man or woman. These variously tinted plumes are beautiful to look at as they wave gently back and forth in the rippling water. The moment they are taken from the water, all their beauty disappears as suddenly as the rainbow vanishes when the rain ceases to fall.

We turn our backs with regret upon this beautiful view, returning to it again and again afterwards, to gaze in wonder at a scene which changes and seems to present new charms at every new position of the eye, and at every new angle at which the sunlight strikes it.

We now climb terrace after terrace and reach plateau after plateau, all old, worn out, and disintegrated. Soil has been formed upon them, great trees are growing on them, and patches of grass and bright flowers are scattered about. This is the scene of the operation in former times of just such springs as those we have seen below, but now nothing more than a remnant of their working remains. Here a deep hole is encountered, up through which the sound of gurgling waters reach the ear; there a small vent through which hot steam issues forth.

Wandering along, we come suddenly upon a structure which at once arrests the attention. In the midst of a clump of large pine trees, and with some small dead ones imbedded in its surface, stands a rocky structure six or eight feet high, say twenty feet long and half as broad, looking like a great rough jelly-mould turned upside down. From the top and down the sides of this are running in every direction little streams of water, depositing their rocky material and building the mound still higher and broader, as they have been building it probably for thousands of years before Columbus told the world there was such a place as America. We climb upon the top of this oval-shaped mound, and find along the axis of its length a row of apertures of all sizes, from that of a quill to one of an inch in diameter, and from each one of these steam mingled with hot water is rushing forth with a noise which threatens to blow the whole structure to pieces. Each aperture is surrounded with delicate little porcelain finger-nails, beautifully colored; and the mingling of sounds produced by the hissing steam, has suggested the name which has been given to this singular spot, "The Beehive." An engine whistle placed over one of the vents of "The Beehive" might well impress the visitor with the idea that the iron horse had invaded these solitudes.

Our rambles at length brought us to the foot of a high steep bluff, covered with dense timber, where we were shown into a cave excavated by water trickling from above. We crawled down into it, enjoyed the cool atmosphere, lit a candle brought along for the purpose, and gazed in admiration at the thousands of stalactites and stalagmites which flashed back their rays to us. The formation of the rocky structure in which the cave was hollowed out was the same as that about the springs below. In fact the whole valley, four miles long and from two hundred yards to a mile and a half broad, is filled with the same material which abuts against the solid rocks of the hills at the sides.

Returning we walked for half a mile or more along the top of a ridge, stretching like an immense backbone over the plateau, and formed evidently by the water boiling up through the top and depositing its material from openings which we passed at every step. The waters have long since found some outlet at a lower level, leaving the former channels now empty. At one point we came to a wide opening, down which we looked into a great cave some twelve or fifteen feet deep, where countless bats, disturbed by the sticks and stones we threw down, flew from side to side in wild dismay at their solitude being so roughly invaded. The materials of which this great backbone is made are evidently identical with the hot springs deposit. They rest in layers, and the slightest break serves to show the manner in which the deposit was made. The rippling of running water is still there, but with none of the freshness of the recent formation lower down the valley. In fact nearly all this portion of the valley bears evidence of operations long since extinct. There was a little time, however, when the disintegrating masses around us presented all the fairy forms and brilliant colors seen to-day at a lower level. Now quite a soil has formed on top, and in this are imbedded the roots of lofty trees. Taking into account the incalculable length of time which must have elapsed to form this great deposit, layer by layer, of almost inappreciable thickness, like leaves of paper piled one on top of the other, the period, after the water ceased to flow, required by disintegration and other causes to produce the soil necessary to support vegetation, and after that the time for these trees to grow up, one may form some vague estimate by the thousands of years which have probably elapsed since the active powers were at work on the space where we are now standing. Here and there a faint trace, as if a mere draining of the former system, exists in the form of a little pool, out of which boils water strongly impregnated with mineral substances, dyeing with beautiful colors the little basins which it seems to form as naturally as the leaves form on a tree or flower.

The number of charming views, beautiful forms, novel structures, and curiosities of all kinds to be seen here, seems to be limited only by one's amount of physical endurance; for whichever way we turn something new and strange is sure to meet the eye. Weeks might be spent in exploration, and every hour furnish a new wonder. Our time was limited to hours, and we found them only too short to explore the springs themselves, without attempting much in the surrounding country, which contains some magnificent scenery. From the top of the hill near the head of the valley, we obtained a fine view, which made us yearn to explore the deep cañons of the three forks of Gardner's River and the highlands intervening between them. Each of the three forks before reaching their junction in the valley below the springs, passes through a deep, dark, rugged cañon with almost perpendicular sides, and directly before us, far up on the eastern fork, we see a magnificent waterfall, with here and there a patch of snow, so hidden in the gorge that the warm August sun has not yet succeeded in melting it. Of this fall we shall obtain a closer view when we come to resume our rambles towards the Great Falls of the Yellowstone, but for the present we have to content ourselves with a distant one. Far off to the south of us can be seen great mountain peaks towering to the skies and covered with perpetual snow. These, we are told, are around the head-waters of the Madison, and with the wings of a bird we might reach in a few miles what on horseback will consume many difficult days' marching.

Making our way back down the valley we linger about the great hot spring, admiring anew its formation and colors, and as we pick our way down the steep slope we stop to examine an impromptu shower-bath, which some enterprising individual has improvised half way down the slope, where the water has cooled sufficiently to render parboiling improbable. A pretty little arbor of pine boughs has been constructed over one of the basins, in which a board seat has been placed. A wooden trough, with one end so placed against the bank above as to catch the water, conveys it so as to strike the neck and shoulders of a bather seated on the bench. We did not stop to try the bath, but since bathing in warm milk is considered the height of luxury, we can readily imagine what a bath here would be, especially since the bather, if dissatisfied with the temperature of the stream he was under, could satisfy the most fastidious taste by doing as the thermometer does—rising for more heat, falling for less.

Returning towards our bivouac, we met and conversed with some of the visitors, some thirty of whom, men, women, and children, are here for the benefit of the waters. They are taken both externally and internally, and one old man we saw seemed to have made a mistake, and fancying his stomach a bath-tub, was trying with all his might to fill it at the earliest possible moment with water a good deal hotter than any coffee ever drunk in more civilized regions. He was seated by a spring with a quart can in his hand, with which he dipped up the boiling fluid and poured it down his throat as fast as he could swallow, stopping only now and then to lick his lips and utter a grunt of satisfaction. I looked at him in astonishment, and asked him if he liked it.

"Oh, yes," he replied, "it is better than any of your coffee, tea, or such truck."

On his invitation I tried it, and it is no exaggeration to state that the first mouthful scalded me; the second one, taken with the usual precautions, I managed to swallow, and did not try a third. The old man regarded me with that silent look of pity with which a habitué of Saratoga regards the first attempt of a novice to enjoy a glass from Congress Spring. The water is strongly impregnated with sulphur and other substances, smells like an old hen-house after the setting season, and I have seen *iced* drinks I like better.

Most wonderful stories are told of the cures produced by these waters. Persons so weak as to be held on their horses to get here are in a short time strong enough to move about and take all sorts of exercise. There is no question that with easy means of reaching these springs, and accommodations for visitors on the spot, which last would soon follow the first, people would flock there from all parts of the world. The route of the Northern Pacific Railroad, although not yet definitely decided, will, in all probability, go within seventy-five or eighty miles of the springs.

The hotel accommodations at the springs are as yet not very extensive; but there is plenty of space, and if you carry your own blankets, you will meet with a hearty Texas hospitality—permission to spread them under the eaves of a house.

Returning to our bivouac, it was found that our poor horses and mules, tormented beyond endurance by the hordes of flies, had concluded to vacate the country, and seek less objectionable company lower down the river. Parties sent out in search of them found that, as is the custom of animals under such circumstances, they had taken the only route they knew anything about, and gone back on our trail. Rapid pursuit was made, but they were not overtaken till they had reached the cañon of the Yellowstone, some twenty-five miles away. Here the formidable rocky ascent before them probably caused them to pause just before they were overtaken. Had they succeeded in getting through the cañon we should in all probability not have overtaken them before they reached Fort Ellis, sixty-six miles away, which would have caused a serious delay in our ramblings towards the great lake and falls of the Yellowstone, for which we were to start in the morning. Additional precautions were, therefore, taken, and as it was out of the question to picket the animals in the daytime and find them alive at night, a man was detailed to watch them. So troublesome, however, were the flies that the poor creatures could not even eat during daylight, and occupied themselves in crowding together and rolling in the dust, to get rid of their pests. At night they had to be let loose to feed whilst their enemies were asleep, a few only being kept picketed in the best grazing ground, and with the hope that the rest would not desert them. This, however, proved a vain hope, and the horses, remembering how they suffered after the sun got up, concluded to get out of the way in time, and when daylight came all but those picketed were found to have disappeared.

In the Western country when a man loses his horses the first thought is "Indians"; the last one "strayed." But here we were under no apprehension of Indians, for although they sometimes come as high up the Yellowstone as Boettler's ranche, they never, we were assured, visit this section of the country; although it is said there are near the lake region some few poor miserable wretches called "sheep-eaters," they are very seldom seen, and avoid, like any other wild beast, a white man. It is said, too, that occasionally wandering members of the Bannock tribe sometimes pass through the country, but they have a holy dread of it as closely allied with the infernal regions. It is stated to be a fact that should an Indian fail to return from this country, his tribe would never think of attributing his disappearance to murder, but would conclude, as a matter of course, that he had been swallowed up by one of the numerous hot springs or geysers, and gone straight through to report to his Satanic majesty. This renders the passage of white men through the country pleasantly secure.

We therefore had no fears that Indians had "jumped" our stock, and at once made preparations to follow it. Several parties were started out, and as it is best under such circumstances not to stand on the order of going, but go at once, myself and another officer mounted our horses, and ascending the hills back of our camp proceeded to search for the trail. We found it at last, but the horses were then evidently feeding, and much time was lost following the tracks here and there over the dry hard ground.

After some perseverance, and a good deal of grumbling and hard words, we found the trail leading, in as direct a way as the broken nature of the country would permit, in a northeasterly direction towards the home trail. Down into deep ravines and up on to high hills we followed it, slowly picking our way along over the rough rocky places until the tracks led us into the plain well-beaten trail we had followed two days before. Here the footprints were plainly seen in the dusty road, and now commenced a more rapid pursuit as the tracks could be easily seen whilst we were moving at a gallop. A stern chase is proverbially a long one, and we now pushed forward as rapidly as possible with the hope of over-taking our truant animals, at least before they reached the cañon. As we rose the top of each hill we strained our eyes with the hope of catching sight of them, but it was not until we came in sight of the "Devil's Slide" that we caught a glimpse of a single moving object, and that proved to be one of our mounted men going on the same mission as ourselves. We soon overtook him, dismounted to rest his weary horse, and taking the lead we pushed ahead in rapid pursuit. The "sign" fresh-ened, and as the prospect of catching sight of our animals increased we increased our speed as much as the weary condition of our horses would permit. As we neared the gorge of the cañon hope faded away, for in the valley before us no living creature was to be seen. We reached the first rocky point, and picked our way slowly across it, knowing that if the animals once got across the next point we were destined to have a long chase indeed. We moved rapidly across the little valley, looking forward to a climb over the rocky slope before us, when, casting our eyes to the right, we were gratified with the sight of all our animals quietly crop-ping the rich bunch grass on a side hill. As we neared them they looked up with a quiet stare, which said as plainly as words, "Is it possible we are of so much importance that you would follow us twenty-five miles?" We quickly shifted the saddles from our tired horses to some of the estrays, and arming ourselves with long sticks we made those animals "*hump* it" back to camp in a way which was a sight to see. We made the twenty-five miles in a little over two hours, hastily broke up camp, packed our mules, and left the beautiful "frozen cascades" behind us.

We followed across the country due south, crossed the middle fork of Gardner's River, a raging torrent up to our horses' girth, where the animals could scarcely keep their footing on the smooth round boulders which covered the bottom; struck the east fork, crossed that, and followed up its right bank by a steep game trail leading up the side of the valley. From a point on the steep side hill, where we stopped to take a drink from a little ice-cold spring which gushed from the rock, we had a splendid view of the Falls of Gardner's River, east fork, where the water makes a perpendicular plunge of sixty or seventy feet. Still toiling up the slope, we stand at length upon the flat horizontal ledge of rocks through a break in which, worn out by itself, the river makes its plunge.

Halting to rest, and turning back, a sight meets the eye which causes a burst of admiration from the whole party. Far down below us in the gorge through which we have just come, our pack mules are still struggling up the steep pathway. Away off to the left and rear, rising one above the other, are the rocky broken hills surrounding the valley of the Hot Springs, here and there cloven with steep-sided openings for the passage of the branches of Gardner's River, whilst standing like a great white marble castle, in marked contrast with the dark foliage behind, is the prominent point in the "Frozen Cascade," glistening like snow in the bright rays of the now setting sun, a thin misty cloud of steam rising from its top. One might well linger in admiration over such a view, but the sun is fast sinking behind the western snowcaps, and we push on to find a pleasant camp in a grove of pines, with plenty of rich grass for the horses, bright clear water for them and ourselves, and a store of hard dry lodge-poles for our fires. Years ago this must have been a favorite camping-place for Indians, for we find plenty of "tepee" poles, but all old, dry, and partially rotted under the rank grass which has grown up around and over them.

The next morning we encounter our first difficulty, for the trail becomes dim, and as no horsemen have lately passed over it we wander about for a long time searching for it in vain. We are now on the high rolling divide which separates the head-waters of Gardner's River from the Yellowstone, and have nothing to guide us but general directions and the fact that we know the Yellowstone lies to the east of us. We know, however, that one of Professor Hayden's pack-trains has recently passed over the route, for we met it the day before, returning to Fort Ellis for supplies. If we can only strike its trail we will be all right. At length, after a search of several hours, we strike the broad fresh trail of the pack-train. With shouts our party is assembled, and we move confidently forward again towards the Falls of Tower Creek, some eighteen miles away.

That our elevation is now considerable we can plainly see, for along the slope of a low range of hills to the south, long snow-drifts extending well down are glistening in the bright warm August sun. Away off to the eastward the broken rocky mountains on the right bank of the Yellowstone, cut up into deep dark cañons, are in full view, and we pass every now and then clumps of "quaking asp," whose roots are fed by moisture from the melting snow. The country has evidently once been a fine game section, but now, as we move along, we see nothing but a few antelope, which scamper away as fast as their fleet legs can carry them, evidently well acquainted with the crack of a rifle.

Our route leads us through some beautifully wild wooded valleys, and at length we stand on top of a hill looking once more down upon the Yellowstone. In the valley below us stands the first and only bridge which has ever yet spanned the virgin waters of the river. It was built by miners, to enable them to reach the gold diggings on the head-waters of Clark's Fork, a stream which empties into the Yellowstone several hundred miles below the point where we are now standing. Our trail leaves this bridge to the left, and we follow it till it enters a thick and matted wood, where we meet with our first difficulty in the way of fallen timber. It lies in almost every possible direction, and we twist and turn in all ways to avoid it, sometimes losing the trail, and now and then encountering a hill so steep as apparently to preclude the idea of our pack-mules scrambling up it. Rising all the time, we reach the edge of an immense chasm, standing directly across our path. The trail seems to lead to the left across a rocky ledge, along the steep edge of which I follow until the view opens a little, and a cry of alarm escapes me as I call to the rest of the party to halt, and hastily spring from my saddle. My horse and I are standing upon a projecting ledge with scarcely room enough to turn round, and I have a sort of feeling that at length I have reached one of the *ends* of the earth. The spot is an overhanging ledge of rock, the disintegrating edges of which render it uncertain at what moment the whole thing may go toppling over into the depths below. You cannot get close enough to the edge to see the bottom of the abyss before you, and from it, far down below you, comes up the hoarse roar of falling waters. This is Tower Falls, so deep down in this great rent of the earth, and so surrounded by tower-shaped masses of rock, that from this point no sight of it can be obtained. The tops of great trees can be seen far, far below where we now stand. On the other side of a vast amphitheatre the steep, almost perpendicular, rock rises up for hundreds of feet, cut into all sorts of fanciful forms by the action of water in former ages. At the foot of this wall, far off below us, the Yellowstone comes tumbling along with its characteristic sea-green color, here and there worked up into milk-white foam, as ledges of rocks interfere with the

current. We are now looking into the very mouth—the lower opening—
of the Grand Cañon, and its slopes near the water's edge are tinged with
the bright colors which we are to see in all their glory at the other end of
the cañon, some twenty-five miles above, to which point the Great Falls
of the Yellowstone have worked their way back after, who shall say how
many, centuries of labor.

The trail ends where we stand. There is no place for it to go, except
into empty air. After gazing with that feeling of admiration and awe
which a sight of magnitude and splendor always produces, I carefully
picked my way back along the perilous ledge, and started to search for
the trail which was to lead us down to the bed of Tower Creek. After a
long hunt we found it, and commenced the descent by a path so steep
that we had to dismount and lead our horses down. Down, down we go
for hundreds of feet, passing by the tops of great trees, until we finally
reach where their roots are imbedded in the banks of the creek, a foam-
ing mountain torrent, rushing over a bed of boulders towards the Falls
below. Crossing this we turn down the narrow valley, and obtain a fine
view of the "Devil's Den," a wild, narrow, dark gorge, through which the
stream rushes boiling, to make its fierce leap before it mingles its waters
with those of the Yellowstone far down below. The country is here
exceedingly broken. Wild and beautiful high hills rise in every direction
around the point where the two streams join, the enclosed space being
also broken up with steep rounded hills, clothed in a luxuriant growth of
grass, flowers, and trees. To the top of one of these hills we mounted, to
enjoy a sight of the Tower Falls. The stream, after passing through the
"Devil's Den," enters a still narrower gorge, with great pinnacle-shaped
towers rising on each side, and, bending slightly to the right, plunges
over a perpendicular precipice, fifty or sixty feet high, and in a sheet of
foam strikes below with a roar, sending up clouds of cool spray, which
makes the chasm below feel like an ice-house, compared with the heated
air above. From a point lower down we get a side view, which, concealing the channel of the creek, makes the water appear as if plunging out
of a hole in the solid rock. Far above is the projecting point of rock upon
which we stood an hour ago, and we can now appreciate what a tumble a
false step there would have given us.

The path down to the river is too steep for our horses, so, tying
them to a tree, we pursue our way on foot, and climbing down to the
very edge of the surging waters of the Yellowstone, put our rods
together, and prepare to test the truth of the assertion that the speckled
trout from that stream will not take the artificial fly. We stand at the
mouth of a little stream whose warm water and sulphurous smell tell of
hot springs near by, and no fish rise to our flies. We wander lower down,

and where Tower Creek comes plunging in with a roar, forming eddies, which we feel sure must entice the trout to lie in them, we try again. I select a large brown-winged fly with yellow body, and scarcely has it touched the surface of a deep pool, just above the mouth of the creek, than a pair of jaws, large enough to take in your hand, opens at the surface of the water, and immediately my reel commences to sing and my rod to bend, as if a whale were tugging at the line. What with the trout's surprise and fright, and my eagerness, it is a hard struggle to land such a monster through the rushing torrent, but, at length, my fingers are in his gills, and the great fish, with spotted sides of the color of liquid gold, lies panting on the shore. Another and another soon follow him, and in a time entirely too short, we have a string of three and four-pound trout, enough to supply the whole party, and entirely too large to carry up the steep ascent behind us with any sort of comfort. Our camp is pitched in a little valley close by, where we enjoy our feast with travellers' appetites, and are lulled to sleep by that most delicious of all sounds to the sleepy senses, falling water, provided always it does not come in the shape of rain.

Our next day's trip was over a rough and rugged path. We first had to climb the rough, steep, and wooded slope which bounds the valley of Tower Creek on the south. Here one of our pack-mules slipped, fell, and got rid of his load, which had to be repacked. Then the country opened out into rolling prairie, and as we reached a high point, a magnificent view opened to us. The whole surface below us, as far as the eye could reach in every direction, was covered with dense masses of pine timber. On the left was the Grand Cañon of the Yellowstone, beyond which mountain rose beyond mountain, until in the far distance to the south peaks covered with perpetual snow appeared. On our right we could trace the deep cañon of Tower Creek running far to the westward, whilst to our front Mount Washburne (named after the late Surveyor-General of Montana, the first modern explorer of the wonders of the Yellowstone) rose up as if to bar our further progress south, its long sloping sides striped here and there with long deep snow-drifts. Along the northern face of Mount Washburne the trail led us over a rough country; now passing through dense masses of timber, now threading our way through intricate meshes of fallen trees, and now deep down into great gulches washed out by streams running from the melting snow-banks above, we at length reached the top of a divide to the west of the peak, from which we looked down and over an immense wooded district, with the now far-famed Yellowstone Lake glistening in the distance. Here and there over the landscape rises a column of white steam, serving to remind us of the hot springs, geysers, and other wonders we have before us. We climb down the steep slope in front of us along a path well beaten by recent horse-tracks, and enter a pleasant region of thick timber, alternating with pretty little valleys well watered and covered with grass and flowers. In passing through one of these we missed the trail, and whilst searching for it came across a great bank of white plaster-of-Paris-like substance, in which our horses sank up to the fetlock. It was evidently a deposit similar to that made at the hot springs, and along its base sulphurous water was boiling up, and bubbles of gas rising through the stagnant pools.

Our directions were to follow along the southern face of Mount Washburne to obtain a fine view of the Grand Cañon and the Great Falls, and, as we were now fast leaving the mountain, we decided to halt for the night, and made camp in one of the bright little valleys alongside of a clear stream.

It being early in the afternoon, myself and a companion started out to search for the Falls, and, guns on shoulders, we plunged into the deep forests. Our provisions were growing scarce, at least the fresh meat part, and we were not without hope of finding game of some kind. We proceeded, therefore, very carefully, walking lightly, and every now and then halting to listen. The stillness was almost oppressive, not even a breath of air seemed to break the monotonous quiet of the pine woods, when suddenly, as we rose the slope of a hill, and stopped as usual to listen, a startling sound broke upon the ear, of so singular a nature that we looked at each other in alarm. Again it sounded, with a dull sort of thud easily magnified into a growl.

"Listen; what is that?"

"A grizzly!" comes back in a hoarse stage whisper from my companion.

Now a grizzly bear is an awkward kind of an animal to meet sometimes, especially in a lonely wood with the only help within a hundred miles of you a mile or two away. The trees fortunately furnish one means of escape if resorted to in time, and we both instinctively picked out the most convenient one near. But neither of us contemplated such an ignominious retreat before an invisible foe, and now eyes and ears were eagerly bent in the direction of the sound, with the hope of obtaining some definite clue to its origin. For an instant it seemed to me that I was all turned into eyes and ears. Again and again did the sound come booming through the otherwise silent wood, and in the absence of any bodily presence light commenced to break in upon our frightened senses. It was observed that the sound came at regular intervals, did not vary at all, and did not sound like the voice of an animal. This set us to thinking, and in a moment the woods resounded with a shout and a cry.

"It is a mud volcano!"

The mere suggestion was enough to carry conviction, and we pushed forward in the direction of the sound, as eager now to go forward as we had been before to go back. We travelled in this way for nearly a mile, the sound being our compass, and at last, pushing our way through a thick piece of wood, stood in an open space, on the far side of which rose a steep bare hill. At the base of this was a circular pool of dark muddy water in an active state of ebullition. At regular intervals, a few seconds apart, a column would shoot up from the centre of the pool to the height of six or seven feet, scattering the dirty-looking water in every direction, and giving out the sound we had heard. At every burst of the volcano the water would rise slightly and a little run off through a channel, the depth and worn appearance of which showed that the flow at some periods was much more copious than at present. Near by was another pool, but of clear water, and in place of shooting up like the other it was quietly boiling, the surplus water flowing off in a drain. The side hill above was filled with vents, from dozens of which hot steam and water hissed forth as though eager to escape from the pressure below. In one place, in a sort of pocket half-filled with well-mixed mud, the steam bubbled through and reminded one of boiling mush.

We stood, long wondering at this singular spectacle, the sounds given forth from the vents in the side hill reminding one of those heard in a railroad depot when half a dozen engines are hissing forth steam from their partially closed valves.

As we turned to leave the place we quietly laughed at the recollection that we came very near taking to trees to avoid a mud volcano.

Continuing our ramble, and with our eyes now open for new wonders, we entered one of those pretty little prairie-like openings which seem to be so common here. Talking as we walked, and thinking only of the singular phenomenon we had just witnessed, I suddenly became aware of a great pair of bright eyes surmounted by a long pair of ears, both of which were turned eagerly towards us from the other side of a pile of dead trees lying one on top of the other not thirty steps from us.

"Stop! What is that?" and I had to look twice before I could make out that the eyes and ears belonged to the head of a deer, whose body was concealed by the pile of fallen timber. Our camp was out of fresh meat. I was but an indifferent rifle-shot. If the deer ever made a spring she would expose her body, but in motion she would be safe from my bullet. These thoughts passed rapidly through my mind. As if by instinct, my rifle came down; a moment, and the woods resounded with a shot; and before my companion had even seen what caused my exclamation, the game disappeared behind the logs. A few steps forward, and there almost in the very bed from which she was startled by the sound of our voices, lay a fine fat doe with a bullet through her eye. Of course it was a splendid shot, of the William Tell order, and, of course, I accepted with becoming modesty all sorts of compliments about snuffing candles at fifty paces, etc.; but I could not conceal my exultation at our good luck, and exhibited an excitement entirely inconsistent with the aplomb of an old hunter.

The deer was quickly disemboweled, one leg cut off, and shouldering this, the liver, and our two guns, we commenced a rapid movement towards camp, giving up for the time all hope of seeing the Falls, and filled only with the idea of what a welcome sight we had for the rest of the party, and what a feast we should have when we got back. Oh, what a trip that was! I don't think I ever saw mosquitoes more numerous or more bloodthirsty. They swarmed around us in myriads, covering our faces, our meat, and our hands, and pushing in their bills wherever they could find an unguarded spot. We cut branches of trees to whip them off, but all to no purpose; for both of our hands were constantly occupied, and no sooner were they driven from one spot than they reappeared at another. But as night came on, and it commenced to grow cool, which it always does as soon as the sun sets, they gradually lessened their attentions, and allowed us to enter camp in triumph and comparative comfort. Our appearance was hailed with delight, and our little camp resounded with good cheer and merriment. This was the only deer we saw upon the whole trip, and although we saw plenty of "signs" of both deer and elk, we failed to catch even a distant glimpse of the animals themselves, and concluded that they, during the summer, resorted to the highest mountains, where, in the vicinity of the snows, they were comparatively safe from both heat and flies.

Seated around our bright camp fires we ate, drank, and were merry, planning our expedition to the Great Falls the next day, neither knowing nor caring for the disappointment in store for us.

We supposed ourselves camped on what was called Cascade Creek, and that the Falls were only a mile or two off. The next morning, therefore, we were in our saddles by six o'clock, and our first care was to find and secure the rest of our deer. We started for the place with many misgivings, for wild beasts, such as bears and wolves, are almost certain to find game a few hours after it is slaughtered. As we approached the spot, after taking a second view of the mud geyser, I caught sight of a large wolf which rapidly disappeared in the woods, and I failed to get a shot at him. We found the deer, which we had drawn up on a fallen tree, safe and unmolested, but the entrails were carefully covered up with leaves and grass scraped together for the purpose, and doubtless by the wolf found lurking near the spot. The deer was quickly cut up and distributed amongst the party; and now to find the Falls was the question.

For six mortal hours did we wander through the dense forest, stumbling and pushing through masses of fallen timber, twisting and turning to get out of its way. Several times we reached the edge of the Grand Cañon, and looked down its almost perpendicular sides at the river rushing along hundreds of feet below us. The scene was grand beyond description, but the Falls were nowhere to be seen. Sometimes we would fancy we could hear their roar beyond a projecting point ahead of us, and in trying to make our way to that, we would encounter lateral cañons so steep and rugged as to render necessary long detours before we could reach the other side, and when we did reach there, it was only again to be disappointed. At length we gave up the fruitless search, returned to camp about twelve, packed up and resumed our journey with a sad feeling of disappointment that one of the principal objects of our trip, a sight of the Great Falls, had been defeated by imperfect maps and incorrect information. In places, the trail being very indistinct, we lost our way, but at length an opening appeared in the dense forest, and we could see a short distance before us. For some time we had noticed a peculiar noise which, when in the dense timber, sounded like the wind sighing through the trees. It appeared, however, to grow louder as we advanced, and when we entered the open space it increased in volume, and appeared to come from the left. Joy lighted up all faces as the fact suddenly broke in upon us, and with a cry of "The Falls! The Falls!" we spurred forward in the direction of the sound, now heard in thundering tones, proceeding from the other side of a strip of timber in our front. A couple of horses saddled and tied to trees in the edge of the timber told us we were in the vicinity of one of Professor Hayden's surveying parties. Hastily dismounting and tying our horses we pushed forward on foot through the timber. For a moment we stood looking in silent admiration and awe, and then, as the thunder of the cataract struck upon our ears in contrast with the previous silence reigning around us, and our previous disappointment recurred to us, each one uttered a yell of triumph and delight, and rushed ahead to obtain a better view of the scene.

Now it so happened that just at this time a young assistant of the surveying party was engaged in taking the height of the Falls, and had his instrument set up upon a projecting point of rock, towards which this yelling, rough-looking party was rushing. Travellers in the Western country do not generally dress in the height of fashion. Dressed buckskin and ragged fustian take the place of broad cloth and "good clothes"; and straggling beards, matted hair, and bronzed faces are apt to be the result of rough Western life. The young assistant was a new importation, as yet unused to Western life, and his feelings on having his quiet labors suddenly interrupted by an Indian-like yell and the apparition of half a dozen wild-looking creatures, with rifles in hand, rushing towards him, when his only retreat was by a spring five or six hundred feet down a perpendicular precipice, can be more easily imagined than described, and were pretty plainly depicted in his face as we neared him. His relief must have been correspondingly great when he discovered by our language that we were not the ferocious redmen or "road agents" we looked.

The position chosen for a view of the Falls was the finest possible one. Looking up the river a deep, narrow rocky gorge was seen, its sides composed of black volcanic rock, towering hundreds of feet above the water and into the dense timber above. At the bottom of this gorge is the river, moving along in its majesty faster and faster as it rushes towards its leap, its bright sea-green surface flecked here and there with white. Reaching the mouth of the cañon, in a smooth, unbroken green sheet from shore to shore, it plunges over, and is at once converted into a mass of creamy white. Down, down, down it goes, the spray becoming finer and finer, until when it strikes the bottom, three hundred and fifty feet below, with a roar and a shock which makes both air and earth tremble, the whole space is veiled in a thick mist, on which the rays of the sun strike, spanning the gulf with a bright rainbow. The bow seems to reflect the colors which, on both sides of the cañon below the falls, light up and beautify the disintegrating slopes, from the deep-green pine forests above, down to the very edge of the water, which, looking like a waving ribbon of green flecked with pure white, rushes along far beneath our feet. Below the Falls the river, a narrow green ribbon, rushes along between shores, whose steep slopes, of a Milwaukee brick-yellow, contrast strongly with the black volcanic rocks above. To add to the novelty and beauty of the scene these slopes are colored with the most brilliant hues, not one particle exaggerated by the brush of Moran in his view of the Falls already referred to. In fact the artist on viewing the scene with an artist's enthusiasm is said to have remarked, with a tinge of sadness in his tone, "No brush can do justice to it."

Looking down at the river almost under our feet it is seen that we stand upon the edge of a perpendicular cliff of rock which descends for hundreds of feet to join the steep yellow slopes of the river shore. We amuse ourselves by hurling over immense pieces of rock. The ear catches no sound from below, but looking over, after waiting some seconds, the eye detects far down in the lower depths a fragment, apparently the size of a fist, bounding from side to side in water-worn gulches, and finally splashing into the river at the bottom. Short of the river there is no possible stopping-point.

Half a mile above the Great Falls, in a bend of the river, is the Upper Falls, where the water makes another perpendicular plunge of one hundred and twenty-five feet, and, between the two falls, Cascade Creek, a considerable stream flowing through a deep gorge and filled with beautiful cascades, joins the Yellowstone. We cross this, ascend the steep hill beyond, enter a bright, grass-covered valley, and strike the river again at the rapids above the Falls, where it rushes over a steep incline, at one point of which stands a huge mass of rock, which divides the rushing waters like an island. Further above, the river flows through grassy meadows, with a gentle though rapid current which a steamboat could with little difficulty stem, and from this point to the lake, a distance of eighteen or twenty miles, the river is said to be navigable. Perhaps at some future day a landing will be established here for steamers conveying passengers from the Great Falls to a tour of the lake.

For thousands of years (how many thousands, who can say?) these falls have been working their way back to their present position, and in the course of ages the water has worn out the Great Cañon of the Yellowstone, some twenty-five or thirty miles in length, from its mouth, near Tower Creek, to the present location of the falls. Like the falls of the Niagara River, they will eventually work their way back to the waters of the lake above, and drain it. But this will not be in our day.

From a high point on the trail we had a fine view of the river as it flows through a picturesque landscape, and then crossing another steep, wooded hill entered upon a broad, flat, uninteresting, greasewood-covered plain, from the far side of which columns of steam can be seen rising.

Crossing a bright, clear stream, a foot and a half wide, and an inch or two deep, which my map informs me is Alum Creek, I requested a little negro boy belonging to the party to dismount and hand me a drink, tasting it first to see if it was cool. He raised the cup to his lips, took one mouthful and with a cry of disgust ejected it from his mouth, with an expression strongly reminding us of our younger days and experience with green persimmons.

"What is the matter?'

"Why dat's de queerest water I ever tasted."

"Is it cool?"

"No, sir; it's bitter."

I put the cup to my lips, and found it filled with a bitter, saturated solution of alum.

We were now approaching the "Seven Hills," an interesting group of hot springs, the steam from which we had noticed from a distance. We dismounted to examine them, and found two large boiling springs, with all the beautiful formations and colors of the Gardner's River group, and a number of other lesser ones and mud-tanks. The surplus water from the springs flows over a long slope, which it has itself built up, and, as the hot steam escapes at several points along this slope, we step rather carefully, not yet being fully used to our ground, and not knowing at what moment we might plunge into a boiling bath. The feeling is not a pleasant one, but we get more accustomed to the ground after awhile, and learned to pass anywhere, even on horseback, with perfect confidence.

Standing by the largest one of this group, you might very naturally, from the noise made, fancy yourself in the room of a high-pressure engine, and hence the name given to it, "Locomotive Jet." The imitation of the impulsive puffing, and noise of wheels turning in water, is perfect. The aperture of the jet is about six inches, is in a kind of raised chimney, and all round it are numerous small vents, each one most elegantly lined with bright-yellow sulphur. In the springs, where sulphur exists in the greatest abundance, the beauty of the scolloped edges, bordered by pearl-like bead-work, and colored with every tint, from a deep, rich yellow, through straw to a delicate cream, is something beyond the power of words to describe.

The mud-tanks are curious affairs, and seem to be boiling springs simmered down and nearly extinct. The muddy water loses in time the fluid part, the mud becomes thicker and thicker, and finally reaches the consistency of mush, and through that the escaping steam slowly makes its way.

We spent an hour looking over this interesting spot, then the party getting separated lost each other and the trail, and it was sundown before all but one member got together again and established camp on the bank of the Yellowstone, where plenty of grass and a supply of driftwood invited us to stop. The absentee wandered about till after dark, contemplated a supperless bivouac by himself, and was rejoiced when our pistol shots called him to camp.

In the meantime I had put my rod together, to try, with little hope of succeeding, a cast for a trout. One, two, three throws, without result; but at the fourth the water broke, a fine fellow took the fly, and in a few minutes three or four golden-yellow trout, enough for the whole party, were safely landed in the grass. Other rods were produced, and for half an hour trout were landed almost as fast as we could make the casts, and until we became actually ashamed of the cruel waste of catching more. These trout were all of a nearly uniform size, about three pounds in weight, and at the time we entirely forgot all about the stories we had heard of the worms which afflict those inhabiting the lake. I fear, however, it would make no difference, for we were tired and hungry, and when after appeasing our hunger we recalled the worm-stories, we consoled ourselves as did the Western toper in regard to whisky, and complacently reflected that "all trout is good, some is better than other trout, but none is *bad.*"

Just as the night was closing in and we had ceased fishing, the whole air was suddenly filled with an immense number of large flies, called by one of the party "trout flies." These were swept across the river by a gentle breeze, and immediately the whole river seemed alive with trout, eagerly springing for those nearest the water. The turmoil, kept up long after dark, gave us a better idea than we had yet had of the immense number of trout in the river.

During the night a heavy rain fell, and, as the sun began to redden the east the next morning, I crawled from between my blankets, and, before the rest of the party were awake, had several more fine trout landed for our breakfast. The time of day does not seem to make much difference with these fish. They are always hungry, and always ready to appease their hunger and your own.

Leaving the main body to dry the things in the sun, myself and two or three others started ahead to examine a mud geyser, some miles up the river. After crossing several broad, open meadows, in the valley of the river, we approached a wooded point, where the columns of steam rising above the trees pointed out the object of our search. We wandered about in quest of the curiosities belonging to this interesting group, and whilst doing so, started a drove of black grouse, the finest game-bird in the Western country, and dismounted at once to shoot off their heads with our rifles. At the third or fourth shot a shout was heard from the hill above us, and two men, as rough-looking and ragged as ourselves (which is saying a good deal), came towards us, to ascertain who the strange party were. They proved to be a portion of one of Professor Hayden's parties, left here to observe the operations of the principal mud geyser of the group. Under their guidance we made a very satisfactory examination of the different localities. The first consisted of a group of large tanks, half-filled with mud, in a most perfect state of mixture, some of about the consistency of brick material, some as thick as fresh mush, others thinner, and others again like thick, muddy water. Up through all of them the hot steam was pushing its way in bubbles, continuing the admixture of the materials, and working them up as it had been probably working them for long ages before. In some of these tanks the appearance was exactly that of boiling mush, where the bubbles came thick and fast after each other. In others the gas worked more slowly and seemed to have just power sufficient to push its way through the thick, stiff mass. In some of these last a curious and novel feature was observed. As the bubbles slowly and laboriously worked their way up, the surface of the mud rises in a blister, which, growing thinner and thinner as it rises, finally bursts. As the broken blister sinks slowly down towards the general surface of the mud, the most beautifully accurate rings are formed around the opening, and these finally disappear, to be followed by other bubbles, blisters, and rings, and so on indefinitely. We lingered a long time about these mud tanks, where thousands of tons of mud appear as if yearning for brick-moulds to press themselves into. The tanks are of all sizes, from twenty or thirty feet across down to a few inches; the larger ones boiling up all over the surface; the smaller ones sometimes with but a single bubble forming blisters and rings on its own account.

These tanks are all situated at the foot of a hill on a plateau, which bears the appearance of being itself formed of the same material, hardened, as the mud in the present tanks. Nearly all the tanks have a depressed passage-way leading from them to lower ground, which formed in former times, when there was an overflow of fluid, a waste weir to carry off the surplus, resulting from eruptions. In the boiling springs of muddy water a little still makes its way out through these channels.

Under the direction of our guides we passed from this group of immense "brickyards" to another of a different kind, higher up on the side hill. Here we were shown the site of the great mud geyser, an immense tank with a boiling pool of muddy water in the centre, and gorges, six or eight feet deep, leading from it through the plateau in which it stands down to the river, which runs close by. The dirty mixture is quietly simmering, now and then spurting up into boiling, preparatory to an eruption, which we are told, takes place with great regularity about once in every six hours.

Not far from the mud geyser is the spring which has been named the "Devil's Grotto," where a vast column of steam issues from a cavern in the side of a hill with an opening five feet in diameter. The roaring of the clear waters in the cavern, and the surging of the waves up to the mouth of the opening, remind one of the surf on the sea-shore, although but very little water is thrown out. So hot is the steam from the mouth of the Grotto that it is only when the wind wafts it aside one dares to look in.

Close by, but higher up the hill, is the "Devil's Caldron"—a great conical basin, forty feet across at the top and thirty feet deep—where a dense column of steam is constantly escaping with a roar which shakes the ground for a considerable distance around. When the wind blows the cloud of steam aside you look down upon a mass of thin mud, boiling violently like an immense caldron of mush. At times it must act with still more violence, for the trees standing around within a radius of one hundred feet or more are bespattered with mud to a height of seventy-five or one hundred feet; and this kind of an explosion has evidently occurred within a year or two, for some of the trees are still alive.

By the way, I have never yet been able to account for the disposition shown to name so many beautiful places after the Devil, unless on the presumption that he has the exclusive right to everything in the vicinity of hot water—an admission I am not willing to make; for, although we got into plenty of hot water on the trip, we saw nothing of the Devil, and had very little time or disposition to even think of him whilst contemplating the beauties placed there by the All-Beneficent Power.

On visiting the camp of the surveying party we were assured that the geyser would certainly "go off" in a few hours, and that it was a sight well worth seeing. We therefore decided to await here the arrival of our packs and witness the eruption. We were shown a number of specimens of natural history collected on the trip, and amongst the rest a bottle filled with long, white, tape-like worms, taken from the river trout, the sight of which made us shudder at the recollection of our last night's feast. In vain we protested there were none of these in the ones we had eaten. We were met by the startling assertion, "There are very few without them!" To prove the fact we were invited to catch some of the fish from the river close by, which we at once proceeded to do. The first one landed was taken possession of by one of our informants, who, scraping his knife down along the bright golden side of the fish, called our attention to a puffy spot, a little lighter in color than the rest of the surface, and looking like an incipient boil about the size of a dime. Into this I was invited to insert the blade of a penknife, upon doing which out came a long, whitish-looking worm, and we were all convinced against our will. We caught a number of fish, but few of which were without the outward manifestation of these parasites. They all have them to a greater or less degree, but it is only when they exist super-abundantly that they make their way from the entrails of the animal into the surrounding flesh, on entering which they produce a kind of mortification, which would probably prevent any but a starving man from eating it. The fish suitable for food can be readily selected by the absence of the light protuberances on the side. I afterwards found in a trout, caught in Sun River, in the northern part of Montana Territory, a similar worm, but of darker color. To indemnify ourselves for any mistakes we may have committed at our supper of the night before, we cut great slices from a fine fat quarter of elk hanging in the camp, and, roasting them at the fire, made a hearty lunch, whilst waiting the pleasure of the geyser.

At length, after waiting through a pelting storm of rain and hail, our watches told us the hour for eruption was approaching, and we assembled around the geyser crater, the party being increased in the meantime by the arrival of the rest with the packs. Seated on the rim of the basin, at a safe distance, we awaited the advent of the phenomenon. The water was still slowly bubbling about a foot below the edge of a rocky ledge which appeared to form the edge of the crater proper. All at once a great commotion suddenly takes place in the basin, the water boils rapidly up, rises above the rim of the crater, and then with a loud report the whole volume is thrown six or eight feet into the air. Before it has time to descend another explosion takes place, and then another and another in rapid succession, until there is a constant flow of a fountain-like mass of dirty water and white steam projected into the air. Now and then an explosion of more than usual force takes place, throwing the water a foot or two higher, and each additional effort is hailed by the audience with a shout of applause, as if a living animal were exerting its powers before us. This scene continues for twelve or fifteen minutes, when, as suddenly as they commenced, the explosions cease, the water is no longer thrown into the air, it boils violently for awhile, then slowly recedes until it reaches its former level, when it quietly settles down into its old simmer, and bubbles away for six hours again, until the next explosion.

We resumed our trip well satisfied with the gratification afforded us by the few hours' delay, and, continuing up the river through pleasant meadows diversified with groves of pine, we in a few miles reached the far-famed lake. It does not break upon us suddenly, but the river, as we approach the lake, grows wider and wider, with broad flat shores, and here and there a flat island, near which flocks of wild ducks, plover, and the staid white pelican are feeding. Occasionally we ran into a flock of wild geese feeding on the grassy meadows, but they rise wildly as though fully aware of their danger in the vicinity of man. We soon come in full view of the lake, which opens out to the southward as far as the eye can reach, its banks heavily wooded on all sides to the very edge of the water.

We halt to rest, get a view of the lake, and take a shot at a flock of ducks near the shore. Looking to the south the waters stretch far off in the dim distance, broken in one place by an island wooded like the projecting points of the mainland to the very shore, whilst beyond, in the distance, mountain peaks covered with snow bound the horizon. To the eastward "Steamboat Point" juts boldly out into the lake and, with columns of steam rising up from it, looks what its name implies, a busy landing-place for steamers. We continue up the shore of the lake, and camp directly on its shore in a pleasant grove, where the abundant grass furnishes full forage for our hungry animals.

Here on a small scale is seen forming the secondary shores described by Elisee Reclus, in *The Ocean,* as constructed on the line of equilibrium between the marine and fluvial waters. From a point near our camp, and stretching across an inlet of the lake, a broad causeway of sand extends, thrown up on the one side by the gentle waves of the lake, arrested on the other by the accumulation of waters from a tributary of the lake. This causeway extends nearly across to the opposite point, where a deep channel is left for the escape of the waters of the tributary. This we ford with difficulty, for the waters come up to our horses' shoulders, and beyond is another causeway across another inlet, with a deeper channel, which we do not care to try, although the tracks in the sand show that a party ahead of us has gone that way. We observed a number of these singular sand-spits, or secondary shores, as we passed along the shore of the lake, and also evidence of their existence at a higher level. For, as we proceeded, we now and then entered upon marshy ground which we found best avoided by keeping close down to the lake shore, where the footing was dry and sandy. In times past, when the lake was at a higher level, similar sand-spits were formed, and in time the space between them was filled up by the sediment brought down by the tributaries, but the water which continued to run down was prevented from escaping by the solid bars of sand, and bogs were formed into which our horses sank as we tried to push through them. The only solid ground we could find was along the solid sand barriers of former days, but the trouble was that the whole space had been overgrown with timber, which had been blown down or fallen from old age, until it lay in an intricate mass where the trees were piled on top of each other in every conceivable direction, sometimes so thick and matted together that after wandering for a long time trying to get through it, we would be compelled to turn back and seek another outlet. When we left the solid basis of the old sand barriers we were compelled to encounter both the fallen timber and the boggy ground too, and had a difficult and tedious time of it. Time and time again were we compelled to turn back from some interminable maze of fallen timber and boggy ground to seek an outlet, our poor horses worn out with the constant labor of twisting and turning, and scrambling over fallen timber.

To avoid this fallen timber and boggy ground we attempted the next morning to keep away from the lake shore and travel by the compass through the woods, and to a certain extent we improved the route, but we were glad to catch sight of the lake shore once more, and so follow along it until we reached our camp late in the afternoon, near another group of hot springs on the western shore of the lake.

This group is one of the most interesting we have yet seen, and in it all the magnificent colors of the "Frozen Cascade" are reproduced. Within sight of our pretty bivouac is a formation which attracts attention at once. In a space of not over fifteen or twenty feet in diameter is a group of twelve or fifteen vents, each of which shoots out its pellet of mud, exactly like a Roman candle ejects its star. The vents are close together, and each one has built up around it a sort of cone two or three feet high. Each one throws out every few seconds, with a sound exactly like that of a Roman candle, a pellet of mud, which falls in some cases on its own cone, in others into the face of its neighbor. In this latter case it is again ejected only to fall into the mouth of some other vent, and this goes on indefinitely. We dubbed it our great *political machine,* on account of its facility for throwing mud. But this mud is clean and of a beautiful variety in color. The aim, too, is a good deal like that used in politics, where the mud is directed against purity of character; for, instead of striking always in the face of a neighbor, it will fall upon the cone, and build that higher, as the character of a pure man is built higher, and appears brighter to the rest of mankind by the filth that is thrown at him by political opponents.

The mud thrown up by these puny volcanoes is of endless variety in color, and at a little distance the collection of cones looks like a great mass of party-colored cream candy. Pink, olive, cherry, blue, or creamy yellow, shading off almost to pure white, all appear, and intermingling, form an effect delightful to the eye and impossible to describe adequately in words. The activity of the different vents is as varied as the colors of the mud. In some the pellet flies up two or three feet with a report like a pop-gun. In others the explosive force is less and the mud appears to have just force enough to reach the top of the cone, and sometimes falls back again and is ejected over and over again. On the outer edge of the group new phenomena occur, if possible, more interesting than the little volcanoes themselves. Here small pools of the soft, pliable, and variously colored mud are formed, and having been worked to a degree of fineness suitable for the manufacture of the finest kind of delicate porcelain, the stream, as it comes up through, forms the blisters and rings described as existing in the mud tanks near the mud geyser. But here the varied and delicate color of the material, and the state of fineness into which it is worked render the rings more delicate and the sight more beautiful. Fancy one looking all day long at an infinite variety of beautiful rings done in mud, which resembles liquid porcelain of varied colors.

But still a more beautiful sight meets the eye of the visitor as he continues to walk around the group; for he now approaches a point where the jets of gas are more active than where the rings are found, but not so active as in the little volcanoes, and here the result is a medium between the two actions. The mud is still of various colors, and still thoroughly intermingled and worked up into a sort of pasty-looking mass; but the gas, instead of rising slowly as when forming the rings, comes up with a sudden spurt. This throws the mud up in a little column three or four inches high; the gas breaks its way out at the top dividing that into numerous parts, each one curving gracefully outwards by the force of the explosion, and as the mud sinks slowly down, a most exquisite representation of a tulip is formed. This has scarcely sunk out of sight before another springs up in its place like a "Jack in the Box." Each time the details of the form are varied, and here you can stand all day long, and look at an infinite variety of tulips of varied colors, done in mud, forming and disappearing at every moment. To have pressed for preservation, some of these beautiful flowers would have been the height of our ambition, but their forms were as fleeting as the tints of the rainbow, and nothing short of a brick would have served the purpose.

We returned again and again to enjoy this novel scene, and could not help reflecting how many thousands, perhaps millions, of these beautiful flowers had been born to "blush unseen, and waste their sweetness on the desert air," away up here in the great wilderness at the top of the American continent.

We tried to put some of the soft pliable mud to practical use, and one of the party gathering a quantity at the imminent risk of scorching his hands, plastered our deer-head thickly over with it, and placed it in our camp-fire, with the idea of roasting the head in the Indian fashion. Very much to our disappointment, the plan did not work, for in the morning it was found that the plaster, after baking hard, had cracked, and our deer-head burnt to a crisp was lying in the embers surrounded by bits of baked clay, and we had wasted a deer's head which a day or two afterwards would have furnished us with a feast. The afternoon was occupied in wandering about and discovering new curiosities at every step.

The whole shore of the lake in the vicinity is filled with numerous hot springs which by their deposits have built up a long gentle slope, extending from the springs down to the edge of the water. Over this slope the hot water from the springs flows, and, continuing to make its deposit, the slope is gradually encroaching upon the lake. Small hot springs are bubbling up at different points all the way down the slope, below the main springs, to the very edge of the lake. Even under its surface the presence of springs is shown by the gas, here and there, bubbling up through the water, so that the rocky deposit is now being formed at the bottom of the lake at some distance from its edge. Were there any doubt upon this point, it would be solved by the existence of a very curious structure which stands like an island *in* the waters of the lake, and a few feet from the main land. This is a flat, cone-shaped, and truncated deposit of the usual material, about ten or twelve feet in diameter, which stands near the point where the principal part of the water from some of the largest springs enters the lake. Inside of this is an opening, or well, two or three feet across, filled with hot water which is slowly simmering. The water seems to have built up its wall to the highest point, for it now does not run over, and the surrounding conical surface is perfectly dry. Surrounding this little island is the cool water of the lake. A log laid across from the main land enabled us to pass dry shod from the shore to the island. Here seating ourselves, we could have placed a foot in the cool water of the lake, and a hand in the hot waters of the well behind us. From the appearance of this structure, there can, I think, be no question as to the manner of its formation. A vent under the surface of the lake formerly existed, and through this the heated water came to deposit its rocky material. This deposit went on until the surface of the lake was reached, and above that until the flat cone-shaped island was finished as it appears to-day.[1] From the description of this well of boiling water, it will readily be seen that the feasibility of performing the Munchausen-like feat of the early explorers depends simply upon the existence of trout in the lake, and the ability of a hungry man to catch them. I had no desire, however, to leave the question an open one. My rod was soon put together, and one or two casts of the fly ended in the landing of a fine large trout. I was not hungry at the time, nor

---

[1]We were advised before starting for the Yellowstone region, by one who had been there, not to open our mouths after we got back about the wonders we had seen there, *for nobody would believe what we said.* Mankind is naturally prone to exaggeration, and so wonderful were some of the stories told in regard to the wonderful sights to be seen in the Yellowstone country, that a spirit of incredulity was the result with many whose imagination was not equal to the occasion. Amongst other stories one was told, with various embellishments, to the effect that trout could be caught in one pool, cooked in another without the sportsman moving from the spot, and eaten without being taken from the hook. Of course, such a story of a life-sustaining locality was received with many "grains of salt," winks, and nods of incredulity, which plainly placed it in the same category with the Irishman's account of the blessed country where roasted pigs ran about begging to be eaten.

disposed to reproduce the qualms resulting from the trichina-like investigations of two days before. But a great question was to be solved, and picking up the struggling fish, still upon my hook, I dropped him into a boiling pool a few paces behind me. His death was instantaneous, and with the softening of the muscles he broke loose from the hook, and disappeared from view. I did *not* eat him, but demonstrated the practicability of the feat, for during the half hour that I lingered about the pool, watching for his reappearance, the smell of boiled trout was sufficient to satisfy any skeptic on the question.

We slept soundly to the tune of the constant puff, puff, of the little volcanoes by our side, and woke up to find the sun just rising above the snow-capped peaks to the eastward, and casting his long slanting rays over the broad smooth surface of the lake, where an occasional great lazy-looking pelican was gently rocking in the little waves raised by the morning breeze. A horizontal band of white clouds, the product probably of the heat and moisture generated in the vicinity, rested over the lake, but was soon dissipated by the rays of the sun, and the bright morning scene appeared in all its beauty. Near us, the numerous columns of white steam, slowly rising in the cool air, created the impression of the neighborhood of some busy manufacturing mart, whilst in front, the broad beautiful lake stretched out far to the eastward, and away off on the opposite shore "Steamboat Point" loomed up in the distance, and with its puffs of steam reminded us of more civilized regions where half a dozen steamers are blowing off, preparatory to a start. With a very little imagination it was an easy matter to fancy the appearance of a steamer starting out from there to come here and take us off, for a trip around the lake and to the Great Falls below. Fancy a busy crowd awaiting her arrival on a dock built out, we will say, upon one of the cone-like structures I have described, each one eager to be the first on board. Let us pursue the fancy to its possible crisis. As you and a crowd of fellow-passengers rush along the narrow structure—each seeking to be *first,* as is usual in America—a loud scream pierces the air, and before you can interfere to prevent it, your wife's favorite lap-dog—or preferably somebody else's wife's favorite dog—is being rapidly converted into soup far down in the boiling caldron beneath your feet.

Visiting the Park in all its virgin wildness we were not afflicted with the tribe of professional guides to mar our pleasures with their senseless jargon, but the absence of all guides rendered our movements uncertain and threw us upon our own resources, and we had now reached a point in our travels where we were obliged to strike out into a wilderness of thick timber with nothing but the compass to guide us. We had been told that a direct western course for twenty-five miles would take us to the Great Geyser Basin, to visit which was the main object of our trip.

On the morning of the 10th of August, therefore, after a delicious bath in the waters of the lake, near the mouth of one of the warm-water streams, where any temperature to suit could be had, we plunged into the dense forest to the west of us, and followed, by the compass, as direct a course as the fallen timber would permit. Travelling along blindly in this way for about twenty miles our eyes were at length greeted by an opening, and we descended into a beautiful little grassy valley with a bright, clear stream running to the southward. Before us rose a high, steep, and rugged range of hills, and looking down the valley to the left, nestling in the hills there was a bright sheet of water, which we concluded must be Lake Madison, put down on the maps as the head of Madison River.

The hills in front of us looked forbidding and impassable, and the lake, as it glistened in the sunlight within its grassy banks, invited a closer inspection, so we concluded to accept the invitation, and moved down in that direction, with the hope of being able to pass down along the shore and get round the end of the range of hills in our front. But the high grass of the shores was filled with fallen timber lying two or three deep, underneath which the ground was not unfrequently boggy, and after struggling along through this for some distance we found ourselves shut in on the one side by the impassable shore of the lake, and on the other by the rugged range of hills. And of the two evils we were finally compelled to choose the lesser and climb the hills, which we did along a sort of trail where I doubt if anything but a mountain sheep had ever been before. After incredible labor, during which one of our pack animals lost his footing and rolled down a steep incline, we reached the top only to find the opposite slope worse than the one we had mounted. It was so late in the day when we succeeded in getting down this that it was concluded to camp here for the night, and to make an early start for the geyser region the next morning. We were fortunate enough to strike, near our camp, the trail of the engineer party of the preceding year, which was recognized by the little wheel-track of an odometer machine they had with them. The next morning we followed this trail, still in the midst of dense timber, and passing many beautiful falls of the Firehole River finally reached the head of an open valley, which from the description we recognized as the Upper Geyser Basin.

The first view of the valley produces a singular impression. In the midst of hills clothed with a dense growth of deep-green pine is a wide, open space of desolate ashy whiteness, with columns of white steam rising in every direction, some large, some small, so that one feels as if standing in the presence of an immense, old steam-boiler, with jets of steam hissing from every pore.

We select a camp in the edge of the timber, and then sally out, map in hand, to locate and examine the different geysers. Away off to the front, its marble whiteness contrasting with the deep-green of the pine forest beyond, rises the "Castle Geyser," fourteen feet high, looking like the ruins of some old castle, jets of steam and showers of water rising almost constantly from its top. Directly below us is the "Beehive," three feet high and seven feet through at the base, which we recognize from its form, and in every direction the surface rises into an innumerable number of truncated, cone-shaped structures, from each one of which rises a cloud of steam, like smoke from a chimney on a frosty morning, and in the midst of it all the bright, blue waters of the Firehole River tumbling along on their rapid descent, receiving numerous streams of hot water as it flows.

The "Giantess" is close by our camp; its crater at the top of a wide, gradually sloping cone, up the sides of which we walk with some trepidation, for there is no knowing when she will "go off." We are not yet much accustomed to geysers, and when she spouts, it is said she throws water two hundred and fifty feet high. She is quiet enough now, however, and, approaching the edge of her crater, we find it a deep, irregular basin, thirty feet across, filled with hot water, of a beautiful green color. This is usually simmering, but now and then it starts to boil up violently, and, until one becomes accustomed to this feature, a very strong disposition to step hastily back is developed in anticipation of an eruption. Standing on the cone of the "Giantess" and looking around, lesser ones of almost every size are seen, capped in some cases with the most beautiful forms of marble-white structures, some of which resemble those flower-stands formed in tiers, with a central stem, surrounded, lower down, with a circular basin, which has most beautifully scolloped rims, and is filled with warm water and white pebbles almost as round as marbles, formed evidently by the conglomeration of the material held in solution by the water, and constantly rolled about by the falling waters during eruptions. These formations are all similar in their nature, but there is such a variety in color, shape, and minor forms, that new beauties arise at every step we take in our explorations. Here a little vent, no bigger than a quill, is sending forth a jet of steam; the edges of the vent being polished as smooth as glass, and colored with the most beautiful tints, sulphur-yellow on the inside, growing gradually lighter outward, and merging on the exterior into a delicate straw, now and then tinted red or brown and other shades. There was a great basin, with its magnificently scolloped edges of pure flint-like porcelain, more delicate and perfect than any art can imitate. Here is a great caldron of boiling hot water, bubbling up every now and then with vigor, as if some power below was heaping on fuel. There is an immense basin filled to the brim, on a level with the ground, with water so clear, bright, and still, that it looks almost as placid as the air above our heads, and down through which you can look to an unknown depth.

Wandering about amongst these beauties, admiring at every step, I had just waded the stream to explore on the other side, when my attention was attracted by a great shout from the men, who were all running to the high ground on the cone of the "Giantess," and looking towards my side of the river. Turning around I caught sight of the cause of all this tumult. "Old Faithful" had "gone off," and was spouting water and steam to a great height in a graceful fountain. Higher and higher rose the column of pure white steam and spray, impelled by successive explosions from below, the steam at times being gently wafted aside by the breeze, and disclosing the column of water gracefully curving outwards at its highest point, and falling in showery spray upon the scolloped basins below. Approaching closer and closer to the beautiful fountain, I stood at length at its very base, just far enough away to avoid the falling waters. Every moment or two explosions far down in the crater, which shook the solid rock around, sent the water fifty or sixty feet into the air, the shock between the ascending and descending waters converting the whole into pure white spray, which, curving gracefully outwards, presented, in falling, a fountain of beauty of which it is impossible to describe in words. After this had continued for five or six minutes the explosions suddenly ceased, the water in the vent receded rapidly, gurgling as it went, and I took a closer view of the crater and its surroundings. The aperture, six feet by two, and irregular in shape, is as smooth as glass and creamy white in color. This throat of the geyser is surrounded by a formation very irregular in shape, and which rises about two feet above the *first platform.* It is formed of the material deposited by the water, and presents an incalculable number of beautiful and singular forms, which, in some cases, resemble the massive coral formations of the sea. The first platform consists of a number of tiny basins with curved and scolloped edges similar to those at the "Frozen Cascade," and these are succeeded by other basins, growing larger and larger, and forming successive steps or platforms as you recede from the crater down the conical slope which surrounds it. Immediately after the eruption the water thrown out by the geyser goes trickling down from basin to basin, just as I have described as taking place at the "Frozen Cascade." On looking into these basins I found that the water had deposited coloring matter of the most delicate tints. In the smaller basins next to the crater this was of a deep saffron, and, as you receded, it grew lighter and lighter, through cream-yellow and straw, until in the outer basins the color was a pure milk-white. I lingered a long while about "Old Faithful," admiring all these beautiful forms and colors, and, although we found similar ones about all the other geysers, none appeared so fresh and bright as these. We had numerous opportunities during our stay of witnessing the eruptions of this splendid geyser, for it acts with remarkable regularity once in about every hour, and got its name from the first explorers from this fact. All that was necessary to bring everybody to his feet, during the day was for some one to say, "There goes 'Old Faithful' "; and, during the night, any one awake could hear him regularly spouting his glories to the silent stars.

We made visits to all the prominent geysers in that portion of the Upper Basin, and, whilst a certain similarity seemed to exist amongst them all, there was such a variety in shape, color, ornamentation, and formation as to call forth exclamations of delight and wonder at every step. The great tube of the "Giant" stands up ten feet high and twenty-four feet in diameter, like the stump of some immense tree, which, however, instead of decaying, is growing larger and higher every year. The "Grotto" is a great mass of deposit with smooth water-worn cavities through which the water and steam rush during the eruptions. Many geysers have received names from the peculiar features which they possess, but hundreds and perhaps thousands still remain without names, and probably will remain so until a more thorough investigation develops their respective peculiarities.

The "Castle" geyser is peculiar, and differs from all the rest in possessing an irregular magnificent cone, one hundred and twenty feet in circumference, which rises twelve feet from the platform on which it stands. This cone is pure white in color and made up of an immense number of masses, globular in form on the exterior, beautifully decorated with beads and ornaments, and at a little distance presents the appearance of an immense pile of cauliflower-heads. I have ventured to modify somewhat the name given this geyser by my friend, Dr. Hayden, and called it the "Cauliflower Castle." The geyser, which has an orifice of some three feet in diameter, is in an almost constant state of eruption, and the falling spray, as it dashes against the exterior of the cone, is constantly adding to the cauliflower-heads, and replacing those which may be broken off. Lying near the base of the cone, I observed what was once the stem of a tree of considerable size. It was now crumbling to pieces, and, on breaking off a portion, the woody fibre was found to be completely replaced by the marble-like deposit from the water of the geyser. Close by the "Castle" is an immense circular pool, twenty feet across, of deep blue, placid water, down which you can look to an immense depth. Around this pool a rim, about a foot in height, has been built up, with the usual variety of bead-like and beautiful forms. To the very top of this the water now rests with a surface as smooth as glass, an outlet through a break on one side giving escape to the surplus water which, as it runs off, deposits a great variety of beautiful coloring matter.

It would take a volume to describe in detail the beauty and variety of the various geysers, hot springs, and pools, which pour their waters into the Firehole River, rolling along through this valley of wonder, a light cloud of steam always rising from its surface. Every step of the explorer brings forth exclamations of wonder and delight, and the sight-seers rush about from point to point, anxious and prepared to find curiosities more wonderful than any yet seen. From "Old Faithful," which stands near the head of the valley, these formations extend for four or five miles to a point where the stream is joined by another coming from the eastward, and flowing through a valley filled with another group of geysers and springs. This latter is called the Lower Geyser Basin, the other being named the Upper Basin. More recent explorations, however, have developed the fact that these are not the only geyser basins in this region. Every year adds to the number of the discoveries, and as yet the country has never been thoroughly explored or mapped. When it is, it is safe to predict that the Great National Park of the United States will be found to contain more great wonders than are known to exist on any other portion of the earth's surface of the same extent. The whole region should be thoroughly explored and accurately mapped, and, in the meantime, observation under a well-devised system should be inaugurated to determine the laws which govern the action of the geysers. So far as observed this action appears to be exceedingly irregular, both as regards the length of the eruptions and the intervals between them. To this remark, "Old Faithful" appears to be a marked exception, though the observations made have not as yet been sufficiently extensive to demonstrate that even he may not have his periods of rest. Observations made during the severe cold of winter would be especially interesting as showing whether or not the action is affected by the season. But little is known of the winter climate of the region, but there is every inclination that the fall of snow is very heavy. The immense quantity of hot water and steam thrown out, it is supposed, would materially moderate the temperature of these geyser basins, and would probably prevent the snows from lying very long in these valleys, and there is every indication that they are resorted to by game of all kinds during the winter. The only game seen by the party in the Park was the single deer I killed near Mount Washburne, but in the Firehole Valley we found numerous tracks of deer, elk, and bear made, evidently, when the ground was soft from snow or rain. In the winter the game would naturally resort to these valleys, in consequence of the modified temperature. In the summer the animals desert them for the highest mountains, to avoid the heat and flies. It was proposed, several years ago, to station a small military party under charge of officers in the Upper Geyser Basin during the winter for purposes of observation, and lovers of the hunt were stimulated with the idea of the probable sport to be had there. Such a party would have to be sent there early in the fall, in order to carry in the necessary stores and provide the necessary shelter before the approach of winter. During several months it could have but little intercourse with the outside world, unless in exceptionally mild winters. The results of the observation made by such a party would be exceedingly interesting to science, in investigating the laws governing the eruptions, which are now but little understood. The geysers are supposed to be the expiring action of volcanic forces of a former age, and, as pulsations of the heart of this great world of ours, cannot fail to be regulated with great interest by science.

As we returned from our ramble of sight-seeing my attention was attracted by a novel scene. Near our little camp, pitched in the edge of the timber, were several boiling springs. Around one of these a party of soldiers was gathered, evidently in great good humor, and engaged in thrusting in and pulling out different articles of wearing apparel, attached to sticks, from the waters of the spring, which looked white and frothy. On inquiry I found they had thrown a piece of soap into the spring, and Dame Nature was called upon to act as laundress in cleansing the clothing from the dust and dirt of travel, and she did the work very well.

Our attention was directed every now and then to the eruption of some of the smaller geysers, but, with the exception of the regular action of "Old Faithful," none of the larger ones seemed to be in the humor to act during the afternoon. The "Beehive" was said to be very handsome but very irregular, and we did not have the pleasure of seeing it act during our stay. The one, however, which all felt the greatest desire to see was the "Giantess," on account of its volume and reported height, but we were obliged to retire for the night without her showing her beauties, and strict orders were given that if, at any time during the night, she was heard to be astir, the alarm should be given. About midnight I was waked out of a sound sleep by a cry, and jumping up looked out upon the night. Everything was dark and a drizzling rain was falling, and satisfied we could see nothing, although the sound of the eruption was very apparent, we crawled back to our blankets, disappointed that the "Giantess" should cover her beauties with the veil of

night. It was supposed, however, that it was not the "Giantess" which
alarmed us during the night, for the next morning, as we were preparing
to depart, we were startled with a loud rumbling report, and the
immense body of water in her crater sprang fifty feet into the air, in the
midst of a great volume of dense white steam with a mushroom-shaped
head, which recalled the explosion of the Petersburg mine. The water at
its highest point curved gracefully outward and descended as a beautiful
water-spout, but before it had reached the earth another explosion came,
and then others in rapid succession, each one with the same mushroom-
shaped head forcing its predecessor up higher and higher, until there
stood in the clear morning air a great column of which I cannot better
describe than by supposing a number of immense umbrellas of dense
white steam piled one on top of the other, each one with its handle
resting on the roof of the preceding one, with heavy showers of rain
falling on all sides, as if dripping from the umbrella roofs. This continued until the whole heavens above were filled with clouds of steam,
which, in the still morning, rose perhaps for a thousand feet straight up
and then gently floated away. How high the water rose it was impossible
to tell, for the dense masses of steam prevented the point where it turned
from being seen; but I formed the impression that in this eruption it did
not rise over seventy or eighty feet. The effect was magnificent in the
extreme, and the impression produced on the mind one of awe, due, I
think, in a great measure, to the sudden exhibition of great *power* developed in what was, a few moments before, a placid powerless body of
water. I approached the crater closely during the eruption and found the
water running off in floods down the slope of the immense cone which
surrounded the geyser. Much of it, of course, returned to the crater, only
however to be again and again thrown up. As I stood on the solid rock
and felt it trembling under my feet at each successive explosion, heard
far down in the bowels of the earth, an impression was produced of
*unlimited* power, and I have no reason to doubt the statement, that the
water rises, in some cases, to the height of two hundred and fifty feet.

After this magnificent spectacle had continued for about fifteen
minutes, the explosions suddenly ceased, the masses of steam floated
away, the water in the crater rapidly sank about twenty feet, boiling
violently, very gradually rose to the top of the basin, and then settled
down into comparative quiet again. About an hour afterwards, just as we
were mounting our horses to leave, the "Giantess" went off in another
eruption similar to the first, and all eyes were turned back in admiration
at what appeared to be a parting salute from the beauty. As though she
had given the signal, the different geysers, as we rode down the valley,
broke out in succession as if bidding us farewell, and riding away we

THE GIANTESS
One of the most impressive geysers in the
Upper Geyser Basin, the Giantess shot upwards
with a series of eruptions that resembled
umbrellas stacked upon one another. *Scribner's
Monthly Magazine,* June 1871.

probably saw the valley under its most magnificent aspect. As we turned northward and got the erupting geysers between us and the sun, then just rising above the tree tops, the falling spray caught the beams of light and spanned each fountain with a rainbow. Again and again did we halt, and turning back our eyes enjoy the magnificent spectacle, with a feeling of regret at having to leave such beauties behind us.

We passed out of the Upper Geyser Basin and entered the lower one, filled with hot springs, mud geysers, and the like; but we saw nothing which would compare in splendor with the glories of the Upper Geyser Basin.

This remarkable region, which has been opened to the knowledge of the civilized world only a few years, has been known for a long time through rumors and the information derived from mountaineers. In 1860 a party under charge of Captain Raynolds, of the Topographical Engineers, approached this country from the south, guided by probably the most noted guide of the Northwest, James Bridger. The party found the passes of the Wind River Range so blocked up with snow in June that it was unable to get through to the Yellowstone Lake region, but succeeded in passing the mountains farther to the west, struck the Madison River below the geyser basins, and proceeded down that stream to the Three Forks of the Missouri.

James Bridger, or as he is universally called, "Jim" Bridger, I believe is still living, and has the reputation of being the best guide in the Western country. He is reported, too, to be in the habit of drawing a very "long bow" in regard to the wonders he has seen during his very extensive travels in the Western wilds. It is said he especially delights in "stuffing" unsophisticated Eastern visitors with stories of diamond mountains so transparent that horsemen can be seen *through* them miles away, and the like, and that when persons express wonder at the height of the slim spire of "Chimney Rock" (a celebrated landmark on the Platte), he assures them that when *he* first saw it, it was some thousand feet higher, but had afterwards its dimensions much reduced by a streak of lightning, which struck and shattered it.

Since the discovery of the wonders of the Yellowstone, it is said, the old man has been heard to say very complacently that people will yet find out he has not been "blowing" quite so much about this country as has been generally supposed, and that now they will probably admit he is not such a "great liar" as they have given him credit for being. Certain it is that even "Jim" Bridger's active imagination is not equal to the task of exaggerating the scenes to be encountered amidst the wonders of the Yellowstone and geyser region.

I have already detained you too long, and will not stop to tell of the minor incidents of the trip—how we fell short of provisions, and had to kill squirrels, blue-jays, and a pelican, and finally to grub for wild roots for subsistence; and what a feast we had when we met a part of Professor Hayden's party and were furnished with a double-handful of sugar and a sack of flour.

I have endeavored to describe to you some of the many beautiful things I saw in the Yellowstone region. There are thousands which I did not see, and probably thousands of others which have never been seen by a white man, and by very few red ones. All these are included in a territory about sixty miles square, in the northwest corner of Wyoming Territory, set apart by Congress as the National Park of the United States.

Americans are sometimes accused of being afflicted with a boastful spirit; and, whilst willing to admit that the charge is not entirely without foundation, I can readily see how anyone raised in this great Western world of ours might very naturally feel some apprehension about going out at night in England, lest by some accident he should *step off*; or imagine that one used to wandering through these snow-capped Rocky Mountains should reply as the American did who was asked, after crossing from France to Italy, how he liked the scenery in the Alps: "Oh, yes, the Alps. Well, now you remind me, I believe we did cross *'rising ground.'*"

But, after all, have we not a great deal to boast of in this country? Have we not the most varied soil and climate within our borders, capable of producing everything from a tropical fruit to the finest Montana wheat, grown right under the snow-line? Have we not the freest government on the face of the globe? Have we not kept up the largest army in the world, squandered more money and spilled more blood in the cause of liberty than any other people? Have we not the highest mountains, the broadest plains, the longest and largest rivers, the handsomest women, the biggest men, and the best revolvers in the universe? And ought we not be proud of all these?

And now, to cap the climax and the continent, have we not the greatest National Park on the face of God's earth, filled with every beauty which the eye of humanity delights to rest upon—great waterfalls for the ladies, ready-made mud pies for the children, spouting geysers for the men, magnificent scenery and heated baths for all the rest of mankind?

# Last Summer's Expedition against the Sioux and Its Great Catastrophe

*Campaigns against hostile Indians occasionally interrupted the frontier routine of scouting and garrison duty. John Gibbon and his regiment were important components of two major Indian campaigns, against the Sioux in 1876 and against the Nez Percé in 1877. The following two articles, "Last Summer's Expedition against the Sioux and Its Great Catastrophe" and "Hunting Sitting Bull," are actually two chapters of the same story. Colonel Gibbon's memoir of the Sioux Campaign of 1876, familiar to readers of today as "Custer's Last Stand" or "The Battle of the Little Big Horn," was published in 1877, a scant year after the events described. Employing his official report, diary entries, and recollections of the events, Gibbon wrote a captivating account of this famous Indian campaign. His first article ends with the rescue of survivors from the Seventh Cavalry and confirmation that Lieutenant Colonel George A. Custer and five of his companies had been killed by Teton Sioux and Northern Cheyenne warriors. Contrary to popular opinion, the defeat of Custer did not bring an end to the campaign, and Gibbon's column remained in the field for another three months in a fruitless search for the elusive Indians.*

*Although Colonel Gibbon titled his second article "Hunting Sitting Bull," it was merely a gesture to his readers. In 1878 he explained that Sitting Bull was not the leader of a great Indian confederation, saying, "Sitting Bull is pretty much of a myth; he has been given, by popular clamor, a prominent position to which he was not entitled. He was not the principal man in that Custer affair at all. He has been noted, however, for a great many years for his intense hostility to the whites."[1]*

*Less than two years after the Custer fight, Colonel Gibbon was asked whether infantry or cavalry was more useful in fighting Indians on the frontier. He replied, "Under favorable conditions, as when operating in a kind of country where the Indians*

---

[1]U.S. Congress, House of Representatives, House Misc. Doc. No. 56, 45th Congress, 2d Session, vol. 4, 1877, serial 1818, "Reorganization of the Army," p. 273.

*are encumbered with their villages, infantry can sometimes overtake them and strike them in their camp, but, as a general rule, and especially when they are on the alert, cavalry is the only arm of the service with which that can be done." Then, perhaps remembering the battlefield of the Little Big Horn, Gibbon continued, "When in contact with the Indians, the infantry is, in my opinion, far superior to the cavalry, and I think that the Indians dread them more than they dread the cavalry, because they are well aware that as horsemen they are the superiors of the white men, and that they are better shots on horseback than white men possibly could be."* [2]

"Last Summer's Expedition against the Sioux and Its Great Catastrophe" appeared in American Catholic Quarterly Review 2 (April 1877): 271–304; "Hunting Sitting Bull" appeared in ibid. (October 1877): 665–694.

*I*n the old geographies of the country an immense tract was left blank except for the words, printed across it in large letters, *"The Great American Desert."* Through a portion of this country I propose to take my readers in the present paper.

The Great Missouri River, heading in the heart of the Rocky Mountains, at about the intersection of the forty-fourth parallel with the one hundred and eleventh degree of west longitude, flows directly north for nearly four degrees, then turning to the eastward continues in that direction for about eight degrees more, and then after its junction with the waters of the Yellowstone at old Fort *Union,* near Fort Buford, doubles on its course and flows southeastwardly for hundreds of miles towards its union with the Mississippi. The northern portion of this great bend of the Missouri River was the scene of events during the spring and summer of the Centennial year, in a search for General Sitting Bull and the hostile bands associated with him, some of which we will describe.

With its head waters only a few miles to the south and east of those of the Missouri, the Yellowstone River also flows directly north for over a hundred miles, passing through the National Park and then turning to the eastward pursues its northeastwardly course for nearly five hundred miles to its junction with the Missouri at Fort Buford. Where it turns to the eastward the Yellowstone is only about twenty miles from Fort Ellis, at the head of the Gallatin Valley; and a few miles lower down it receives the waters of Shields's River, the only *northern* tributary it has throughout its whole course. From the *south* it receives numerous streams, heading in the mountain ranges far to the southward. The largest of these are Clark's Fork, the Big Horn, Tongue, and Powder Rivers, all streams

[2]Ibid., pp. 269–270.

named by the Lewis and Clark expedition of 1806. The largest of them all, the Big Horn, runs for several hundred miles directly north, and joins the Yellowstone at a distance of over two hundred miles from Fort Ellis, and furnishes about as much water as the main Yellowstone. It drains an immense area of country, and has numerous tributaries from the east and west. About forty miles from its mouth, it receives from the southeast the waters of the Little Big Horn, around whose name mournful memories will linger for many years to come.

On the Big Horn, seventy-five miles from its mouth, are the ruins of old Fort C. F. Smith, and eighty miles to the southeast those of Fort Phil Kearny, the scene of the Fetterman massacre in 1866, the perpetrators being the same tribe which ten years later made a spot on the Little Big Horn, not a hundred miles away, mournfully notorious by the slaughter of the gallant Custer and his three hundred men. A few miles below the mouth of the Big Horn and on the left bank of the Yellowstone, stands, or stood, Fort Pease, named after a former agent of the friendly Crows, on whose reservation, extending south of the Yellowstone and far to the eastward of the Big Horn, General Custer's battle took place on the 25th of June. Fort Pease is not, and never was, a military post. It was established as a trading and "wolfing" station, was formed of little log huts connected by a line of stockade, and was occupied by a party of hunters and trappers, whose principal occupation consisted in collecting furs from the numerous wild animals inhabiting the country. The most valuable of these are derived from the wolves, which exist there in great numbers, and those who collect the skins are known in the Western country as "wolfers." The skins are most valuable in the winter season when the fur is heavy and soft, and the method of securing them cruel in the extreme. During the severe weather of winter when the ground is covered with snow the wolves in immense numbers range over the whole country, especially at night, in search of food. The quick nose of the wolf soon discovers the location of any dead animal, and it is at once eagerly devoured by the half-famished animals, whose cries bring others to the scene of the feast. The "wolfer" after slaying a deer, antelope, elk, or buffalo, removes the skin, takes such portion of the meat as he wants, and then taking from his pocket a little bottle of strychnine proceeds whilst the flesh is still warm to impregnate it with the poison. The next morning when he visits the scene he has only to follow the wolf-tracks in the snow for a short distance to discover the bodies of all the wolves which have participated in the feast, lying where the poor animals have expired in the most intense agony. He removes the valuable skins at his leisure, or if the weather is cold waits for a milder day to perform the skinning operation.

So violent is this poison that it is said that another animal eating of the flesh of a poisoned one rapidly falls a victim to the deadly taint, and the stomach of a poisoned wolf will retain its fatal properties for a long time to come, as many a hunter with valuable dogs has found to his cost. This active poison, strychnine, is sold in immense quantities throughout this whole Western country, and is, I believe, the only one used; the more common one, arsenic, producing, as is well known, no effect upon the dog-kind. The Indians are very much prejudiced against its use, and it is said they have a superstition that where it is used on dead buffalo it destroys the grass, and drives the buffalo away. The Sioux in the vicinity of Fort Pease early testified their hostility towards the "wolfer" party, and took occasion to waylay and kill any of them who imprudently wandered too far from the post. They even threatened the post itself with attack, and so beleaguered the little garrison in the winter of 1875 and 1876 that it was with difficulty any of them could get out for procuring the necessary food or fuel. In the early spring of 1876 their cries for help became so loud that in February a command was ordered from Fort Ellis to go to the relief of Fort Pease. Four companies of cavalry started on the 22d, made the march of over two hundred miles down the Yellowstone, crossing the river several times on the ice, and returned to Fort Ellis in less than a month with the rescued trappers, having seen no Indians on the trip.

The Sioux did not confine their hostile acts to parties, like the one at Fort Pease, immediately on the borders of their hunting-ground. For several years, murdering and thieving war parties had invaded the white settlements of Montana, carrying consternation wherever they went. Cattle were slaughtered, horses stolen, and men killed in the settlements east of Fort Ellis, in the summer of 1875, and during August of that year several soldiers, whilst hunting and fishing in the vicinity of Camp Lewis, a post established for the protection of a mail and freighting route from Helena to Carroll on the Missouri River, were killed. These depredations were all supposed to be committed by men belonging to a tribe presided over by a chief called Sitting Bull, a rather notorious Sioux who prided himself greatly upon standing aloof from the whites, never going to an agency and never trading with one personally, although he was not averse to trading with the agency through others. His home camp was supposed to be on the dry fork of the Missouri, a stream which running north empties into that river just above Fort Peck (a trading post and agency for the Northern Indians). These war parties from his camp, operating during the summer season, would pass over vast distances on their fleet little ponies, commit their depredations, and be off hundreds of miles away before anybody but the poor victims would know anything about it.

But Montana was not the only region which suffered from these depredations. Similar transactions were taking place to the southward along the northern borders of Wyoming and Nebraska, and in the Black Hills (a region guaranteed by solemn treaty to the Indians), the "irrepressible conflict" between barbarism and the invading gold-seekers was carried on, and, as may be imagined, did not tend to bring about peaceful relations between the government and the Sioux nation. At length the government, having through its agents *starved* many of the Indians into leaving the agencies in order to get food, ordered them all back there in the depth of winter at the penalty of being proceeded against by the military, and early in March the troops took the field from the south, struck Crazy Horse's camp on Powder River, and returned.

On the very day of this occurrence (17th), five companies of infantry left Fort Shaw, and, in the midst of snow and mud, commenced their march of one hundred and eighty-three miles for Fort Ellis, whilst another company from Camp Baker dug its way through the deep snowdrifts of a mountain range, and proceeded towards the same post. These troops reached Fort Ellis in the latter part of March, probably the most inclement month of the year, and, in the midst of heavy storms of wet snow and sleet, and over roads which were simply horrible, were pushed across the divide which separates that post from the waters of the Yellowstone, under the supposition that they were moving to cooperate with General Crook's column from the south. On the 1st of April, the four companies of the Second Cavalry left Fort Ellis to follow the same road, and overtake the infantry. It proved anything but an April day. The steep and rocky road was intersected in places by streams and marshy spots where our heavily loaded wagons sank to the hub, and on the 3d a furious storm of wind and driving snow assailed us, so that it was midnight on the 4th before the train reached Shields's River, a distance of twenty-eight miles. This was slow progress, indeed, if we wished to cooperate with General Crook's column, the account of whose fight, some four hundred miles away, had just been received by telegraph.

The military was started out to punish and bring to subjection the hostile bands which were defying the government. These were known to be not numerous, and they were, during the summer months, in the habit of roaming at will over the vast uninhabited region I have described in the great bend of the Missouri River, hunting the buffalo, laying up their supplies of skins and meat for the winter, and varying their operations by sending out small war parties to raid upon the white settlements, or fighting the Crows, against whom they were at deadly enmity. If these were all the troops had to contend with it was natural to suppose that the moment General Crook commenced to press them from the south, these bands would move north, and, if not interfered with, would, if the pressure continued, cross the Yellowstone, and perhaps even the Missouri. Hence the necessity for other columns of troops with which to strike these moving bands on the march, or interfere to prevent their crossing to the north of the Yellowstone. For this purpose two columns moved, one from the east the other from the west, and marched towards each other. But two weeks before the Montana column started from Fort Ellis, General Crook had struck his blow, and hence the necessity for pushing forward down the Yellowstone as rapidly as possible, for the Indians, if moving north, would succeed in getting across that stream before the yearly spring rise, and before either the eastern or western column could interfere.

The original intention was to move the Montana column directly on Fort C. F. Smith by what was called the Bozeman wagon-road, then to cross the Big Horn River and move eastward, with the expectation of striking any hostile camps which might be located in that vast region watered by the Little Big Horn, Tongue, and Rosebud, but, on the receipt of the news of General Crook's fight, it was deemed advisable to move this column directly down the Yellowstone, and to keep it north instead of south of that river. This rendered necessary a change of our depot of supplies from the new Crow agency on the Stillwater, one hundred miles from Fort Ellis, to the north side of the Yellowstone River. In a few weeks that stream would be entirely impassable from the melting of the spring snows. A train with a month's supply of forage and rations had already been forwarded to the Crow agency. The troops found no difficulty in fording the Yellowstone River, and on the 7th the cavalry overtook the infantry in camp on the Yellowstone above the mouth of the Stillwater, where the whole command was luxuriating on the delicious trout caught in the greatest quantity from the clear and almost ice-cold waters of the Yellowstone.

I had in the morning sent forward a courier to the agency, calling a council with the Crows with a view to obtaining some of them to accompany the troops as scouts, and had requested Mitch Bouyer, a noted guide and interpreter, to meet me that night in my camp. This man I had never seen, but he had served with troops before, and bore the reputation of being, next to the celebrated Jim Bridger, the best guide in the country. Whilst seated in my tent the next morning, a man with the face of an Indian and the dress of a white man approached the door, and almost without saying anything seated himself on the ground, and it was some moments before I understood that my visitor was the expected guide. He was a diffident, low-spoken man, who uttered his words in a hesitating way, as if uncertain what he was going to say. He brought the news that the Crows were waiting to see me, and mounting my horse I was with a small party soon on the road to the agency, which we reached after a disagreeable ride of eighteen miles through a severe storm of wet snow. The agency, situated amidst bleak and barren hills, was surrounded by the tepees of some three thousand Crows, scattered in family groups all over the little valley of Rosebud Creek[1], a branch of the Stillwater.

The next day, Sunday, the chiefs assembled in council to hear my "talk" and the proposition to furnish us scouts. Somewhat to my surprise the proposition did not appear to be favorably received, and when an Indian does not want to do a thing he resembles a white man a good deal, and has a thousand and one excellent reasons why he should not do it. They listened in silence to the interpreter as he translated, or *appeared* to translate, what I said. For when he came to translate their answer to me he strung his English words together in such a fearfully incongruous way as made me tremble at the idea that my eloquent appeal to the chiefs had been murdered in the Crow tongue, as he was murdering the English in conveying to me their answer.

These Indian interpreters are a peculiar institution. As a class, they are an interesting study, and will bear generally a good deal of watching. A white man, usually a renegade from civil society, takes up his abode with a tribe of Indians, adopts their mode of life, takes unto himself a squaw, picks up gradually enough of their signs and words to make himself understood, and when the Indians come in contact with the whites becomes, in the absence of any other means of communication, an "interpreter." He may not understand the English language, or be able to put together a single intelligible sentence, and it does not mend the matter much if he happens to be a French Canadian, for then broken French, broken English, and broken Indian are mixed up in a hodge-podge which defies all understanding and makes the listener sometimes give up in despair. I suspect many an Indian commissioner would stand aghast could he have *literally* translated to him the perfect jumble of words in which the "interpreter" had conveyed his eloquent and care-fully prepared speech to the ears of his red audience. For this reason it is a matter of some importance in communicating with Indians to make use of the plainest language and the shortest sentences, and even then you are by no means sure that anything like what you intended is conveyed to your listeners, especially if what you say does not happen to meet the peculiar views or interests of the one who, for the want of a

[1]This must not be confounded with the other Rosebud lower down.

better term, is called an "interpreter." The one who officiated on this occasion appeared to try to be making up by gesticulations and a loud voice for any defects in his knowledge of language. I believe he did finally succeed in conveying to the Indians the information that we wanted twenty-five of their young active warriors to accompany us to the field and serve as the "eyes" of the expedition, in spying out the country and giving us information regarding the location of the Sioux camps.

The talk was received in silence, followed by a very earnest discussion among themselves, after which two of the principal chiefs, Iron Bull and Blackfoot, replied to the effect that if the young men wanted to go they could go, but that if they did not want to go they (the chiefs) could not make them; that they were friends to the white man and desired to remain at peace with him; appealed to the Almighty (the interpreter called him *Godalamity*) as to the sincerity of what they said, and ended with what I fear is a very common appeal now amongst Indians, for more flour and beef than was issued to them. But one single man seemed to talk in favor of going to war, but they asked time to talk about it amongst themselves, for such weighty matters are never decided in a hurry, and have to be discussed with due deliberation and the appropriate amount of smoke. So the council broke up without any definite conclusion being reached, and I began to think we should have to enter the Sioux country blindfolded. I soon discovered, however, that only the "old fogies" had spoken in council, and that as soon as "Young America" had a chance to be heard in the camps our chance for obtaining scouts improved, and the next morning the whole number required came forward and were sworn into the United States service. This ceremony was peculiar. We wished to bind them to their contract in some way, and in casting round for a method were informed that the Crow's way to take an oath was to *touch with his finger the point of a knife.* After this solemn proceeding if he failed to stand up to his pledges he was a disgraced man; but what was far more likely to keep him faithful was the belief that a violation of the oath laid him open to direful calamities in the way of disease and misfortune, not only to himself, but to all the members of his family! All the volunteers were paraded, and an officer presented to each in succession a hunting knife, on the point of which each one gravely placed the tip of his forefinger and the deed was done. They thus became United States soldiers for three months, and were to receive soldier's pay, rations, and clothing. After all had gone through the ceremony, one of them took the knife and gravely presented the point of it to me. When asked why he wished to swear me, he said he wished to bind me to do what *they* said; but I told him I could not do that, for the obligation to obey was on their side alone. The officer who swore them in offered to swear that he would see they got all the pay, rations, etc., they were entitled to, and as all they wanted apparently was some kind of mutual obligation, they readily consented to this, and the officer solemnly touched the point of the knife.

I will not burden my readers with the long list of the long names of the twenty-five warriors who thus engaged to join us in our campaign against the Sioux, but will mention simply the names of several who afterwards became noted amongst us.

Ee-suh-see-ush, whose English name was "Show-His-Face," was an old man, who went along with no idea of engaging in the labors of war, but accompanied the party simply to give it character, and bestow upon the younger members the benefit of his advice. He was early looked upon as what in Western phraseology is called a "coffee-cooler," a fellow who loafs around the camp-fire, and whose principal occupation consists in cooling *and* drinking coffee from a tin cup. From his supposed resemblance to a venerable senator from the State of Pennsylvania he soon became known in the camp as "The Senator."

Iss-too-sah-shee-dah, Half-Yellow-Face, was a large, fine-looking Indian, who afterwards became a great favorite with us, and was one of the six Crows who accompanied the Seventh Cavalry and was present with it in its fight on the 25th of June.

Mee-uah-tsee-us, White Swan, also accompanied the Seventh Cavalry, and was badly wounded in the battle.

Shuh-shee-ahsh, Curly Hair, was quite a young man and became noted afterwards as the one single person who, of all those taken into action under the immediate command of General Custer, made his escape.

On the 10th our wagon train arrived from the camp, our supplies were loaded up and ready to start the next morning for the depot to be established on the north bank of the Yellowstone. That night a furious storm of wind and snow raged, and we opened our eyes to find the ground covered with two feet of snow and rapidly deepening. To remain stationary, however, was simply to contemplate the possibility of being snowed up in the mountains for a week, perhaps longer. As soon, therefore, as the harness could be dug out of the snow, and the teams hitched up we started to plough through the deep snow notwithstanding the storm, which still raged directly in our faces. As we receded from the mountains, however, the snow decreased in depth, the storm abated, and the train reached camp late at night, the only mishap being the loss of two mules drowned in crossing the Yellowstone at a ford which was quite a deep and rapid one.

All the supplies and extra baggage which we could not carry in our wagons we now prepared to leave here under charge of one of the infantry companies, and with the remainder of the command and our heavily loaded wagons, we resumed the march down the Yellowstone. The ground was, however, very soft from the melting snow, and the teams labored slowly along. For several days we made but little progress, and only reached Baker's battle-ground, a distance of forty-three miles, on the 15th. This was the scene of an attack made by Indians in 1872 upon a body of our troops engaged in escorting the engineers of the Northern Pacific Railroad Company.

Below this, in order to avoid the rough broken ground extending for miles along the north of the river, we were obliged to cross once more to the southern bank, at a ford which was deep and rapid, and came very near proving fatal to one of our officers. His horse yielding to the force of the swiftly rushing current soon got out of his depth, and in an instant both he and his rider disappeared beneath the surface of the water. Soon the horse's head came up and then the rider's; but to the horror of the lookers-on the horse seemed to be utterly incapable of swimming, and engaged in frantic struggles, without aim or object, in the course of which he nearly fell over backwards on his rider. The current fortunately, as it swept them along, carried them close enough to the river-bank to strike bottom, when horse and rider, the latter still clinging to the bridle, but chilled with the ice-cold water, were pulled ashore.

On the south side of the river there is no longer any road, and we have to make our way as best we can through the thick heavy sage-brush of the valley of Prior's Creek, which we find a deep rushing torrent of muddy snow-water, with high banks. Crossing this delays us so long that the day is far towards its close when we go into camp, chafing at having made only seven miles.

The next day brought us to the far-famed Pompey's Pillar, almost under the shadow of which we camped. It is an irregular mass of sandstone, rising several hundred feet above the level of the valley on the south side of the river, and evidently belonged originally to a corresponding bluff on the opposite side of the river, from which it has been separated by the wearing away of the intervening rock. The account of Lewis and Clark mentions that a fine view of the surrounding country was had from the top of Pompey's Pillar, which was ascended by Captain Clark for that purpose the day the expedition passed the pillar, which is stated in their journal to have been the 25th of July, 1806. I climbed up the not very steep ascent on the eastern side, and whilst resting on one of the ledges read over the names, which, in travellers' fashion were roughly scribbled over the face of the soft sandstone, until I came to this:

Wm Clark
July 25th 1806

My first thought was that some later visitor had amused himself by inscribing the great explorer's name on this landmark; but an examination of the more recent inscriptions showed them all to be light-colored, whilst the lines of this one were of the same tint as the face of the brown sandstone upon which the writing was placed, and I remained satisfied that I stood face to face with Captain Clark's name inscribed nearly seventy years before. I continued the ascent, pondering over the different circumstances surrounding me in this Centennial year of the country, and those under which Captain Clark climbed up when the nation was but thirty-one years old, and this whole region one vast wilderness. On reaching the top I found myself standing upon a grass-grown mound surrounded on three sides by a sheer precipice of perpendicular rock, down which it made one's head swim to look. To the north, across the beautiful clear river, rose a mass of rough broken hills, whilst to the south and west extended the broad flat plain of the river bottom, bordered on the north by a curved line of timber which marked the course of the river, and to the south by a range of bluffs which, opening in one place to allow the passage of Fly Creek, permitted the eye to range far up its little valley towards the mouth of the Little Big Horn, afterwards to play so prominent a part in the history of our campaign.

With a view to the examination of that region the command laid over here one day, and scouts were sent off in that direction. They returned without having seen any sign of Indians, but reported that the whole valley of the Big Horn was black with countless herds of buffalo quietly feeding, the best of signs that no Indians are close about, and yet the best in the world that they are not very far away; for the buffalo herd is the natural *commissary* of the Indians on the plains, and they constantly follow this moving depot of supplies. When they commence to hunt them, the buffalo immediately about the hunting-grounds stampede and run for miles, pushing the rest of the herd before them. Hence, if the buffalo are quietly feeding you may be sure there is no pressure from behind, and no Indians near. But if on the contrary the herd is found to be moving, you may look out for Indians, as surely as you look for cars behind an approaching locomotive.

Ordinarily on reaching camp both officers and men were so tired out with the march that as soon as the evening meal is finished, and the night guard posted, all are ready to seek that sleep, the want of which tells fearfully upon the physical forces the next day, and usually by nine o'clock, frequently earlier, the whole camp except the sentinels are wrapped in deep slumber, which is enjoyed securely, with the knowledge that several pairs of eyes are peering out into the darkness and the same number of pairs of ears eagerly on the alert to detect the approach of any prowling Indians who may be seeking an opportunity to steal our animals. But after a day's rest the powers are recuperated, groups are formed around the blazing camp-fires, and the still night re-echoes with songs sung in full chorus. Such an evening was spent under the tall cottonwoods of our camp at Pompey's Pillar, and long after the camp-fires were out and everything was still, the thoughts of many of us wandered off towards those "true loves," who, in the words of the ringing chorus, still echoing in our ears, were, so far as communicating with them was concerned,

> "Playing the grand in a distant land,
> Ten thousand miles away."

During the next day's march the bluffs on both sides abutted so closely on the river as to force us to ford the stream twice within a distance of two miles, and now haste becomes all the more necessary, for the river is evidently rising, and we must make our last crossing so as to be on the north side before it becomes impassable. Our guide, Mitch Bouyer, is of inestimable value now, for he rides forward to search for a crossing, and is an indefatigable worker, riding his hardy little pony into the ice-cold water sometimes to a swimming depth, testing the crossings where anybody thinks there is a chance to get our wagons over. At last the shallowest point is found, and although deeper than is comfortable we must take to the water, for we cannot afford to wait another day. A company of cavalry, with its old soldier captain at its head, mounted on his old and long-tried favorite, "Dick," enters the ford, stringing out in a long curved line behind as brave old "Dick" breasts the rushing and rapidly deepening stream. Higher and higher rises the water, and just as we begin to think some of the smaller horses will have to swim, "Dick's" shoulder commences to emerge, and the worst is passed. Now the wagons, covered with infantrymen, start in, and as they approach the deepest part some of the smaller mules barely have their backs above the water, but still they struggle on, seeming to understand as well as their drivers that when crossing a river is no time "to swap horses." Suddenly down goes the forepart of one of the wagons, and for a moment it is a matter of doubt whether a wheel is broken or is in a hole. The mules struggle and plunge, fall down and get up again, the drivers, outsiders, and men shout out their loudest yells to encourage the frantic animals, and at last the long line of wagons reaches the opposite shore, water pouring from every crack of the wagon-bodies, which makes us hope that the bottom layer of each load is bacon rather than "hardtack" and bedding. Our dripping teams are given a short rest, mounted officers and men pour the water from their boots, and we all feel relieved that we are on the right bank of the river at last. A few miles further, and from the top of the bluffs bordering the valley of the Yellowstone we catch sight of the walls of Fort Pease, still standing, with a little United States flag fluttering in the breeze.

The next day a courier arrived from Camp Supply, bringing an important dispatch from department headquarters. It had reached Camp Supply just after the departure of two couriers with our mail, and an energetic young son of one of our officers started with it, accompanied by a single soldier, to ride a hundred miles and bring it to me. He followed our trail, saw nothing of the other couriers, crossed, with great difficulty, the river at our last ford, and reached our camp in safety. The dispatch was dated at St. Paul on the 15th (six days before), and informed me that General Crook would not be prepared to take the field before the middle of May, that the third column had not yet started, and directed that I proceed no farther than the mouth of the Big Horn unless sure of striking a successful blow. Our camp was, therefore, moved down to Fort Pease, and for three weeks we were engaged in what to a soldier is the hardest of all duties—*waiting.*

Advantage was taken of this delay to send back our wagon train under charge of a company, to bring up the rest of our supplies, and to thoroughly examine the valleys of Little and Big Horn in the direction of old Fort C. F. Smith. This latter was accomplished by a scouting party of two companies of cavalry, which left us on the 24th and returned on the 1st of May, having seen no signs of Indians during the trip.

On the 30th, some of our Indian scouts returned from the Rosebud, reporting that country free from any signs of Indians, and it began to look as if they had all fled to the agencies. Our Crow scouts are kept constantly on the alert, some of them being out every day, early and late. They appear to be of a nervous, excitable temperament, and some of them came running in one day to announce the approach of a party of Sioux. A mounted party was at once sent out to reconnoitre, and came back with the information that the scouts had seen one of our hunting parties, and took them for Sioux.

Fort Pease is situated directly on the bank of the river, at the edge of a wide open prairie. Directly opposite, on the other side of the river, a steep rocky bluff rises up almost perpendicularly from the edge of the water, and this our scouts were in the habit of using as a lookout, crossing the river in a small boat, several of which were found at the fort when we arrived there. The 1st of May was a bright clear day, and about noon the whole camp was startled by hearing loud and continued yells from the opposite bluffs. Immediately the Crows in camp seized their arms, and started on a run for their pony herd, grazing about a mile from camp. Looking up to the top of the bluff, four Indians could be seen running in single file at the top of their speed, and uttering the most piercing screams. They looked as if about to pitch over the perpendicular bluff into the river below; but just before reaching the edge, the leader commenced circling around, followed by the others, all uttering the wildest shrieks, and then all disappeared behind a projecting point, to reappear soon after at a lower point, still on the full run. The running in a circle was the signal for "an enemy in sight," and word was sent to draw in the herd. In an incredibly short space of time the scouts had crossed the river, and came panting into camp with the information that they had seen a large war party of Sioux coming out of the valley of Tullock's Fork. As I was expecting the scouting party from Fort Smith, I suggested that it might be that; but they declared they were not white men, did not move like them, and were far too numerous to be our scouting party, and altogether were so positive and confident, and more-over apparently so hurt that I should not think they could confound white men and Sioux, that I began to have serious misgivings in regard to the safety of our two little companies of cavalry, and to imagine that they had met with serious disaster, and the victorious Sioux were now coming in to pay their respects to us. Hence I was very much relieved when, a few hours later, our friends, dripping from the deep ford of the Yellowstone, rode into camp and reported the result of their scout. The Crows looked crestfallen at the idea of their false cry of "the wolf," but were soon to learn by sad experience that the "wolf" was even closer than they thought, for the very next day a heavy windstorm set in, and all that night the camp and vicinity were swept with driving clouds of dust, through which objects could be seen only at a few paces' distance. Just such a night do Indians select for their thieving expeditions, and early the next morning one of our white scouts came into camp and exhibited, with a rueful countenance, a picket-pin with two bits of rope cut off close to the pin-head. The night before, that picket-pin had been driven into the ground a hundred yards outside of our line of camp sentinels, the bits of rope were thin lariats, and at their opposite extremities were tied to graze two of his own animals, a horse and a mule. Now, all of his property that remained was this picket-pin and the cleanly severed ends of his lariats. All our own animals were inside the line of sentinels, as his two should have been. We had never been able to bring our Crows sufficiently under military control to induce them to keep their ponies in camp at night, and they were permitted to roam at large night and day in search of subsistence. The lonely picket-pin demonstrated beyond doubt that "the wolf" had come, and that the thieving Sioux had paid our camp a visit. It did not take long to make the discovery that the whole pony herd of the Crows, some thirty in number, had, alas, disappeared, and the scene which followed was absurd in the extreme. The Crows assembled at their camp and *cried* like children whose toys had been broken. There is nothing unnatural in a crying child, and the manly grief of a broken heart excites one's sympathy, but to see a parcel of great big Indians standing together and blubbering like babies, with great tears streaming down their swarthy faces because they had lost their horses, struck every one as supremely ridiculous. Scouting parties were sent out, the trail of the marauders discovered leading down the river, and signs found which left no doubt of their being Sioux.

On the 8th our train, with the two companies, arrived from Camp Supply, and the whole command being now together, with wagons enough to carry all our stores, I decided to move farther down the river. There were evidently nothing more than small war parties about us, and my reiterated instructions were to guard as much as possible against the Indians crossing the Yellowstone to go north. The principal crossing-places were lower down near the mouth of Rosebud River, and on this side. We moved on the 10th, but were delayed by bad roads made worse by a furious rainstorm, and on the fifth day had made only fifty-two miles to a camp a short distance above the mouth of the Rosebud. Here we were visited by a heavy hail and rainstorm, which stampeded our animals, flooded our camp, and rendered the surrounding country impassable for wagons. Both sides of the river were kept well scouted, and on the 17th one of our party reported the presence on Tongue River, some thirty-five miles distant, of an Indian camp. The Yellowstone was now a raging torrent of muddy water; but we had, on leaving Fort Pease, brought along several small boats found there, and with the assistance of these it was determined to throw a force across the river, and by a night march, surprise the camp on Tongue River. Pack saddles were now got out, extra ammunition and rations issued, and preparations made to cross the river with the whole force except one company, which was left at our camp in charge of the train. The crossing-place selected was about a mile above the camp. The boats were pulled up there and used to cross over the men, saddles, etc., of a company. The horses of the company were then brought down to the shore and an attempt made to drive them into the water. They resisted stoutly; but a few finally entered the water, which was cold and rapid. But no sooner did they lose their footing and commence to swim than, turning round, they returned to our shore, followed by the few which had ventured in after them. Again and again were they forced to the water's edge, but with the same result, and finally the whole of them broke from the men around them and stampeded back to camp. Several hours were consumed in these fruitless efforts, and then a different plan was tried. One of the oldest horses was selected, and to his tail was firmly tied the halter of another; to the tail of this one another, and so on till a long line of half a dozen were tied together. A rope attached to the leader was now taken into the boat manned by rowers and the boat pulled out from shore. The leader quietly followed, dragging his trail behind him, whilst the loose horses, seeing so many going in, followed in a body, urged on by the shouting men. Soon the deep water was reached and the leader began to swim, followed in fine style by the others, and everything was looking favorable for the passage of the horses at last, when suddenly the whole scene changed and one of the most indescribable confusion followed. From some cause or other the boats became unmanageable in the swift current, and instead of keeping on a straight course with a taut rope stretching to the leading horse, it floated for a moment at the mercy of the current, the rope became slack, the rear horses continued to swim forward, the third or fourth horse got across the line in front of the leader, and in an instant the water was filled with a tangled mass of frantic animals struggling for life. Most of the hitching halters held, and the longer the poor creatures struggled the worse entangled they became. Some soon became exhausted and sank beneath the ice-cold muddy torrent; some few continued across and landed on the other shore, but most of them returned, whilst one powerful beast waded back, pulling after him a comrade which had fallen exhausted and died in water so shallow that only about one-half his body was covered. Four horses were drowned outright, and the rest so frightened that they could not be again made to approach the water. It was now late in the afternoon, the attempt to cross the river was abandoned, the few men and horses thrown across were brought back, and the troops returned to camp. We were now, perforce, confined in our operations to the north side of the river, up and down which mounted parties were constantly kept on the move, and occasionally two or three of the Crows would cross and reconnoitre the south side, or start on horse-stealing expeditions; but in each case they returned unsuccessful and disappointed.

One day whilst seated in my tent I heard the distant cry of a wolf. Wondering at the bark of a coyote in broad daylight, my attention was attracted by a great commotion amongst the Crows, several of whom with their guns started on the run for the river-bank, repeating the wolf-like cry. It was answered from across the river, and jumping into one of the boats they soon returned with two of their number, who had gone off on a horse-stealing expedition, and now, having been unsuccessful, were coming back, and took this way of informing their friends of the fact.

On the 18th two companies of cavalry were started on a scout to the mouth of Tongue River, and two days afterwards the Crows reported a heavy force of Indians moving towards the mouth of the Rosebud, evidently with the design of crossing the Yellowstone. Leaving one company of infantry in charge of the camp, the remainder of the command was pushed hastily down the river, and bivouacked for the night just below the mouth of the Rosebud. No Indians, however, were seen, nor any indications of a projected crossing, and the next day the remainder of the camp was brought down to the new position, and the two companies from below joined us. They had gone down as far as the mouth of Tongue River, had seen a party of about fifty Indians trying evidently to get across to our side, and not having themselves been seen, had laid in wait for them several hours. But the Indians after several attempts to cross, had evidently given it up, and proceeded up the river on the other side. On leaving, however, they had concealed their extra ponies in the timber, and with the idea that they had left no guard to look after them, Mitch Bouyer and one of the Crows with the scouting party conceived a bold attempt to capture these ponies. Stripping, and without a weapon of any kind, they swam the Yellowstone, and crept through the timber to within sight of the grazing animals which they found under charge of two Indian boys. To get to them they were obliged to pass an open space, and no sooner did their naked forms leave the shelter of the timber than they were perceived by the watchful boys, who with loud shouts hurried the band of ponies off into the hills beyond their reach, and Mitch and his companion had nothing to do but to swim back to their own side of the river.

We had in the command a number of fine shots, and permission was constantly given these men to hunt, and by them the country in the vicinity of our camps and line of march was kept very well scouted. One of these parties reported on the 22d that they had been fired upon by Indians in the hills that day, but they were evidently not in great force, for the scouting parties sent out discovered but few pony tracks, and saw no Indians. The next morning early the pickets reported firing in the hills. Several hunting parties were out, but the firing being continued, and a number of horsemen making their appearance on the bluff about three miles from camp, two companies were at once sent out in that direction, and it was then for the first time discovered that two men belonging to one of these companies and a citizen teamster were absent from camp without authority. Why they should go without permission when all they had to do was to ask for it, I could not imagine, and it is a singular fact that of all the parties out that morning this one of three was the only one to encounter Indians. The cavalry started at once for the point where the horsemen had been seen to disappear on the bluffs. On reaching the foot-hills the party found itself in the midst of a succession of knolls rising higher and higher, and forming a number of narrow valleys. The men appear to have entered one of these blindly without taking any precaution in the way of a lookout. They were doubtless watched from the high ground, and parties of Indians posted out of sight behind the hills on each side permitted the three hunters to advance until surrounded on all sides, and then making their appearance, delivered their fire from several directions upon the doomed men. The bodies were found stripped, shot in several places and horribly mutilated, with heads beaten in, and one of the men had two knives, taken from the bodies of his dead comrades, driven into the sides of his head. The knife of the third man was afterwards recognized and picked up on Custer's battle-field. When the cavalry reached the top of the bluffs, not an Indian was to be seen. The trail was followed for some miles, but the only thing seen of the party was a single horseman rapidly disappearing on a distant hill. The bodies were brought into camp and laid side by side to rest under a large cottonwood tree, upon the trunk of which, after removing the bark, an appropriate inscription was placed and heavy logs piled over the grave to guard against the action of wolves. As the scouting party came into camp about sundown, quite a number of heads appeared cautiously above a distant hill on the other side of the river, and from this time forth our camp was doubtless very carefully watched.

We had now been out nearly two months, and our supplies were becoming short. I had sent back to Fort Ellis for more supplies, and had information that they were on the road. For the double purpose of escorting this train in, and taking back a number of surplus contractors' wagons, two companies left our camp in charge of a train the very morning of the murders (23d), and we now had nothing to do but to await the arrival of our supplies, keeping the river above and below well scouted by parties of cavalry. I had received dispatches from General Terry that he expected to reach the Yellowstone at the mouth of Glendive Creek about the 28th, and on the 27th I called for volunteers to carry a dispatch down the river by boat. Two men who afterwards became quite noted for a deed of great daring, offered their services for the trip. Their names were Evans and Stewart, both soldiers, belonging to Captain Clifford's company of the Seventh Infantry. They were accompanied by a white scout, named Williamson, and just at dark, with muffled oars, they got into their frail bark and noiselessly dropped down the stream on their perilous and uncertain voyage, many of their comrades assembling on the bank to see them off. The very next morning I received by boat from Fort Ellis an important dispatch from department headquarters. It informed me that General Terry had left Fort Lincoln on the morning of the 15th; that he had received information that the hostiles were concentrated on the Little Missouri, and between that and the Powder River; that he anticipated opposition between the Missouri River and the Yellowstone, and directed me to march at once to a point on the Yellowstone opposite Stanley's stockade, to cross the river, if possible, and advance to meet him on Stanley's trail, and to use one of the steamers which I would probably find there for crossing my command. The point designated was some one hundred and fifty miles from where we then were. A speedy movement was evidently expected, and yet with the region about us infested with hostile Indians, how could we leave the large train of supplies now on the road to follow us with its escort of one small company of infantry? All our wagons were at once unloaded, and the next morning under charge of two companies started back to lighten the supply train, and hurry it forward as fast as possible. Notwithstanding a furious *snow*-storm, which raged all day on the 1st of June, our train made good time, and reached camp on the 4th, so that the command was now once more together, and its supplies with it. The morning of the 5th found us on our way down the river once more, everyone eager to push forward and join the Lincoln column. But we were now entering upon a comparatively unknown region, and on the second day encountered a single hill which required four hours and a great deal of hard work to get our train up, and, on the third day, after a march of twenty-one and a half miles, had made only forty-one miles. Mitch Bouyer informed us that the roads passed over heretofore were good compared with those we should have in the next few days, when we should be compelled to enter a terrible section of the "Mauvaise terres."

On the morning of the 8th, our scouts reported Indians in front, and, later on, two who had followed on the trail of two horsemen brought in a package which told us a tale words could not have made plainer. The package consisted of a small sack containing a number of army cartridges, some small round crackers, such as are kept for sale in the subsistence department, and a piece of *cheese.* The last-named article Indians seldom, if ever, use, and would never carry on a trip, so that the contents of this little sack told us as plainly as if the news had been received in a letter that General Terry was close by, and was trying to communicate with us by couriers, and that the couriers were white men. We camped that night in the open prairie on the bank of the Yellowstone, and about two o'clock in the morning, I was waked out of a sound sleep by loud shouts. Jumping up, I reached the picket-line in time to receive a white man and an Indian, who brought dispatches from General Terry at the mouth of the Powder River. He had reached that stream without encountering any Indians, and invited me to meet him coming up the river on the steamer *Far West* the next morning. I learned too that the sack and its contents picked up by our scouts the day before had been correctly interpreted. It had been dropped by one of two white men who had been sent to communicate with us. They had seen from a distance our Crow scouts, had taken them for Sioux, and had fled back to report the country filled with hostiles, and lose a reward of two hundred dollars which had been promised them if they got through to me with their dispatches, dropping in their flight the articles which were picked up the day after by my scouts, who had never even seen the men who dropped them.

The morning of the 9th I proceeded down the valley with a company of cavalry, and soon had a specimen of the bad lands referred to by Mitch Bouyer as existing in the vicinity of Powder River, north of the Yellowstone. We climbed up an almost inaccessible mountain, being several times obliged to dismount and lead our horses, and on reaching the top had a fine view of the valley of the Yellowstone beyond far down in the direction of Powder River. The muddy rapid stream wound around the foot of the mountain almost directly beneath us, and through the fringe of timber on its banks little puffs of white steam rose up and revealed the presence of a steamer slowly making her way up against the strong current. It was the most civilized scene we had witnessed for more than two months, and as the deep hoarse voice of the steam whistle broke upon the still morning air, the top of what we afterwards named "Steamboat Point" resounded with a loud cheer of welcome from our little party. Following a buffalo trail down the steep side of the Point we were soon on board the steamer and on our way back to camp, where the men flocked down to the bank to welcome the second steamer which had ever been so far up the waters of the Yellowstone.

The existence of any large camps of hostile Indians in this region was now more than ever a matter of doubt; for General Terry had discovered no trace of any on his march from Fort Lincoln to the Powder River, which he had reached at a point twenty-five miles above its mouth. He informed me that he had heard nothing from General Crook, and intended on his return to Powder River to send a cavalry command on a scout up that river and across it west to the Tongue and Rosebud. If no Indians should be discovered then the only remaining chance would be higher up the Yellowstone, where from my observation there must be some Indians, and if General Crook should strike them from the south, it would be all the more necessary for us to guard the line of the river and prevent any escape to the northward. He therefore instructed me to retrace my steps and await his arrival at the mouth of the Rosebud, and as dispatch was now of more importance than ever I agreed to start the cavalry part of my command that afternoon. The General had no guide at his disposal acquainted with the country south of the Yellowstone, and I suggested that he take Mitch Bouyer, who had proved so valuable to us, and was I knew well acquainted with that country. Mitch, always ready and willing, assented at once, and as soon as he and his horse were on board the steamer started down the river, and preparations were at once made to commence the march back. Before, however, the cavalry was ready to move one of those terrific rain-storms, of which we had had so many, set in. The whole alkali flat around us became one immense quagmire, and a gulch back of our camp, which was dry when we came, was soon a torrent ten or twelve feet deep. This rendered any movement out of the question until the afternoon of the next day, when the cavalry succeeded only in making a few miles, and the next day (11th) were overtaken by the infantry, having been delayed to build a road and pull up a very steep hill, it being impossible to follow the road used coming down on account of Sunday Creek being impassable from high water. All the bridges built and crossings cut during the trip down were found washed away by the heavy rains, and the low grounds were filled with driftwood brought down from the hills through the gulches, which, except during heavy rains, are entirely deprived of water.

Finally, the whole command was reunited on the 14th at the mouth of the Rosebud, where we waited for the arrival of General Terry, keeping in the meantime the country well scouted up and down the river. Four days afterwards (18th) a party of horsemen was reported by our scouts as coming down the Rosebud, and riding to a point about three miles above our camp. I started a couple of Crows to swim across the river, then higher and more rapid than ever, with a note to General Terry. The Indians stripped and commenced their preparations for their cold swim by rubbing themselves all over with red paint. I had the curiosity to inquire the object of this, and was surprised to learn that it was to protect them against the attack of *alligators*. As the alligator is an animal unknown to the waters of this region, the fact referred to is a curious evidence of the southern origin of the Crows, at the same time that it shows how traditions are transmitted for long ages in a barbarous tribe. Having completed their preparations against the attack of an animal of which perhaps their progenitors long ago had a wholesome dread in more southern waters, the note to General Terry was tied in the scalplock of one of them, and the two men started on the run for a point higher up the river. There providing themselves with a log of dead wood, they plunged into the water, and singing to keep up their courage, they were swept past us down the swift current, and after a swim of nearly a mile landed safely on the other side, and were seen through our glasses to approach the party opposite. All this took time, and being curious to know who was in the party, one of our officers tied a handkerchief to a stick, and commenced waving it from side to side as a signal. It was soon answered in the same way, and before our Crows had reached the opposite bank, the army code of signals was spelling out for us the information we wanted. In this way we learned that the party was composed of six companies of the Seventh Cavalry under command of Colonel Reno, which had been on a scout up Powder River and across the Tongue to the Rosebud, and had seen no Indians, though signs of camps had been discovered on the last-named stream and a large trail leading up to it. Our Crows swam back to us with a note from Colonel Reno, and the poor fellows were very much exhausted when they reached us. Could we have known what had taken place only twenty-four hours before on the head waters of the very stream at whose mouth we stood, the information would have been invaluable to us, and probably have given a different shape to our whole subsequent operations. As it was, we were still groping in the dark in regard to the location of the hostile camps, and had every reason to believe that the Sioux with their women and children were solicitous only to avoid us. General Terry was understood to be at the mouth of the Tongue River, and the next morning Colonel Reno started with his command to join him. Our scouts reported seeing large fires in the direction of the Little Horn, and now every one was anxious for the arrival of General Terry, for our last chance for striking the Indians appeared to be in the direction indicated.

Anticipating a move up the river, I ordered, on the 21st, three companies of infantry to proceed up the road to replace the bridges, and repair the crossings over the various streams destroyed by the recent rains. During the morning General Terry reached our camp on the *Far West*. After conferring with him, the whole command was at once started up the river, and at his request I accompanied him on the steamer to meet General Custer, who was coming up on the other side with the whole of his regiment. The steamer was run up to the mouth of the Rosebud, and afterwards dropped down to a point below, where Custer had arrived in the afternoon, and gone into camp or rather bivouac. As soon as we were tied up to the bank, he came aboard, and seated in the cabin with a map before us, we discussed the proposed operations. The large trail found by Colonel Reno leading up the Rosebud and the fires seen in that direction by my scouts led to the belief that the Indians, if overtaken at all, would be found somewhere on the Little Big Horn, a favorite resort, where the grazing was good and game close by. It was therefore arranged that General Custer should start the next day with the whole of his regiment, take up the trail on the Rosebud, and follow it; that my command should march to the mouth of the Big Horn, something over sixty miles distant, be there ferried across the Yellowstone, and march from there to the valley of the Little Big Horn, and up that stream to cooperate with Custer's command. An examination of the map showed that the course of the Rosebud approaches that of the Little Big Horn nearest at a point about as far distant from where we then were as the mouth of the Big Horn was from us. Were then Custer, whose command was exclusively of cavalry, marching with pack-mules, to follow the trail directly into the valley of the Little Big Horn, he would probably strike the Indians long before I could be anywhere in the vicinity with my command, part of which was infantry, and to prevent the escape of the Indians, which was the idea pervading the minds of all of us, it was desirable that the two commands should be as near each other as possible when they approached the supposed location of the camp. The Indians, if struck, would probably not retreat *west*, for in that direction was the formidable Big Horn, beyond which was the whole Crow nation, the deadly enemies of the Sioux. They could not go north without running into my column, nor east without doubling on their course, and exposing themselves to attack from both columns. They would, therefore, in all probability, go south; for, in addition to its being their natural and only practicable line of retreat, was the fact that in that direction lay the Big Horn range of mountains, in the fastnesses of which they would be comparatively secure, and could live on the game and wild berries which abounded there. But if, as we had good reason to expect, General Crook's column was somewhere in that direction, there was a third column against which the Indians encumbered with their families were liable to run. Hence it was agreed that Custer, instead of proceeding at once into the valley of the Little Big Horn, even should the trail lead there, should continue on up the Rosebud, get closer to the mountains, and then striking west, come down the valley of the Little Big Horn, "feeling constantly to his left," to be sure that the Indians had not already made their escape to the south and eastward. General Terry, applying a scale to the map, measured the distances, and made the calculation in miles that each command would have to travel. My command having already started, was to be at the mouth of the Big Horn prepared to cross the Yellowstone on the third day.

The scouts with Custer's regiment were entirely ignorant of the country he was to pass through. Mitch Bouyer, who knew all about it, was to go with him, and in addition, by direction of General Terry, I assigned to duty with him six of my Crow scouts who volunteered for the service. Besides this, General Terry expressed a desire that Custer should communicate with him by sending a scout down the valley of Tullock's Fork, and send him any news of importance he might have, especially as to whether or not any hostiles were on that stream. As he had no one with him suitable for this service, I engaged, by General Terry's order, a white man named Herendeen, who had been with my column for some time, was a good scout, and well acquainted with the country he would have to pass over. Herendeen stipulated that in case he was called upon to incur the additional risk of carrying dispatches his compensation should be increased. This was agreed to, and he accompanied General Custer's troops.

At noon the next day, General Terry, accompanied by myself and General Brisbin, rode to the upper end of the camp to witness the departure of Custer and his fine regiment. The bugles sounded the "Boots and Saddles," and Custer, after starting the advance, rode up and joined us. Together we sat on our horses and witnessed the approach of the command as it threaded its way through the rank sage-brush which covered the valley. First came a band of buglers sounding a march, and as they came opposite to General Terry they wheeled out of the column as at review, continuing to play as the command passed along. The regiment presented a fine appearance, and as the various companies passed us we had a good opportunity to note the number of fine horses in the ranks, many of them being part-blooded horses from Kentucky, and I was told there was not a single sore-backed horse amongst them. General Custer appeared to be in good spirits, chatted freely with us, and was evidently proud of the appearance of his command. The pack-mules, in a compact body, followed the regiment, and behind them came a rear-guard, and as that approached Custer shook hands with us and bade us good-by. As he turned to leave us I made some pleasant remark, warning him against being greedy, and with a gay wave of his hand he called back, "No. I will not," and rode off after his command. Little did we think we had seen him for the last time, or imagine under what circumstances we should next see that command, now mounting the bluffs in the distance with its little guidons gayly fluttering in the breeze.

A very heavy cold wind was blowing from the north, and our steamer did not start until 4 o'clock in the afternoon. We ran on till near dusk, when we tied up for the night and took in wood. The next day (23d) we ran steadily all day, and just before night we tied up, the captain stating that he was unable to reach Fort Pease before dark. We

GENERAL GEORGE A. CUSTER John Gibbon last saw Custer on June 22, 1876, when he cautioned the impetuous cavalryman not to be greedy while fighting the Teton Sioux and Northern Cheyenne. Photo courtesy the Little Bighorn Battlefield National Monument.

arrived there, however, early the next morning, and my command being in position was at once ferried across the river, and at 5 o'clock started on its march up the Big Horn. I had been attacked with very severe illness the night before, had remained in bed all day and was unable to move. General Terry accompanied the command in person, leaving me on board to meet the column at the mouth of the Little Big Horn. The next day at noon (25th) we entered the mouth of that stream, the *Far West* being the first steamer that ever ploughed its waters, and running till dark tied up for the night, little dreaming what a disastrous day had closed over the gallant Custer and his command. The next morning we were early under way again. The river, which was very full, began to be intersected with numerous islands, and the boat experienced some difficulty in finding a navigable channel. We had just finished pulling over a bar, and were approaching a difficult rapid, when two horsemen were seen on the bluffs coming towards us. They were soon made out to be one of my staff officers and an orderly. He came aboard and informed me that the infantry part of the command was only a few miles up the river;

that they had had a terrible march the day before over the rough mountainous region lying between the Big Horn and Tullock's Fork, during which the men suffered very much from exhaustion and the want of water, and that General Terry, with the cavalry and Gatling guns, had started ahead for a night's march the evening before. This looked as if he anticipated meeting with Indians, and as I now began to be impatient lest the boat would be unable to reach the mouth of the Little Big Horn that day, I determined to mount my horse and overtake the command at once. It was lucky I did so, for the command was not again in communication with the boat until four days afterwards. After a brisk ride of four or five miles I overtook the infantry marching over a plateau not particularly rough, but intersected by numerous deep ravines, which must have rendered the march of the cavalry the night before very tedious and slow, as the night was dark and rainy. Later in the day we overtook the cavalry as it was leaving the place where it had bivouacked at midnight, and on reaching the head of the column and receiving the command from General Terry, I was informed that our scouts reported Indians in front in the direction of the Little Big Horn. Soon after, the officer in charge of the scouts reported that several Indians had been seen to whom the Crows gave chase, and that they had fled across the Big Horn. In their flight they had dropped articles which showed them to be Crows and not Sioux, and our scouts declared them to be some of the Crows which I had lent General Custer at the mouth of the Rosebud for scouting purposes. They were directed to communicate with their friends across the Big Horn, bring them back, and ascertain what news they brought from Custer. For, of course, the inference was at once drawn that these Crows had been sent out by Custer to communicate with our column. We were utterly unprepared for the startling report which our Crows brought back after calling across to their friends on the opposite bank of the Big Horn. Our best interpreter had been left sick at the mouth of the river, and from what we could make out by the indifferent one with us, who appeared very much excited and demoralized by the news, Custer's command had been entirely cut to pieces by the Sioux, who, so said the interpreter, "were chasing our soldiers all over the hills and killing them like buffalo."

This startling piece of news was received with incredulity by everyone, and the absconding Crows were again sent for, to come back that we might question them, and try to ascertain something near the facts. Whilst the head of the column was halting for the infantry to close up, General Terry and myself walked over to the edge of the bluff overlooking the valley of the Big Horn to await the return of the scouts, and ascertain from them such news as we could. The broad river intersected by numerous wooded islands was spread out at our feet, and from the edge of a piece of timber nearest us our scouts were soon seen emerging, and approaching a buffalo trail which led up the bluffs to the spot where we were standing. As they came nearer we detected signs of grief; and as old "Show-His-Face" (The Senator) mounted the steep slope on his pony, he was seen to be crying as if his heart was broken, with great tears streaming down his old weatherbeaten face, and uttering every now and then the most doleful exclamations. We had become used to this after seeing them cry at the loss of their horses, and therefore did not attach much importance to it; but when the others arrived and confirmed the previous report, with the information that their friends declared their horses and themselves were too exhausted to cross the river again, and positively refused to come back, it became manifest that the Indians themselves believed in the truth of the report as they heard it.

Of course there was but one thing for us to do, which was to push forward as rapidly as possible and try and clear up for ourselves the terrible uncertainty; for, at all events, the fact seemed undoubted that Custer had come in contact with the Indians, and the sooner we could reach him the better. The march was at once resumed, and we shortly reached the bluffs overlooking the valley of the Little Big Horn, some distance up which huge columns of smoke could now be plainly seen. As we wound along over the rough broken hills seeking for a place to get down into the valley, I observed that all our Crows, instead of travelling well to the front, as was their custom, stuck close to the column. I ordered the interpreter to take them to the front and report for duty with the advanced guard; but he declared his inability to get them to go, and was evidently himself so badly scared that he produced a bad effect upon the Indians. Finding I could not get them to the front I angrily ordered them to the rear of the column, an order which they obeyed with so much alacrity under the lead of the white interpreter that we saw them no more; and they never stopped till they reached their agency a hundred miles away. This, of course, we ascertained afterwards. They were evidently very badly stampeded, but I attributed this more to the demoralized condition of the white interpreter than to any want of courage on their part; and they afterwards assured me, when they rejoined us at the mouth of the Big Horn, that the interpreter had told them that I said I did not want them any longer.

We had to remain for some time on the high bluffs overlooking the valley of the Little Big Horn, up which the smoke of fires continued constantly to increase in volume, which gave rise to the hope that, as our guides expressed it, Custer had "got away" with the camp and was destroying it. Such a hope was in consonance with our ideas, for I do not suppose there was a man in the column who entertained for a moment the idea that there were Indians enough in the country to defeat, much less annihilate, the fine regiment of cavalry which Custer had under his command. Distances in this clear, rarefied atmosphere are very deceptive, and, as we moved on, the distance to the smoke which at first appeared to be only a few miles seemed to lengthen out and grow greater under the weary feet of our men, and when we did finally make our way down into the valley and cross the stream at a deep ford we were still some twelve or fifteen miles from the nearest smoke. To afford rest and food to both men and animals the command was halted here; the animals permitted to graze for an hour and a half and the men to make coffee. In the meantime efforts were made to communicate by courier with General Custer, General Terry offering a large reward to anyone who would carry through a dispatch. Two of our guides, Bostwick and Taylor, although unacquainted with the country volunteered for the service, and, shortly after they left, the column resumed its march up the broad open valley. After we had proceeded several miles some stray ponies were picked up by the advance guard, which were evidently estrays from an Indian camp. On our left ran the stream bordered with timber and brushwood, and some distance on our right the valley was bounded by low rolling hills. In our front the stream after cutting into the bluffs crossed the valley from right to left, the timber shutting out all view beyond, save above its top appeared a sharp mountain peak, on the edges of which could now and then be indistinctly made out a few moving figures, and just beyond this peak the smoke appeared to have its origin. Up to this time no Indians had been seen, but shortly after one of our couriers came riding in from the front, and reported that in attempting to reach Custer's command he had run into a number of Indians in the hills, and was unable to proceed farther. A company of cavalry was now thrown out to the hills on our right, and the column pushed forward as rapidly as the men could march, the infantry responding with alacrity and almost keeping up in pace with the horses. Small scattered bands now began to make their appearance on the tops of the distant hills up the river where the latter began to deflect its course to the northward, and as it grew dark more of them could be seen in the distance.

The condition of affairs regarding Custer's command was now more involved in doubt than ever. If he had defeated the Indians and destroyed their camp, as the fires seemed to indicate, it was difficult to account for the presence of these Indians in our front, who were evidently watching us; whereas, if the report of the Crows was correct, and the Indians had defeated Custer, their bearing was equally inexplicable. This state of doubt was only increased when our other courier came in and reported the result of his attempts to get through to Custer. He had struck into the hills to the southward, and had encountered Indians, who appeared to be friendly, and responded to the signals he made them. He approached some of them on foot and leading his horse, when one of them he said treacherously fired a shot at him, and he fiercely declared he had recognized him as one of Custer's Ree scouts, and that he would kill him when he met him for firing at him. As night closed around us the command was halted and bivouacked in the open prairie; the scouting parties were called in, who reported seeing quite a large number of Indians on the distant hills, but in the gathering darkness nothing could be plainly made out. After watering and grazing the animals they were all carefully picketed inside the command formed in a square, guards established just outside, and the tired men sank to rest eight miles from the brave little band of fellow-soldiers which, unknown to us, was watching and waiting on those bleak bluffs of the river above.

Everyone was astir at the first appearance of day, and after a hurried breakfast of hardtack, bacon, and coffee, the march was resumed up the valley. The trail, forced into the hills on the right by the encroachment of the river, led through rough ground around a bend in the stream, and as the view opened into the valley beyond, we caught sight through the scattered timber, of a couple of Indian tepees standing in the open valley. The advance guard with flankers out on the hills to the right now moved rapidly to the front, whilst a party of mounted infantry, which had crossed the river, scouted the hills on that side. As soon as the Gatling guns were passed over the rough portion of the trail, the whole command, well closed up, moved in compact order up through the open valley beyond, every one eagerly pressing forward and anxious to solve the dread doubt which seemed to hang over the fate of our comrades. Silence reigned around us, only a few distant horsemen had been seen, and, but for the presence of a few scattering Indian ponies, the valley seemed to be entirely deserted. The company of cavalry in the advance was seen to push more rapidly to the front, past the Indian tepees, which showed no life, and on beyond at a gallop, whilst our more slowly moving column seemed merely to crawl along. At length we reached the tepees, found them occupied by dead Indians laid out in state, and surrounded in every direction with the remnants and various odds and ends of a hastily abandoned camp. Tepee poles, skins, robes, pots, kettles, and pans lay scattered about in every direction. But we had little time or inclination to comment on these sights, for every thought was now bent upon the possible fate of our fellow-soldiers, and the desire was intense to solve as soon as possible the dread doubt which now began to fill all minds. For, in searching amongst the rubbish, some one had picked up a pair of bloody drawers, upon which was plainly written the words, "Sturgis's 7th Cavalry," whilst a buckskin shirt, recognized as belonging to Lieutenant Porter, was discovered with a bullet-hole passing through it.

It was plainly to be seen now that a conflict had indeed taken place, but of its extent or results we were still in as much doubt as ever, when a report came to me from the scouting party in the hills to our left that several dead horses had been discovered in a ravine in that direction. Every eye was now strained to the utmost in search of information, and whilst looking up the valley I caught sight of something on the top of a hill far beyond the sharp peak before referred to, which at once attracted my attention and a closer scrutiny. I sprang from my horse, and with a field glass looked long and anxiously at a number of dark objects which might be either animals or stubby cedar trees. The closest scrutiny failed to detect any movement amongst them, and yet I could not divest my mind of the idea that they were horses, and called upon a pair of younger eyes to try the glass. One of General Terry's staff officers took the glass and seating himself on the ground peered long and anxiously at the spots, but finally said "they are not animals." But scarcely had the words escaped him, when we both noticed a very apparent increase in the number of objects on the highest point of the hill, and now one doubt was solved only to give rise to another. Were the objects seen friends or foes? Had we come in time to save some of our friends, or were the objects on the hill simply a party of Indians watching our approach after having, as the Crows said, destroyed them all? The feeling of anxiety was overwhelming and the column seemed to crawl along more slowly than ever. The advance was moving ahead fast enough now, and I dispatched a staff officer in haste to ascertain and bring back any information it may have picked up; for I had observed on the peak before spoken of, and opposite which the advanced guard had now arrived, three horsemen evidently observing our movements and watching us closely. They could scarcely, I thought, be white men, for our troops were marching up the valley in two columns, in plain sight of where they sat on their horses, and if friendly they surely would have come down and communicated with us. They did finally come slowly down to a lower hill standing nearer to the river, but there they halted again and seemed to question us with their eyes.

Whilst watching these lookouts and wondering at their strange movements, the officer in charge of the mounted infantry party, in the hills to the north of us, rode up to where General Terry and I sat upon our horses, and his voice trembled as he said, "I have a very sad report to make. I have counted one hundred and ninety-seven dead bodies lying in

the hills!" "White men?" was the first question asked. "Yes, white men."
A look of horror was upon every face, and for a moment no one spoke.
There could be no question now. The Crows were right, and Custer had
met with a disaster, but the extent of it was still a matter of doubt; and
as we turned our eyes towards the lookouts on the hill above us, as
though to question them, we saw them moving, still slowly, however,
down closer to the river. Then as they reached a gentle slope they rode
on a little faster, and were seen to approach the advance guard, and
someone in our anxious group exclaimed, "They are white men!" From
out of the timber near the point, a horseman at full speed was now seen
coming towards us. It was my staff officer coming with news, and as he
approached us on the full run he called out, "I have seen scouts from
Colonel Reno, who report their regiment cut to pieces, and Colonel
Reno fortified in the bluffs with the remnant." We were still some
distance, probably a mile and a half from the objects we had been
observing on the hill, and now pushed forward more eagerly than ever,
the advance guard being already opposite their position. After we had
gone about a mile a party of horsemen was seen approaching, and as we
rode forward to meet them we recognized two young officers of the
Seventh Cavalry, followed by several orderlies. Hands were grasped
almost in silence, but we questioned eagerly with our eyes, and one of
the first things they uttered was, "Is General Custer with you?" On
being told that we had not seen him, they gave us hurriedly an account
of the operations of the past two days, and the facts began to dawn upon
us. No one of the party which accompanied General Custer when the
command was divided, about noon on the 25th, had been seen by the
survivors, and our inference was, that they were all, or nearly all, lying
up in the hills where our scouting party had found the dead bodies.

Whilst General Terry accompanied the officers to Colonel Reno's
position on the hill, I proceeded to select a camp for the command.
Nearly the whole valley was black and smoking with the fire which had
swept over it, and it was with some difficulty I could find grass sufficient
for our animals, as it existed only in spots close to the stream where it
was too green to burn. Except for the fire, the ground presented but few
evidences of the conflict which had taken place. Now and then a dead
horse was seen; but as I approached a bend of the creek (for it is little
more than a creek), just below the hill occupied by the troops, I came
upon the body of a soldier lying on his face near a dead horse. He was
stripped, his scalp gone, his head beaten in, and his body filled with
bullet-holes and arrows. Close by was another body, also close to a dead
horse, lying, like the other, on its face, but partially clothed, and this
was recognized by one of our officers as the body of Lieutenant McIn-

tosh. More bodies of both men and horses were found close by, and it was noted that the bodies of men and horses laid almost always *in pairs,* and as this was the ground over which Colonel Reno's command retired towards the hills after its charge down the valley, the inference was drawn, that in the run the horses must have been killed first, and the riders after they fell.

The command was placed in camp here, and details at once set to work to haul away the dead horses and bury the men, both of which were already becoming offensive. Then mounting my horse I proceeded to visit Colonel Reno's command. As I rode a few hundred yards up the river towards the ford, bodies of men and horses were seen scattered along at intervals, and in the river itself several dead horses were lying. The banks of the river at the ford were steep and some six or eight feet high, with here and there an old buffalo trail leading down to the water. The water itself was not over a horse's knee, and close to the bank, on the other side, a series of steep bluffs, intersected at short intervals by steep and narrow ravines, rose up for probably a hundred feet. Up the sides of these ravines, winding about to make the ascent more gradual, numerous paths led, now tramped hard and smooth by many animals which had recently passed over them. My horse struggled up the steep path, wide enough only for a single animal, with difficulty, and on emerging from the ravine up which it led, I found myself on a sort of rough broken plateau, which sloped gradually up to the curved summit occupied by the troops. I soon came to a line of rifle-pits facing the space I was crossing, and running from the summit of the ridge down to the bluff overlooking the river, whilst behind this and facing the other way was another line, running in a similar way along the summit of an almost parallel ridge. Between the two were standing and lying, almost motionless, the horses and pack-mules of the command. As I approached the summit of the main ridge which overlooked all the rest of the ground I have described, the evidences of the severe struggle which had taken place here began to manifest themselves. Dead horses and mules were lying about in every direction, and in one little depression on the other slope of the main divide I counted forty-eight dead animals. Here and there, these had evidently been made use of as breastworks, and along the top of the ridge holes and rifle-pits extended, connecting the two lines before referred to. On the far side of the ridge, the ground gradually fell away in lower ridges, behind which the Indians had sheltered themselves and their ponies during the fight.

Standing on top of the main ridge with my back to the river, I overlooked the whole of the ground to the front; but on turning to my left, the ground was seen to rise higher and higher in successive ridges which ran nearly perpendicular to the stream, until they culminated in the sharp peak referred to in my description of the previous day upon which we had seen objects at a great distance down the valley. Several of these ridges commanded in reverse the position occupied by the troops, and we were told had been occupied by the Indians during the fight of the 26th, their long-range rifles covering all the space within the lines. Turning again to the left so as to face the river, the broad open flat where Colonel Reno had made his charge at the commencement of the battle on the 25th lay directly at our feet, whilst off towards the south the bluffs which bordered the valley rose up abruptly, and were succeeded by a gently sloping country intersected by several small valleys, with brushwood lining the now dry beds of the streams at the bottoms, while in the far distance the rugged range of the Big Horn Mountains rose, their tops partially covered with snow. One of the little valleys referred to was pointed out to us as the place where at dusk, the evening before, the last of the Indians disappeared in the distance after passing over, in admirable order and in full view of the command, the rolling plateau which bordered the valley of the Little Big Horn to the southward. Looking down the river in the direction we had come was a point of timber jutting out into the plain, where for a portion of the time the cavalry had fought dismounted; and beyond this, in plain sight from where I stood, was located the village where the fight began; and opposite that, hidden from sight by the high peak so often referred to, was the scene of Custer's fight, where his body was found surrounded by those of his men and horses.

On the highest point of the ridge occupied by the troops, and along what had been the northern line of defense, were pitched a number of shelter tents, and under and about these were lying some fifty wounded men, receiving the care of the surgeons and their attendants. The cheerfulness of these poor fellows, under their sufferings, and their evident joy at their rescue was touching in the extreme, and we listened with full hearts to their recital in feeble tones of the long anxious hours of waiting and fighting, during which every eye was strained, looking for the coming succor, hoping for its arrival, yet fearing it would be too late. At one time, so strongly did the imagination affect the judgment, the whole command was convinced that columns of troops could be seen moving over the hills to their assistance, but in directly the *opposite* direction from which they actually came. So strong was this delusion that the buglers of the whole command were assembled and ordered to sound their bugles to attract attention. When we finally made our appearance down the valley, the same thing was done, and it is supposed that it was the gathering together of the buglers on the highest point of the hill which finally decided in our minds that we were looking at men and horses, and not clumps of cedar trees. But we heard nothing of the bugles, for the wind was blowing from us.

Standing on the scene of the conflict, we heard from officers and men the story of the struggle and their experience for the past forty-eight hours. The battle commenced some time about noon on the 25th by the charge of the three companies down towards the village. They reached the point of timber I have referred to as jutting out into the plain. Here they were dismounted for a time, and fought from the timber, and then when the Indians came swarming around them from the ravines in the bluffs, they mounted again, and then commenced the race for the bluffs bordering the river. It must, from their description, have been a race of life against death. Look up the stream, and you will see the ford where Reno's command crossed to enter the fight. The one it crossed to reach its present position lies directly at your feet. Turning now to the left again so as once more to place your back to the river, and looking up to your right and front, you can trace with the eye a little valley winding its way up into the broken ground to the northeast. It was down this valley that Custer's command approached the Little Big Horn, and near where it joins the valley of that stream is the ford where Reno crossed before the battle. Before reaching that point, Custer, it appears by his trail, turned to the right with his five companies, skirted along through these hills to our front, passed to the right of the sharp peak, and still on, beyond it and out of sight of where we stand. His trail is all that is left to tell the story of his route, for no white man of all those who accompanied him has since been seen alive. To us who stand upon the ground, and make these observations, his fate is still a matter of doubt, and is now to be solved. One of Colonel Reno's companies is mounted and started for the scene of Custer's fight. It leaves our position, and winding along the rolling hills, ascends the high ground to the right of the high peak, and disappears beyond, just as Custer's command would have vanished probably from the sight of an observer standing where we are now.

Whilst this company is away we are busy preparing to remove the wounded down from the hot, dusty hill where they are lying to my camp, where they will be more comfortable and can be better cared for.

After being absent a couple of hours the detached company is seen winding its way back, and as it approaches we all collect round General Terry to hear the report of its gray-haired captain, who won such praises by his indomitable bearing in the fight. He comes forward, dismounts, and in a low, very quiet voice, tells his story. He had followed Custer's trail to the scene of the battle opposite the main body of the Indian camp, and amid the rolling hills which borders the river-bank on the north. As he approached the ground scattered bodies of men and horses were found, growing more numerous as he advanced. In the midst of the field a long *backbone* ran out obliquely back from the river, rising very gradually until it terminated in a little knoll which commanded a view of all the surrounding ground, and of the Indian camp-ground beyond the river. On each side of the backbone, and sometimes on top of it, dead men and horses were scattered along. These became more numerous as the terminating knoll was reached, and on the southwestern slope of that lay the brave Custer surrounded by the bodies of several of his officers and forty or fifty of his men, whilst horses were scattered about in every direction. All were stripped, and most of the bodies were scalped and mutilated. And now commenced the duty of recognizing the dead. Of Custer there could be no doubt. He was lying in a perfectly natural position as many had seen him lying when asleep, and we were told, was not at all mutilated, and that, only after a good deal of search the wounds of which he died could be found. The field was searched and one after another the officers were found and recognized, all except two. A count of the bodies disclosed the fact that some twenty-five or thirty were missing, and we could not, until sometime afterwards, form even a surmise in regard to their fate.

The great mystery was now solved, at last, of the destruction of that part of Custer's command. It was possible that some few individuals might have escaped the general massacre; but so far as we could judge all had fallen; and the particulars of that sad and desperate conflict against overwhelming numbers of the savage horde which flocked about Custer and his devoted three hundred when Reno was beaten back, will probably never be known.

# Hunting
# Sitting Bull

*T*he poor wounded claimed my first care. They were lying on the hot dusty hill under inadequate shelter, and steps were at once taken to remove them to my cooler, pleasanter camp on the creek-bank below. The majority of them had to be carried, and there was not a single stretcher or litter in the command. These had therefore to be improvised. A quantity of light tepee poles were collected from the Indian camp, and by means of these, old pieces of canvas, and blankets, a number were made, and by night all the wounded were carried down the steep slope of the bluffs, across the creek, and down to our camp, the men working by relays.

The Seventh Cavalry remained upon the bluffs during the night, and early the next morning moved down to the scene of Custer's conflict, to perform the mournful duty of burying the remains of their slaughtered comrades. This would have been an impracticable task but for the discovery, in the deserted Indian camp, of a large number of shovels and spades, by the aid of which the work was performed.

The formidable question of the transportation of the wounded now came up and had to be met. The mouth of the Little Big Horn to which point the steamer *Far West* had been ordered was about twenty miles distant, and couriers had been dispatched to communicate with her, ascertain if she had reached there, and warn her to await our arrival. In the meantime, we set to work to construct the necessary litters with what rough material could be collected. Lieutenant Doane, of the Second Cavalry, volunteered to construct *horse*-litters out of rough cottonwood

SITTING BULL
Although he was a prominent Sioux medicine man, Sitting Bull was not a war chief and did no fighting in the Little Bighorn battle. Photo courtesy the Smithsonian Institution.

poles, rawhide, and ropes, but the process proved a very slow and tedious one, and other details were set to work collecting tepee poles and manufacturing hand-litters out of them and such old canvas as was to be had. Late in the afternoon, but four or five of the horse-litters had been finished, and the necessary number was completed with hand-litters. But on trying the mules in the horse-litters (all of them animals taken from baggage-wagons, unused to carrying packs, and sore from their few days' service under the saddles), most of them proved so refractory in the novel position assigned them, that grave doubts arose as to whether the suffering wounded could be safely carried in this way.

It was to be feared that any show of precipitancy in leaving our position was calculated to invite an attack from the overwhelming number of our enemies, and we should probably not have started that day at all, but for the report of the surgeons that it was indispensable that the wounded should be removed at once to avoid the ill effects of the heat, and the flies that swarmed around them in immense numbers from the dead bodies in the vicinity. It was therefore decided late in the afternoon to commence the movement, and as the sun sank behind the western hills, the wounded were transferred to the litters and the sad cortege moved out of camp.

At first two men were assigned to each hand-litter, but it was soon found that this was not sufficient, and the number had to be doubled, and, besides, two men had to be assigned to each horse-litter to steady it. Infantrymen and dismounted cavalrymen relieved each other every few minutes, but our progress was slow and laborious, and before we had made more than a mile from our camp, darkness overtook our straggling and disorganized column, completely broken up by the repeated halts and constantly recurring changes of carriers.

As we moved through the darkness, the silence of night broken only by the tramp of men and horses and the groans of the suffering wounded, I could not help contrasting the scene presented with that gay spectacle we had witnessed only six days before, when Custer's splendid regiment moved out in solid column, with its guidons fluttering in the breeze as it disappeared from our sight over the bluffs at the mouth of the Rosebud.

Long, tedious, and slow, the hours of that sad night wore on, and it was past midnight before we reached camp at a distance of only four and a half miles.

A company of the Second Cavalry had been sent out in the morning to make a reconnaissance on the trail of the retreating Indians. It was followed some ten or twelve miles, leading directly south towards the Big Horn Mountains, and was there found to divide, one portion going to the southeast, the other to the southwest, and the whole country in those directions was filled with the smoke of fires, lit either as signals or to burn the grass in rear of the retreating camps. In returning to our camp, the scouting party struck across to the Little Big Horn, coming down which was discovered a large lodge-pole trail, only a day or two old. From this it was inferred that General Custer had fought not only the party whose trail he had followed over from the Rosebud, but also the warriors of another large camp which before the fight had formed a junction with it, by coming up from the south, in which direction, as we afterward learned, General Crook had had his fight on the 17th, only eight days previous to Custer's battle. The concentration of superior numbers, thus effected, demonstrated very clearly that the Sioux leader, whoever he was, was not lacking in those strategic ideas justly deemed so valuable in civilized warfare. From these indications it would appear that, after the check given General Crook on the 17th, the whole hostile force concentrated against Custer, who by an almost unheard-of rapidity of movement had precipitated himself against their main camp. We know absolutely nothing of the details of the conflict, as relates to that portion of the command under Custer's personal supervision, but so soon as his part was annihilated, the whole hostile force turned upon the balance of the command, and laid siege to that upon the bluffs, where it was closely confined until the afternoon of the next day, when, upon the approach of our column, the whole Indian force decamped.

From the top of the peak, overlooking Colonel Reno's position, an observer could see far down the valley of the Little Big Horn, and the Indians probably had early news of our approach, and no doubt knew of our coming when we were fifteen or twenty miles away.

They were doubtless much elated by the total annihilation of Custer's part of the force, and made repeated and persistent efforts to complete their victory by destroying the rest of the command. But these were manfully and desperately resisted, and the Indians, encumbered with their camp equipage and families, doubtless felt no desire to continue the struggle with fresh troops, although these numerically were only about as strong as the force they were then fighting. Our arrival, therefore, was opportune; although, had it been possible to anticipate it by thirty-six or even twenty-four hours, the result doubtless would have been even more satisfactory. As it was, we were joyfully hailed as deliverers, and many did not hesitate to express the opinion that but for our arrival they would all have shared a common fate. This was especially noticeable in the wounded, who appeared to feel that they were stepping from death back to life again. Poor fellows! an impression had, in some way, gained a footing amongst them during the long weary hours of the fight on the 26th that, to save the balance of the command, they were to be abandoned. Hence, *their* joy at our arrival can better be imagined than described. I have seen in the course of my military life many wounded men, but I never saw any who endured suffering, privations, and the fatigue of travel, more patiently and cheerfully than those brave fellows of the Seventh Cavalry.

Our march of four and a half miles on the 28th demonstrated that it was practically out of the question to transport the wounded in anything like a reasonable time in the hand-litters, and, as the command laid over the next day for the purpose of destroying the large quantity of property left behind in the Indian camp, the delay was taken advantage of to construct, under the superintendence of Lieutenant Doane, an additional number of mule-litters, the few he had made the day before having worked satisfactorily. Ash poles were obtained, several dead horses lying about the camp were skinned for rawhide, and by the afternoon nearly the requisite number was completed, the full number being made up by structures called "travois," or "travailles," in imitation of the Indian method. These consist of a couple of lodge-poles, having one end fastened to the saddle of a packhorse, and the other trailing on the ground, the two being fastened together just behind the tail of the horse by a wicker-work platform, on which the patient reclines. The light flexible poles act as springs, and, except over very rough ground, the movement is far from disagreeable or rough. All the animals of the pack-train were now picked over, and the most gentle and best broken of these were turned over to Lieutenant Doane for service with the litters.

A number of companies were now sent out, scattered all over the site of the camp, to collect and destroy the property left by the Indians, and soon columns of smoke were seen rising in every direction from burning lodge-poles, upon which were thrown vast quantities of robes, dressed skins of different kinds, and other inflammable objects, while such pans, kettles, cups, and *crockery,* as were not needed by the troops were broken up.

Up to this time I had no opportunity to personally visit the scene of Custer's battle, and taking advantage of our delay in camp, which was situated just below and beyond the limits of the old Indian camp, I that morning rode up to the spot, and went over most of the ground.

The Little Big Horn is a stream with some singular features. It winds through its valley in a very crooked bed, bordered in many places with high precipitous bluffs, and is generally through this part of its course very sluggish, and wherever this is the case the water is deep enough to swim a horse. At various intervals between these sluggish parts the water becomes shallow enough to admit of fording, and goes rippling along to form the next deep spot below. About a mile below the bluffs occupied by Colonel Reno's command the river makes a considerable bend to the northward, and, sweeping round towards the south again, cuts in its course well into the bluff on the north bank, and leaves all the valley on the south bank. In this curve the Indian camp was located, and on the river just below its site, and at the most southern point on the curve, our present camp is situated. Close by us are two such fords as I have described, and crossing one of these we move up the right bank of the stream which here runs nearly due south. On our right is the wooded bank of the river, the intervening space between the cottonwood trees being filled up with brushwood. On our left the valley opens out into a grass-covered prairie, fringed on its southern side, and again on its western side, where the stream curves to the north again, with timber and brushwood. Riding along up the stream we come to the point where, after cutting the bluffs skirting it on the north, it turns sharply to the south. Here the ground commences to rise before us in gently sloping hills separated by little valleys, one of which seems to lead in about the direction we want to take. Just before this valley joins the valley of the river, the bottom has been cut into a gulch some eight or ten feet deep, and this is filled with brushwood nourished by the moisture of the rain-water, which doubtless cut out the gulch. Struck with the fact that this little valley seemed to be a natural outlet from the scene of the fight, and the possibility that individuals might have sought shelter in the gulch on their way to the timber below, we closely examined the place up to the point where the gulch headed, but found no "signs." As we proceeded up the valley, now an open grassy slope, we suddenly came upon a body lying in the grass. It was lying upon its back, and was in an advanced state of decomposition. It was not stripped, but had evidently been scalped and one ear cut off. The clothing was not that of a soldier, and, with the idea of identifying the remains, I caused one of the boots to be cut off and the stocking and drawers examined for a name, but none could be found. On looking at the boot, however, a curious construction was observed. The heel of the boot was reinforced by a piece of leather which in front terminated in two straps, one of which was furnished with a buckle, evidently for the purpose of tightening the instep of the boot. This led to the identification of the remains, for on being carried to camp the boot was recognized as one belonging to Mr. Kellogg, a newspaper correspondent who accompanied General Custer's column. Beyond this point the ground commenced to rise more rapidly, and the valley was broken up into several smaller ones which lead up towards the higher ground beyond. Following up one of these we reach a rolling but not very broken space, the ground rising higher and higher until it reaches a culminating knoll dominating all the ground in the immediate vicinity. This knoll, by common consent now called Custer's Hill, is the spot where his body was found surrounded by those of several of his officers and some forty or fifty of his men. We can see from where we are numerous bodies of dead horses scattered along its southwestern slope, and as we ride up towards it, we come across another body lying in a depression just as if killed whilst using his rifle there. We follow the sloping ground bearing a little to the left or westward until we reach the top, and then look around us. On the very top are four or five dead horses, swollen, putrid, and offensive, their stiffened limbs sticking straight out from their bodies. On the slope beyond others are thickly lying in all conceivable positions, and dotted about on the ground in all directions are little mounds of freshly turned earth, showing where each brave soldier sleeps his last sleep. Close under the brow of the knoll several horses are lying nearer together than the rest, and by the side of one of these we are told the body of Custer was found. The top of the knoll is only a few feet higher than the general surface of the long straight ridge, which runs off obliquely towards the river, in the direction of that ford at which it is supposed Custer made the attempt to cross.

Before leaving the prominent point from which probably Custer surveyed his last battle and took his farewell of earth, let us look around us. There is no point within rifle range which we do not overlook, but the surrounding space, which only a few days ago resounded with the sharp rattle of rifles and the wild yells of savages, is now silent as the grave, and filled with the fetid odor of decaying bodies.

Looking first along the ridge, which, almost level, runs off as straight as an arrow, the eye catches sight on both slopes of dead horses lying here and there, and little mounds showing where the riders fell and are lying. Beyond the end of this, in the direction of the ford, the ground becomes more broken, but still only in gentle slopes as it descends towards the river. Far beyond, a little to the left, rises that peak so often referred to, which with its neighboring heights hides from our sight the bluffs where Reno was besieged. Turning now to the right and facing the river, the ground is seen to be broken up into rolling hills and valleys, the sides formed of gentle slopes, but now and then where these valleys approach the river their bottoms are washed into gulches sometimes ten or fifteen feet deep. One is especially noted, to the right and front, running in a direction nearly perpendicular to the river, and at the bottom of this one were found some forty or fifty bodies. The general surface of the ground does not slope off towards the river, but continues high up to the very bank and above it; here and there the eye catches sight of the tops of the trees bordering the stream, and, beyond, the site of the Indian village. Turning now our backs upon the river, we see the ground sloping off rapidly behind the position into a long open valley, the lower part of which, as it runs off to join the valley of the Little Big Horn, far below, is seen to be fringed with brushwood, and an examination of this discloses the presence of innumerable pony tracks. More to the right, and beyond the little valley which borders on the north the straight ridge referred to, the ground rises into another ridge, and beyond this, as far as the eye can reach, extends a mass of rough broken "bad lands." Had we only known what dread secret those bad lands were hiding, we probably should have been able to perform the mournful duty of interring the remains of our twenty-five or thirty missing comrades. But we knew nothing of this then, and, turning our horses' heads, rode slowly along the top of the main ridge, stopping now and then to examine the place where some poor wounded animal, struggling in its death throes, had worked its way down the slope to the valley below. Arrived at the end of the ridge the ground opens out where several other ridges join it into a kind of level platform. Here evidently a severe struggle took place, for the bodies of men and horses are thickly strewn about. Moving to the far edge of this irregular plateau the ground is seen to fall away in a gently sloping valley towards the ford over which Custer is supposed to have attempted a crossing. I have stated that the top of Custer's Hill dominates over the whole surrounding country. Standing upon that he must have had a full view of the struggle taking place around him, and of the Indian village lying at his feet, but not within his power. And when forced back by overwhelming numbers, only to find the valley behind filled also with yelling hordes of savages, he must, whilst straining his eyes in that direction from which alone help could come, have recognized when too late the courageous-born error he committed in dividing his force in the presence of so numerous an enemy.

The body of our poor guide, Mitch Bouyer, was found lying in the midst of the troopers, slain, as the Sioux had several times reported they had slain him, in battle. He was a half-breed Sioux, and they had often tried to kill him. He was the protegé and pupil of the celebrated guide Jim Bridger; was the best guide in this section of the country, and the only half-breed I ever met who could give the distances to be passed over with any accuracy *in miles.*

The bodies of all the officers but two were found and recognized, and those of all the men, except some twenty or thirty, accounted for. The probable fate of these will be hereafter referred to. By the burial place of each officer was driven to the head a stake, in the top of which a hole was bored, and in this was placed a paper having upon it the name and rank of the officer.

On leaving the battle-ground we bore obliquely to the right, and making our way over the steep bluffs down to the river, near the mouth of the deep gulch mentioned as containing so many of our dead troopers, pushed our way through the brushwood of the river-bank, and, crossing the river at a shallow ford, entered the site of the Indian camp, where our working parties were still busy searching for, collecting, and destroying the Indian property, part of which was found concealed in the brush.

Riding across the valley towards the bluffs, we passed the site of the two tepees filled with dead Indians, now a mass of charred remains, and approached a clump of small trees, in and near which the Indians had buried a number of their dead, the ponies slaughtered in their honor lying about the remains of their dead masters, now tumbled upon the ground from the destruction of the scaffolding by those human ghouls whose existence seems to be inseparable from a fighting force, *after* the fighting is over, and whose vandal acts painfully impress one with the conviction that in war barbarism stands upon a level only a little lower than our boasted modern civilization.

The bodies lay upon the ground, the hideous display of their mortal corruption contrasting strangely with the gay robes and tinsel trappings with which they had been carefully, perhaps lovingly, decked. Turning from this revolting spectacle, we rode back to camp to find the work of litter-making going on bravely and successfully. About the camp numerous mules in couples, between the rude shafts of the litters, were being led about to get accustomed to the awkward movement, and under the direction of the indefatigable Lieutenant Doane, the men as well as the mules were being instructed how to turn, how to advance, hold back, etc., so that the poor suffering burdens should neither be thrown out nor shaken more roughly than was necessary.

At length all was ready; the wounded were lifted as tenderly as possible into the litters, and at six o'clock in the afternoon we started, expecting to make a short march, more to test the litters than anything else. But we had not gone more than a few miles and had just crossed the river a second time when two horsemen made their appearance on the bluffs on our left, and our couriers rode into the column bringing us news that the *Far West* was waiting for us at the mouth of the Little Big Horn. Our failure to obtain news of these couriers, started from our camp on the morning of the 29th, had caused serious apprehension that they might have fallen into the hands of the hostiles; for the distance they had to travel was only twenty miles, and if unmolested they should have been back to us before. Their return with the good news they bore solved the mystery of the delay. Leaving us late in the afternoon, they rode all night, and just at daylight mounted a hill overlooking the mouth of the Little Big Horn to look for the steamer. She was nowhere to be seen. Then, in accordance with their instructions, they started down the Big Horn to find her, following the bank of the river up and down over the deep gulches which all along the right bank lead into that stream. But their anxious search was without avail, and finally, late in the afternoon, they reached the mouth of the river, communicated with our supply camp there, obtained some food and forage for their horses, and the next morning started back up the Big Horn, and early in the afternoon when they rose the hill at the mouth of the Little Big Horn, a glad sight met their eyes, for there lay the steamer moored to the bank. They were quickly on board, and there learned that the officer in charge of the boat, uncertain as to whether or not he had reached the mouth of the Little Big Horn, directed the captain to run further up the river, which he did for about ten miles, and during the absence of the boat our couriers reached the point where they expected to find her. Resting on board the boat for an hour, the two indefatigable riders mounted their horses again, and finally reached us after a ride of about one hundred and forty miles in the course of forty-eight hours. Their names deserve to be preserved in the records of the campaign. One of them was an orderly of mine, Private Goodwin, of the Seventh Infantry, the other, Bostwick, the post-guide of Fort Shaw. They had a wonderful story to tell us of a Crow Indian, named Curly, whom they found on the boat, who asserted his escape from the Custer massacre, who had given many particulars of the fight, and even drew a rough map of the ground. The story of this man was found on examination to be consistent and intelligible, and the faithful fellow had ridden from the battle-field, immediately on his escape, to the mouth of the Big Horn, and not finding General Terry there, had followed up the stream to the boat, where he carried the first news of Custer's disaster. There is nothing very remarkable in the fact that a friendly *Indian* should have succeeded in making his escape from the general massacre in the midst of the turmoil of battle, however difficult it might have been for a single *white* man to do so, and Curly removed any lingering hope that any of the troops escaped, by stating that when he left, a party of twenty-five or thirty of our men had succeeded in getting away into the hills, several miles distant, but that they were entirely surrounded by a numerous band of Indians; that he could hear the firing there when he left, and that they were undoubtedly all killed. He described how he threw his blanket over his head, pretended to be a Sioux, and even fired his pistol towards the body of a dead soldier, as the Sioux were doing, and then slipped away from the fight.

Assured now of the close proximity of the boat, and anxious to get the wounded as soon as possible within its comfortable shelter, General Terry decided to push forward at once for the mouth of the stream. The mule-litters were working beyond our most sanguine expectations, both as regarded comfort and rapidity of movement, and all felt that Lieutenant Doane, by his energy and skill, had relieved us from a difficult dilemma, and our wounded from prolonged suffering. We therefore pushed rapidly down the valley, keeping near the bluffs, for Bostwick informed us that we must mount these and cross a high, wide plateau, before we could reach the boat. Darkness overtook us before we were able to reach this part of our road, but we had a young moon to light us on our way, and pushed ahead, hoping to reach the boat by eleven o'clock or midnight. But on reaching the plateau, the sky was overcast with heavy clouds. It became dark as pitch, and rain commenced to fall. We had now nothing to depend on but our sense of direction, and the skill of our guide, who had come over the ground in the daylight. Now and then the moon broke through the clouds to assure us of our direction, but the slow moving column was liable to separate at the slightest change of direction in front, and finally, pushing ahead with too much eagerness to find the path down from the plateau to the river, the advance found itself separated from the rest of the column, and we had no recourse but the sound of our bugles to get the command together again. This was finally effected, but amid the darkness and rain, our guide failed to discover the ravine down which our path lay, or to be sure even of his direction, and whilst we were pondering over the difficulty, there came moving to the front one of our Crow scouts, "Half-Yellow-Face," leading behind him a pony with a "travois" on which was travelling a wounded Crow.

Instinctively, for he could understand no English, and we had no interpreter, he seemed to divine what was wanted, took the lead, and we followed him with childlike faith in his skill. But even the Indian's skill was baffled, and he sought in vain in the midst of the rain and darkness to find the pathway down to the river bottom. We followed him closely, for otherwise the column would have been lost amid the windings in and out of the heads of the ravines, and we once found ourselves upon a point bounded on each side by gulches of unknown depth and steepness, and were obliged to countermarch the whole column, at the imminent risk of upsetting the litters, or having them run into each other. In the confusion, indeed, one of the men, a poor fellow whose leg was amputated, had a narrow escape, for one of the mules of his litter stepped into a hole and fell, and brought him with violence to the ground. Our search finally brought us in sight of a light, which would have aided us much, provided we could have gone directly to it, but this we were debarred from doing by the ravines and broken ground, and as the moon went down and the darkness increased, it began to look as if we were not going to reach the boat that night, after all; but the prospect of halting within sight of our harbor of rest, bivouacking on that bleak hill, with such scant accommodations for the wounded, prompted us to renewed efforts.

The column was now halted, and in company with a staff officer I rode forward to try and pick out a way. I was soon compelled to dismount, but we finally succeeded in making our way down to a lower level, and whilst going towards the light were hailed by a challenge. In answer to our call, "Who are you?" came back the welcome words, "Captain B., of the Sixth Infantry" (the officer in charge of the boat), and in a few minutes he was mounted on my horse and on his way back to the head of the column, whilst I reached the boat and started men out to build fires along the route. They were all up and expecting us, on the boat; and the lower deck, inclosed with canvas, was prepared with beds to make our wounded as comfortable as possible. It was now long after midnight, the side of the hill was soon ablaze with a line of fires, and by the light of these the litters made their way down, and when dawn commenced to streak the eastern sky, our poor patient sufferers were comfortably at rest on the deck of the *Far West.*

The next day she started down the river, and on the second day thereafter I reached the Yellowstone with the command, and, being ferried across the river, went into camp around our supply train. Here we remained until the 26th of July, receiving in the meantime supplies from down the river by steamer, and mails from Fort Ellis by small boats and carriers. Communication with the main Crow camp near Pompey's Pillar was opened, and on the 7th a party from there brought us the first news we received of General Crook's fight on the Rosebud on the 17th of June. It was carried to the camp by the Crows who were with General Crook's force in the battle, and two days afterwards we received further news about the fight, in a mail brought by scouts from the mouth of Powder River.

General Terry had been very anxious for some time to communicate with General Crook, and a message was dispatched to the Crows to try and induce them to go through, but none could be found willing to take the risk, although a large reward was offered. Their horses were tired, and they wanted to be with their families, they said. The real reason was, they regarded the trip as too hazardous, from the large number of Sioux known to be in that part of the country. Hearing of what was wanted, one of our citizen teamsters came forward and volunteered to carry a dispatch through. He possessed one thing in an eminent degree—a full knowledge of the law of trade so far as regards supply and demand. For knowing the demand was great, and the supply of couriers small, he thought he had a "corner" on couriers, and placed a very high estimate on his services, demanding in the first place fifteen hundred dollars. Being informed that this would not be paid, he dropped to six hundred, and the use of a horse, a rifle, and a field-glass. On the evening of the 4th of July he was put across the river, and four days afterwards he was back to us without horse, rifle, glass, hat, or shoes, and with a wonderful story of his narrow escape from Indians, and his vain attempt to cross the Little Big Horn on a raft, in which attempt he had lost everything. As his account was not very clear, and the Little Big Horn was known to be an insignificant stream in which it would be difficult to find water enough to float a raft, his story was looked upon with suspicion, and it was even strongly insinuated that he had never left the timber on the south side of the Yellowstone. Volunteers from my command were now called for to go through to General Crook, and in answer twelve men came forward and offered their services. Amongst them were the two men already mentioned as carrying the dispatches to General Terry by boat down the river on the 27th of May, Evans and Stewart, and with them came a third belonging to the same company, Bell, Company E, Seventh Infantry. I called all these twelve men up, told them what was required, what risks would probably have to be run, and questioned each in regard to how he proposed to make the trip. I knew nothing of the qualifications of any of them, so far as their knowledge of wood-craft was concerned, a knowledge so essential to a successful trip through an entirely unknown region. But the answers and bearing of the three men, all from one company, and proposing to go together, finally decided the matter in their favor, and they were told to get ready at once. Evans and Stewart were both tall, gaunt, lank specimens of humanity, and looked as if a hard day's ride would use them up completely. Bell was short, and more stoutly made. All of them appeared to be very quiet men, did not light up at all in conversation, and exhibited no enthusiasm whatever. Evans was apparently the leader of the party, and to him I gave full instructions as to how he was to travel. I also placed in his hand a section of a map of the country he was to pass over, marking upon it the supposed location of General Crook's camp. He looked at this in a stolid sort of way, and I began to think he did not even know the object in giving it to him. But he quietly stowed it away in his pocket, and after he came back to us, told me with a little smile he believed he could go anywhere in an unknown country if he had a map to travel by. They all three provided themselves with moccasins, so as when on foot, to make Indian instead of white man's "sign," and being provided each with a good horse, rifle, plenty of ammunition, and three days' rations, they were put across the river on the afternoon of Sunday the 9th, being accompanied some miles up the valley of Tullock's Fork by a company of cavalry, which, as night came on, left them to pursue their perilous route, and for sixteen days we heard not a word of news in regard to them.

On General Terry's invitation, some fifty or sixty Crows came down and joined us, and with them came back all the scouts who had left us the morning we heard of the Custer disaster. They all appeared much mortified at their conduct, especially as the Crows who had remained with us had been given a number of Sioux ponies picked up on the trip, which they had exhibited to their companions as trophies of the expedition. I was satisfied on talking with them, that their defection was entirely due to the white interpreter who was with them, and who did not return until some time afterwards. Soon after their arrival four of them were induced, after considerable persuasion, to start for General Crook's camp with a duplicate of the dispatch sent by the three soldiers, and on the 17th, having, in the meantime "prepared their *medicine*," they set out, and we heard no more of them for eight days.

The weather during the summer's operation became a matter of comment with all. Accustomed as we were to the exceedingly dry climate of Montana, where, during the summer months, anything more than a slight sprinkling of rain is almost unheard of, and the sound of loud thunder almost unknown, we were unprepared for the perfect deluges of rain which repeatedly overwhelmed us, and seldom selected our camps with any reference to water, regarding each rainfall as a phenomenon not likely to be repeated. Our present camp was located in the flat open bottom between the river and the bluffs, through which last, just above camp, a large dry gulch ran, having at its mouth a quantity of large driftwood. Where this gulch opened out into the valley the waters in times past, instead of cutting a channel out of the soil, as is usual, seem to have been in the habit of spreading themselves over the whole face of the valley. On the afternoon of the 13th we were visited by a severe storm of rain, accompanied by heavy thunder and lightning, and the next night a terrific rain commenced falling, and during nearly the entire night the whole atmosphere was lit up by vivid flashes of lightning, and resounded with constant peals of thunder. As daylight approached, a stir was heard in camp, and it soon appeared that all the campground, except a few elevated points, was under water, and the men busy removing their bedding and provisions to the higher ground. Wherever ditches were of any avail, men were set to work to dig them, but most of the ground was entirely submerged with some six to eighteen inches of water, and this, far from decreasing when the rain ceased, grew rapidly in depth as the water accumulated from the drainage of the surrounding gravelly hills poured in upon us from the gulch, which was now a raging torrent. It is not pleasant to be flooded out of your blankets at any time by a stream of muddy water from the "bad lands," and we soon changed camp to a more favorable location below Fort Pease.

A mournful incident occurred on the morning of the 19th. One of our officers who had for years suffered with a painful disease, the seeds of which were laid in Libby Prison during the war, rendered, it is supposed, desperate by his sufferings, put an end to his existence by shooting himself through the heart with a pistol. We laid him to rest in the afternoon on the top of a hill overlooking our camp, and piled up stones over his grave to prevent the depredations of wild animals.

Although no Indians had been seen since leaving Custer's battleground, we had reason to suspect we were watched, and on the night of the 19th two were fired upon whilst approaching our pickets, evidently with the design of spying out our camp, and attempting to steal our stock. The country was kept well scouted, too, and evidences were discovered that a party of twenty-five or thirty was prowling about in the vicinity. Having Indians from two different tribes, the Crows and Rees, in our camp, great care was necessary to avoid collision between these and the resultant alarms in camp. One evening whilst quietly resting in camp, someone called attention to a number of horsemen on a distant hill, apparently watching our camp. The Crows, on having their attention attracted to them, immediately became very much excited. They at once stripped for the fight, leaped upon their ponies without saddles, and with rifles in hand started on a helter-skelter run for the bluffs, yelling as they went. We watched them as they crossed the valley on their fleet little ponies, and in an almost incredibly short space of time they were seen rapidly climbing the hills a mile or two away. They disappeared over the top, a shot or two was heard, then all was still, and shortly afterwards the whole party was seen slowly coming back, accompanied by several Rees who had been imprudently permitted to leave camp on a scout, contrary to orders. They had been fired upon by the excited Crows, and found some difficulty in convincing them they were not *hostile* Sioux.

So great a length of time had now elapsed since the departure of Evans, Stewart, and Bell, that all began to look upon it as a matter of course that they had failed in their mission, and to mourn the brave fellows as so many more victims to the barbarous contest. When, therefore, on the 25th horsemen were reported as appearing on the bluffs south of the river, everyone was on the alert as to who they were; for they might be either hostiles, taking a view of our camp, or couriers from General Terry, who had gone down to Powder River some days before. Scarcely anyone entertained a hope that they were our absent couriers. They soon showed us they were not hostile, and coming down to the bank of the river a boat was sent over to meet them. Then a hope was expressed that they might be our absent men, and as the boat neared the opposite shore the conduct of the crew was narrowly watched through our glasses, for although some of the strangers were seen to be Indians at least two were recognized as white men. When the boat finally reached the shore, and the men in it were seen to cordially grasp the hands of the two white men, we felt sure they were our long-absent couriers and brought us news from General Crook, and when they landed on our shore and presented me with dispatches from General Crook I greeted them almost like men risen from the dead. Bell's horse had broken down on the trip, and Evans and Stewart only returned, accompanied by the Crow scouts, who had also succeeded in getting through to General Crook's camp. The modest recital of these men of their trip through a region swarming with hostiles, was interesting in the extreme. Their conduct was, enthusiastically, commented upon by the whole press of the country, and the Department commander published a highly complimentary order, thanking them for their services.[1] The news they brought decided the plan of our future operations, and two days after their return we commenced the march to the mouth of the Rosebud, where for the present was to be our depot of supplies. The hostile Indians were evidently still in the vicinity of General Crook, near the base of the Big Horn Mountains. We could no longer use the Big Horn River as a line of supply, for the waters were falling, and soon that stream, as well as the Yellowstone, adjacent, would be impracticable for steamboats. Hence the necessity of a depot and starting-point lower down the latter river. Besides which, the valley of the Rosebud could be made practicable for wagons, and led in the direction of the location of the hostiles and of General Crook's position. Starting on the 27th the command joined General Terry at the Rosebud on the 30th, he in the meantime having proceeded there by steamer, to locate the supply camp and the reinforcements known to be coming up the river.

Our new camp was in a flat sandy bottom interspersed with groves of trees. Directly opposite was the mouth of the Rosebud, below which, on a rocky point, were the remains of an old trading post, and on a hill just above it the remains of an old Indian grave, the scaffold of which was tumbling to pieces.

Indians always keep with the greatest care every scrap of writing they can get hold of, believing, I presume, that as white men scrutinize closely all such documents they must be *good medicine,* and such things are frequently deposited in the grave-clothes of the dead. A number of articles were picked up about this grave, and as it is possible some of them may serve to clear up the fate of some poor frontiersman, whose family never heard of him after his disappearance in the far West, I will

---

[1]They afterwards received "medals of honor" from the War Department for their service.

describe what they were. First was a copy of "The Soldier's Hymn-book," such as were distributed among our men during the war. With this was an envelope, addressed

"MRS. M. BETTS,
"Toledo,
"Jama Co.,
"Iowa."

On this there was no postmark, and it evidently had never been mailed; and a second envelope, much soiled and torn, with a stamp, a portion of the Toledo postmark, and this portion of an address:

"BETTS,
"Co. F., Sixth Iowa Cav.,
"Sioux City,
"—ase forward."

A letter which was probably enclosed in this envelope, was dated "No. 3, June 20th, '64." It commences "Dear husband," is signed "wife," speaks of "Jimmy" having gone to the army, and calls her husband "Duke." Besides this there was a scrap of letter-paper, upon which was written in pencil, "he has 2 pieces of gold, he says it is worth 20 drs. I cannot talk with them so am at a great loss on that account this man has been kind to me but am compelled to do their bidding
"FANNIE KELLY,[1]
"Captive white woman."

A round piece of something which resembles iron pyrites was picked up, and is probably one of the pieces of "gold" referred to.

On the 1st of August six companies of the Twenty-second Infantry arrived by boat, having had a skirmish on the way up at the mouth of Powder River with a party of Indians, and the next day six companies of the Fifth Infantry arrived, and went into camp. All the reinforcements expected immediately having now arrived, the movement across the Yellowstone commenced on the 3rd, and was completed on the 7th, and the following morning the movement up the Rosebud commenced; the command having been divided into two parts, one of cavalry, the other of infantry, the latter composed of the battalions of the Fifth, Sixth, Seventh, and Twenty-second. We started at 5 A.M., but the day was exceedingly hot and our march was very slow, as heavy parties had to be

---

[1]"Fannie Kelly" was, I believe, surrendered by the Indians at Fort Rice about 1864, and she, if living, would probably know who the man is, referred to in this scrap.

constantly engaged repairing the road for our wagons, so that we made only between nine and ten miles. The next day the weather turned very cold, overcoats and fires were comfortable, and we made only nine miles and a half after working all day on the road.

Crow scouts had been sent out on the 8th to try and communicate with General Crook, but they showed great reluctance to go far from the column, and on the 10th came running into the command uttering loud yells and saying the Sioux were coming. The scene was striking, and soon became exciting. Along through the valley, here wide and open, our straggling train was making its way flanked on each side by a line of infantry skirmishers. The advance had just passed over a hill from the top of which a good view of the surrounding country was presented. The Crows in parties of twos and threes came riding down the valley at full speed, uttering the most piercing yells, and every now and then circling around to announce the enemy in sight. They presented every appearance of running away, and nothing could stop them until they had passed considerably to the rear of the advance troops. But on the top of the hill where I was standing they met their pack-horses, extra ponies, conducted by their squaws and the hangers-on of the camp, and now was seen the object of their hasty retreat. Leaping from his panting steed each warrior commenced to strip for the fight. Shirts, leggings, saddles, etc., were rapidly pulled off and thrown upon the ground, to be hurriedly picked up by the now equally excited squaws, who, with loud cries, packed them away on the backs of the already loaded horses here, there, or anywhere, and in an incredibly short space of time the men, mounted horseback and rifle in hand, were off like the wind for the front again. On our right was the brush-fringed bed of the stream, beyond which the ground sloped gradually up towards a high ridge which ran obliquely across our front towards a point projecting out into the valley. Beyond this point where the stream (if that can be called a *stream* which is composed of stagnant pools of dirty alkali water) appeared to bend to the right, the Indians pointed excitedly to a column of smoke or dust rising above the hilltop. Whilst looking at this and speculating as to what might be causing it, my attention was attracted by two horsemen coming at full speed down the slope of the ridge on our right. On reaching the more level ground below, their horses suddenly changed direction, and wheeling twice in a circle still at full speed continued on towards us, the riders' shrill cries echoing over the valley. These discordant sounds startled a deer from his quiet bed in the valley, and our attention was for a moment attracted by a splendid buck, who went bounding across the valley before the two horsemen, as if dear life depended on his speed. These two scouts coming from the top of the ridge where they could command a view beyond, seemed to decide the question in regard to the near presence of a foe; and preparations were at once made to meet him. The train was rapidly closed up and parked in a convenient place, the leading cavalry deployed in line and pushed forward up the valley, and the infantry in lines of skirmishers on each flank. As the cavalry moved out, opening like a vast fan across the valley, General Terry moved with his staff to the front, and almost immediately a ringing cheer, reminding of war-times long past, broke from the whole line. Still no shots were heard, and we were not long left in doubt, for the Crows came riding back, calling out at the top of their voices, "Maschetee, maschetee" (soldiers), and we knew that all this dust and turmoil was caused by friends instead of foes, and that General Crook and not Sitting Bull was approaching. As the cavalry was deployed to the front the line encountered a single individual riding towards it at a gallop, his long hair streaming in the wind, and as the men recognized "Buffalo Bill" they broke out in loud cheers of welcome. He announced the near approach of General Crook's troops, and soon afterwards the junction between the two forces was accomplished.

General Crook's column was on a large Indian trail which had been followed for some distance down the Rosebud. Just where our two forces joined, the trail left the valley of the Rosebud, and turned eastward towards Tongue River. Several rains had fallen upon the trail, and the guides differed in regard to its age. But the fact was apparent that the whole hostile force had eluded the two columns, and made, for the present, its escape eastward. The presence of Indians at the mouth of Powder River during the first of the month now became strongly significant, and it was to be feared that, as they had gotten such a start, they would succeed in getting across the Yellowstone, and proceed north before we could catch them. Once across the Yellowstone, they would make for the Missouri River, and if pressed across that, it was but comparatively a short distance to safety, beyond the British line. Hence it was decided to push on in pursuit with the main body, sending a portion hastily back to the Yellowstone to get on board of a steamer, and patrol the lower part of that stream, and sending back also our wagons after taking from them the pack-mules and supplies needed for the trip. The force for patrolling the river started that afternoon, and the next morning our long column stretched itself out to the eastward on the Indian trail.

The well-organized pack-train of General Crook's column, with its skilled packers and trained mules, excited our admiration and envy as the well-broken animals trotted along to the sound of the bell tinkling in their front. This bell was certainly to them "good medicine," for no well-trained pack-mule will ever permit himself to be beyond the sound of that bell, and it is only necessary to sound it to assemble every mule belonging to that particular train. Very different was it with the packs belonging to the Dakota column. Most of our mules were draft animals, and had never been packed before. Our saddles were of an inferior kind, and our packers, the men themselves, generally without any experience in what is always a very delicate and skillful operation. Each individual mule had to be led by a soldier, and the obstinate traits of the animal as developed under the new and novel circumstances of the work he was called upon to perform, would have been amusing had they not been so costly. They took anything but kindly to the loosely fastened, rattling packs, threw their heels into the air, their packs over their heads, and, having thus relieved themselves from boxes of hard bread and sacks of bacon, in several instances galloped back to the wagon train, testifying by their loud and characteristic brays as they rejoined their comrades, their preference for pulling, over packs. I saw one poor fellow going down a very steep hill, his pack almost touching his long ears as the loosened fastenings permitted it to slip forward. At last, tired of his disagreeable burden, he added to the mischief by kicking up behind. The load was in such a condition as to need just this additional incentive to take its departure, and with a bound a box of hard bread broke loose, and, striking upon a corner, went rolling end over end down the steep descent until, hitting a rock harder than its contents, the box flew into a number of pieces, and a layer of "hard tack" was strewn for twenty yards down the slope.

We crossed the high rolling divide separating the Rosebud from Tongue River, and crossing the latter stream proceeded some miles down its valley. The guides report a separation in the trail, but that of a large portion still leads down the valley, and most of the country has been recently burnt over, whilst smoke of still burning fires are seen to the eastward. We found, however, a spot where the grass was green and luxuriant, and bivouacked for the night in it. By the order regulating the movement, no canvas was permitted, no cooking utensils except tin cups, and no clothing or blankets except what each officer and man carried on his person or horse. Such deprivations would not amount to much usually in a dry, clear atmosphere like that of Montana, but old Nick himself seemed to have seized upon the weather-gauge, and that night, after making our bivouac under a clear sky, the rain commenced to fall in torrents, and it was not long before each one, from the general to the private, found himself lying in a puddle of water. It rained on the just and the unjust, on the high and the low, but so far as concerns the latter, inches in altitude were of far more importance than grades in rank, and happy was he who had chosen his bed wisely, and placed his blanket on an elevation and not in a depression. I was not among the wise ones, and had, like most others, to turn out, or rather *up,* light a fire (no easy matter), and shiver soaking by it till daylight. I scarcely ever saw it rain more heavily anywhere than it did on us during our trip down the Tongue River. For three nights in succession everything was thoroughly soaked, and the command got but little sleep. We still pushed on down the river, cheered by the news from the scouts that the trail grew fresher, but as we neared the mouth it turned eastward again, and proceeded towards Powder River. We pushed on in pursuit, having communicated with the steamer on the Yellowstone, and ascertained that as yet no Indians had crossed the river so far as was known. We reached Powder River on the 15th, after passing over a very rough broken country, only to find the whole country burnt over, and no Indians in sight. Twenty miles down the river we followed the trail to a point where General Terry struck it when he came from the east in June, and went into camp in the midst of a rain which came down as though a second deluge was in order. Late in the afternoon the sun burst through the thick clouds, and lighting up the still falling rain, spanned the eastern hills with a magnificent rainbow, as if giving promise of clear weather, a prognostic we were only too ready to accept as true. An incident occurred on this day's march (August 16th) which will serve to show one of the many difficulties under which military operations are conducted in a wild region like this. One of the officers, a fine young captain of infantry, suddenly fell down at the head of his company in a fit of apoplexy, or paralysis, and for weeks afterwards never spoke a word. He was perfectly helpless, and the matter of his transportation became a question of serious importance. Fortunately it was near the close of the day's march, and the distance to our camping-place was not great. But how to carry him at all was the question to be solved. The rearguard was halted, and luckily with this was Lieutenant Doane, whose services with the wounded of the Seventh Cavalry had proved so valuable. He set to work, and in a couple of hours constructed a litter upon which the poor sufferer was carried to camp in the midst of a pouring rain. The next day he was carried in the same way to the mouth of Powder River, and placed on board of a steamboat.

We still followed the Indian trail down Powder River, but twelve or fifteen miles from its mouth the trail suddenly turned to the eastward, and now our guides and scouts seemed to be in still greater doubt than ever regarding its age or, in other words, our proximity to the Indians. There were no indications leading to the belief that we were anywhere close to them, and whilst scouting parties were sent far ahead on the trail, the command marched to the mouth of the Powder to obtain supplies, more especially forage for our animals, many of which were becoming worn down and weak from hard travel and the lack of sufficient food.

The mouth of the Powder is a bleak, desolate region, with poor grass, much of which had been burnt off by the Indians, but by scattering the command along the valley some grazing was obtained, and, with what grain we could get, our horses and mules began to pick up their strength. Here we remained a week, our wagon train and supplies being brought down in the meantime from the mouth of the Rosebud. Of these seven days, we were deluged during three with heavy rains, notwithstanding our promising bow on the 16th.

During the latter part of this march our Crow allies began to show signs of impatience, and a desire to leave us and return to their tribe. This, in view of our future operations, and their excellent qualities as scouts, would prove a serious loss to us. But they had already served a longer time than they had originally engaged for, and it was difficult to see if they demanded their discharge how it could be refused.

One day, seated with my back against a post, pencilling a letter, the whole delegation, squaws and all, approached the spot, but with no interpreter, and whilst I was wondering what was going to take place, the party formed a circle round me and the leader advancing, gravely took my cap from my head and placed it in my lap, solemnly placed one hand upon my scalp as though blessing me, and with the other grasped my hand, shook it and retired. This ceremony was performed in solemn silence by each of the warriors belonging to the band, and I came to the conclusion that they were going to leave us, and were desirous of securing my scalp upon my head for the future. An interpreter being summoned, they expressed through him their desire to return to their people to make provision for the coming winter, by killing buffalo for their women and children, and I found that the ceremony they had gone through signified a *petition* that I would grant their request and discharge them. They expressed great and sincere devotion to our service and a desire to join us again in fighting their enemies, the Sioux. I promised to intercede with General Terry in their favor, and two days afterwards (August 20th) they were discharged and left us with the regrets of all, for we had become much attached to them, and deplored the loss of such faithful and intelligent scouts.

On the 24th, the recuperated command started up Powder River, to take up again the abandoned Indian trail; but the next day "Buffalo Bill" overtook us with a dispatch announcing the approach of steamers with more troops on board, and that they had been fired into by Indians lower down the Yellowstone. This, coupled with the report, received two days before, that Indians were crossing the river above Fort Buford, gave rise to the impression that they were endeavoring to escape to the north, and caused a change of programme. Hence it was decided to divide the command, and, whilst General Crook followed the Indian trail, our column retraced its steps, struck across the country, and the next day (26th) reached the Yellowstone lower down, near the mouth of O'Fallon's Creek. The next morning two steamers arrived, and the command was at once ferried across the river, and late in the afternoon, with pack-mules and in light, very light, marching order, started out for a night-march to the northward. Now it was that we felt the great want of our Crow allies, for this region of country was totally unknown to us. We had no guides with us who knew anything about it, and those we had declared that in all probability, from the lay of the country, we should find no water. The peninsula lying between the Missouri and Yellowstone Rivers, here something over one hundred miles wide, is known to be a high rolling divide, intersected by but few streams, and these generally dry in summer. But Big Dry Creek, a tributary of the Missouri, to the westward of us, was known to be the favorite location of Sitting Bull's camp, and running to it along on the south of the Missouri River, a lodge-pole trail was known to exist. Should the hostiles succeed in crossing the Yellowstone, they would, in all probability, use this trail. To strike it, and if possible any Indians who might be moving on it, was the object of our present movement.

We marched till a late hour of the night, bivouacked in the hills without water, and early the next morning resumed the march without breakfast. The luxuriant growth of grass in the country we passed over, probably the result of the unusually copious falls of rain during the summer, encouraged us in the hope of being able to find water for drinking purposes, and we had not proceeded many miles before the scouts reported they had discovered some pools in the bed of Bad Route Creek, a short distance ahead. Towards these the march was at once directed, and although the first pools discovered were merely small *mud-puddles,* preparations were at once made to utilize these for the manufacture of coffee. Further search, however, developed the existence of a plentiful supply of clear water in large pools, and the whole command enjoyed a hearty breakfast with coffee, for without the latter a soldier's breakfast is but a poor concern. Then, after a halt of a couple of hours, the march was resumed in a direction due north. The day was intensely hot, and both men and animals suffered a good deal for want of water, but we succeeded in finding some small pools from which the men eagerly drank and filled their canteens. During the day the scouts reported buffalo in sight, and this was cheering news, for the presence of buffalo not only indicates the existence of water in the vicinity, but is a pretty good sign generally that Indians are not far off, just as the presence of a commissary train in time of war indicates the near presence of troops. The vicinity of buffalo, however, brought us a torment in the shape of immense numbers of buffalo-gnats, which swarmed around us like bees, stinging men and horses in a way which rendered both almost frantic with pain. As the day approached its close, anxious search was made for water in every direction. The few spades with the command were produced, and with these and the invaluable trowel-bayonets carried by some of the men, holes were dug in the low places where water evidently had been at no very distant period. Not a drop, however, rewarded our labors, and our thoughts began to be seriously directed towards another dry camp, when one of the scouts reported the glad tidings of water in a ravine a mile or two ahead. That summer's rain had left a supply of water in the country was encouraging, not only in reference to the practicability of passing through the region with a command, but in regard to the probability of finding Indians there, and raised hopes that, after all the long delay, an effectual blow might yet be struck.

The next day our march to the north was resumed over a high rolling country, well covered with rich pasturage, and we began to encounter game in abundance. Hundreds of antelope flocked around the column, and crossing a high divide we came in sight of herds of buffalo. But they were quietly feeding, and showed no indications of the proximity of Indians. Still farther to the north rose a high broken ridge of hills forming the divide between us and the Missouri River, and near this the trail of which we were in search was supposed to run. As we advanced the buffalo became more numerous, and finally the command was halted in a little valley, and permission given for the men to obtain a supply of fresh meat, of which they stood greatly in need.

Now commenced one of the most exciting scenes ever witnessed in the Western country. Groups of horsemen moved out in different directions towards the herds quietly feeding on the neighboring hills. At first but little attention was paid to the approaching horsemen, for the buffalo is not usually a very watchful animal, and with the wind in your favor, you can approach them very closely before being perceived; but at length one of the herd looks up from under his shaggy brows, perceives you are not a buffalo, makes an observation to his fellows, and with a slow lumbering gait, reminding one of the awkward movements of an elephant, the whole herd moves off. The horses now strike into a trot, and then a gallop, in pursuit. The faster the horses go, the more rapid becomes the gait of the buffalo, until both pursuers and pursued are on the full run, the hunted straining every nerve to get out of the way, the hunters every nerve to close upon the prey. If a descending slope is reached, especially a steep and rough one, the buffalo at once shows to his advantage, and rapidly widens the gap between himself and the horsemen, but on an ascending smooth slope or on level ground, the horseman redoubles his pace and soon forges up alongside the herd. As they close up, the frightened herd scatters out, still, however, running in the same general direction; the cows and calves with loud bellows of fear dodging in and about the larger bulls to get out of the way of the dreaded danger. Each horseman now singles out his particular game, and with all speed presses his horse up alongside. A puff of white smoke is seen, followed by the sound of a pistol-shot; but still the mad race goes on; another and another shot follows, and now all the buffalo on the surrounding slopes raise their lazy heads, become aware of their danger, recognize their dread enemy, man, and commence to move off in different directions. But they find new enemies at every step, and wild with fright rush off on any course which seems to offer safety. Ride with me to the top of this little knoll, and take a view of the field of battle. In every direction are small herds of buffalo on the full run, followed or accompanied by horsemen in twos or threes, while puffs of smoke and a constant rattle of small arms produce the impression of a bygone battle-field. Every now and then one of the black objects is seen to fall behind the herd, to stagger, sink down and throw his heels up in the air, whilst a loud shout from the victor proclaims his triumph. See that herd wild with fright rushing directly towards a horseman, who sits quietly waiting his chance with a cocked revolver in his hand. Now they approach him, and recognizing their new danger, turn aside without slackening their gait. But with a sudden dash he is abreast of them on his fresh horse; bang! bang! goes his pistol, and one of the herd rolls in the dust, while the others continue their mad flight. Look at this herd, madly tearing up this slope, directly towards us, intent only upon escaping the fiends at their back, as crazy with excitement as they are with fear. They know not and care not what is ahead, but as they rise the hill and go rushing down the opposite slope, a long line of men and horses is seen to bar their way, and half dead with fright they wheel and scatter. Look out, now, for the hunters are as mad as the hunted, and where men are rushing about with cocked revolvers in their hands there is no knowing where the bullets may go, and one which misses a buffalo may bury itself in you. Bang! bang! go the pistols close to your ear, as the frightened animals rush past you, their long tongues lolling out, and bellowing with fear, and as the field of conflict clears away, several black carcasses are seen lying on the ground close by the column of troops. The herds disappear over the hills, a distant shot is heard now and then, and the buffalo hunt is over, with enough fresh meat lying around us for a week's supply. This is quickly cut up and packed away upon our mules, and the command resumes its march, with the means, if required, of making a longer scout than was at first proposed. A detachment of cavalry is sent off towards the divide to the northward, to examine the trail, whilst the main column turns to the eastward to camp late in the day at some stagnant water-pools, the strong smell of buffalo from which calls forth comments about living on buffalo *straight* in every form. The next day we still continued the eastward course, and were rejoined by the detached cavalry, which found the trail, but with no indications that it had been recently used, so that if any Indians have crossed to the north of the Yellowstone we are still ahead of them, and may yet strike them lower down. Scouts are now kept well out from the column, but failing to discover any signs of Indians, the command was again turned to the southward on the 31st, a large cavalry force being sent still further to the eastward, to definitely decide the question as to the presence of any Indians in that direction, and on the 3d of September, the whole force was once more concentrated on the Yellowstone near the mouth of Glendive Creek, it being now certain that no considerable body of Indians had gone north, and everyone being anxious to hear whether General Crook had been any more successful on the south side of the river than we had been on the north. It was expected that General Crook's troops would come in to this point for supplies, but several days passed without hearing from them, and at length a dispatch came by courier to say that he had found the Indian trail divided, and that he was going to strike still further to the east and southward.

Our stern chase had thus proved a long and fruitless one, and we had no longer even a shifting objective point to move against; for the Indians had doubtless divided their forces in the wilderness to the south of the Yellowstone, and could at any time concentrate again or remain scattered, according to circumstances.

Orders had been received for the establishment for the winter of a large force on the Yellowstone near the mouth of the Tongue, the site of one of the proposed posts, and for the transportation to that point of a winter's supply for fifteen hundred men. The river was now rapidly falling, and the steamboat captains expressed doubts as to whether they would be able to make many more trips up, even as far as the point we were then at. Should this prove true, then all the supplies necessary for the force to be left in the wilderness would have to be brought by wagons from Fort Buford, and in any event sent in that way from this point to the post on Tongue River. Our supply of wagon transportation was limited, and a part of that belonging to the Montana column being left for service at the new post, the Montana troops started on their homeward march on the 6th of September with twenty-five days' rations, and a march of six hundred miles ahead of them.

Our homeward march was devoid of any incident of special note, and after passing over about one hundred miles of it, we reached the point where we met General Terry on the 8th of June, and turned back up the Yellowstone. From here our route was substantially the same as the route followed down the river in the spring, except that on passing the mouth of the Big Horn River we found the Yellowstone still too high to admit of fording, and this compelled us to keep north of the river, and pass through a very rough and difficult country. In making the march the men were in much better condition for it than the horses and mules, which for six months had been hard at work on indifferent food. The men, it is true, were dirty and ragged, but their physical condition was excellent, and they got over their twenty to thirty miles a day with far more ease and comfort than the animals did. The cavalry reached Fort Ellis on the 29th of September, and the infantry striking north from a point sixty miles east of that post, arrived at Fort Shaw on the 6th of October.

During their six months' absence in the field the objects attained by them were not at all proportionate to the efforts put forth, but should any feel inclined to criticize too closely our want of success by indulging in sarcastic calculations as to how many millions of dollars are required to kill one Indian, the only answer that can be made is—the truth of which is well recognized in the army—that war is far more costly than peace, and that it never has been, and never can be, a paying speculation. Wars are always costly, and, like commercial operations, the larger the transactions the more cheaply, generally, are they conducted. And it may be safely asserted that, considering the circumstances, Indian wars are in proportion no more costly than any other kind of wars. It is very certain that in Indian wars the labor performed is far greater than in so-called *civilized* wars (as if war in any shape could be called civilized!), whilst the troops engaged have not even the poor consolation of being credited with *"glory,"* a term which, upon the frontier, has long since been defined to signify being "shot by an Indian from behind a rock, and having your name wrongly spelled in the newspapers!" Hence, if the American people do not wish to spend money, they should not go to war. Doubtless many well-meaning people will say, "That is all very well, but how are you going to avoid it?" This question I will answer by asking another. How do you ever avoid war? It can be avoided sometimes by the exercise of a spirit of concession and justice, a spirit directly opposite to that which has universally characterized the treatment of the red man of this continent by the American people. You cannot point to one single treaty made with the Indians which has not at some time or other been violated by the whites, and you can point to innumerable instances where the Indian has been most outrageously swindled by the agents of the government; and the great wonder is, not that we have had so many wars but that we have had so few. The Indian, although a savage, is still a man, with probably quite as much instinctive sense of right and wrong as a white man, and quite as sensible as the latter when wrongs are perpetrated against him. *He* argues in this way: The white man has come into *my* country and taken away everything which formerly belonged to me. He even drives off and recklessly destroys the game which the Great Spirit has given me to subsist on. He owes me something for this, but generally refuses to pay. Now and then, as we find his settlements closing in around us, we succeed in getting him to promise us a certain yearly amount of food and clothing, that our wives and children may not starve or freeze to death, but when his agents come to turn these over to us we find the quantity growing less and less every year, and the agents growing rich upon what was intended to feed and clothe us. We try to reach the ear of our "Great Father" to tell him of our troubles, and how his agents defraud us, but *he is so far away that our words do not reach him.* We cannot see our wives and children starve, and year by year the danger becomes greater from the constant encroachment of the whites, who insist upon settling upon the land guaranteed to us by solemn treaty. Let us go to war and force back the settlements of these intruders, or if we must die, let us die like men and warriors, not like dogs.

Let the great people of America say whether or not the Indian is logical in his savage way, or whether or not the premises from which he argues are sound. None will dispute that his country has been overrun, and taken from him for less than "a mess of pottage"; and few will deny that the game on which he depends for subsistence is recklessly destroyed by the white men, so that in a few years more it will have entirely ceased to exist. None but Indian agents and their abettors will deny the fact that, with but few exceptions, all such agents retire from their positions enriched by the spoils from the agencies, and that, although exposures of these frauds have been made over and over again, none of these government agents are ever brought to punishment, or made to disgorge their ill-gotten gains, whilst the Indians are left to suffer for the actual necessaries of life. When, then, the Indian, driven to desperation by neglect or want and his sense of wrong, goes to war (and even a Christian will fight before he will starve), the army is called in to whip "these wards of the nation" into subjection, and when the task is successfully accomplished, as it always is in the end, the same old round of deceit and fraud commences again, and continues till the next war opens; but all the blame for these expensive wars is laid upon the military, supposed, by the "Indian ring," to be so bloodthirsty as never to be contented unless engaged in the delightful (?) task of chasing roving bands of Indians for thousands of miles through a wilderness, sometimes with the mercury frozen in the tube, for the purpose of bringing into subjection a people forced into war by the very agents of the government which makes war upon them.

Let the American people remove this foul blot from their record by insisting that the red man shall be treated with something like justice, listening to the voice of reason and common humanity, and seeing to it that all the ample means provided by their liberality shall be expended on the Indians, instead of squandered and stolen under a system which is a disgrace to the age and the country. The small, miserable remnant of a race which once covered this whole continent can be retained in peaceful relations with the whites by simply expending for their benefit the funds appropriated every year by Congress. To feed and clothe them is cheaper in every way than to fight them, and if they are fed and clothed they will not fight. If, however, the people of the United States insist upon pretending to do *both,* let them cease to complain of the expense of one part of their bad system, and lay the responsibility for the results where it properly and justly belongs.

As connected with this subject of making war upon Indians, it may be not only interesting, but instructive, to glance at some of the elements involved in the struggle, and it is possible that a due appreciation of them may be of benefit to the people at large, and aid in inducing them to avert such wars by commencing the remedy at the right point.

Of the ultimate result of the struggle between civilization and barbarism there can be no question. The complete extinction of the red man is, in the end, certain. He may succeed in averting this for a time, and by such temporary triumphs as the Fetterman and Custer massacres postpone the fatal day, but ultimately the result will surely come, and as day by day and year by year the white settlements close in around his hunting-grounds, he is gradually becoming aware of his approaching doom. In the meantime he occupies a vast territory of comparatively unexplored country, into which the troops are obliged to seek him when active hostilities open. Of the geography of this region the troops are almost completely ignorant, and are not infrequently entirely at the mercy of incompetent guides, not only in their movements, but for the discovery of what is absolutely necessary to the success of such movements—water. Civilized warfare is conducted upon certain well-established principles, in which good maps of the country operated in constitute a very important element. In addition to which there is always a stable "objective point" to every campaign which the commander knows cannot be suddenly changed to some other place, and elude his combinations, as an Indian village does. To the Indian, every foot of the country he is operating in is as familiar as are the paths of our flower gardens to us. He has travelled and hunted over it from childhood, knows every path, every pass in the mountains, and every water-hole, as thoroughly as the antelope or other wild animals which range through it. He knows exactly where he can go and where he cannot, where troops can come and will come, and where they cannot, and he knows the points from which he can safely watch the whole country, and give timely notice of the movements of troops, and direct those of his own camps so as to avoid an encounter, or concentrate to meet one. The best horseman in the world, he can, on his fleet little pony, the speed of which is a matter of wonder to the white man, pass over the incredible distances in the shortest time, his mode of life accustoming him to any amount of fatigue, and the greatest deprivations in the way of clothing and food. A piece of buffalo-meat strung to his saddle, and the lightest possible amount of clothing, suffices him day or night for weeks and even months together. With eyes, ears, and even nose always on the alert, like any wild animal, he will discover signs of an approaching enemy more quickly and more certainly than can any white man, and will read the signs he meets with, as a scholar will read the page of an open book. He scents the smoke of a fire from a distance, and at early dawn will patiently watch from some prominent peak, as motionless as a bronze statue, the columns of smoke which at that time of day rise like pillars in the still clear air, and tell him whether a large force is preparing its breakfast, or some small scouting party is out looking for his village. If his quick eye encounters horse-tracks, he can tell with unerring certainty how many are in the party, whether the horses are ridden by white men or Indians; whether they are proceeding at a walk, a trot, a gallop, or a run; whether they are acting cautiously or carelessly; how many of the horses are ridden, and how many are without riders. He can tell whether the horses are tired or fresh, and whether they have travelled but a short distance or a very long one.[1] The system of espionage of the Indians is probably the best in the world, and when time presses, and even the fleet-footed pony is not quick enough to convey information to

---

[1]This is done by an examination of the ordure.

their chiefs, they have a system of signals by using the smoke of fires, or the reflected light of the sun with mirrors, by which the necessary intelligence is given at great distances.

Whilst troops entering the hostile country are watched by such a system, *they* move along almost without eyes, nothing beyond a very short distance from the moving column being seen or known, and the game of war is carried on very much on the principle of "Blindman's Bluff." The Indians can always, in summer, avoid a single column, or select their own time and place for meeting it. And they never do meet it unless they are prepared and have *all* the advantages on their side. The campaign of last year fully exemplified this. Hence there are but two alternatives by which success can be attained. Operate against them in the winter-time, when their movements are restricted, their watchfulness less efficient, and any "signs" left in the snow as plainly read by a white man as by an Indian; or else have in the field a number of columns, so that the moving Indian villages cannot avoid all of them, and have these columns cooperate under some common head. Each of them being strong enough to take care of itself, the Indians, if successful in eluding one, will in all probability be encountered by one of the others. The two posts to be established in the Yellowstone country will serve as starting-points for two of these columns, and as depots of supplies and rest for all.

One other important element enters into this system of warfare, for which, as yet, no adequate provision has been made. This is the care of the wounded, who cannot, as in civilized warfare, be left in hospitals on the field of battle. An Indian is rarely defeated until he is dead, and he not only kills every one of his enemies he can find, but wreaks his vengeance on his dead body. Hence, a very small number of wounded men is sufficient to temporarily paralyze the offensive operations of a considerable body of troops. The Indians are better prepared in every way than our troops to carry off their wounded, and, as they invariably do it, we might very profitably take some lessons from them on the subject.

# The Pursuit
# of "Joseph"

*The next two articles, "The Pursuit of 'Joseph' " and "The Battle of the Big Hole," recount Colonel Gibbon's expedition against Chief Joseph's band of Nez Percé in July and August of 1877. While there is some overlapping of material, the two accounts emphasize different aspects of the campaign and together offer a detailed record of the entire operation.*

*The campaign against the Nez Percé illustrates the conflict within the colonel himself. Gibbon always believed that the tribe had been forced into hostilities by the whites, an opinion he expressed on April 26, 1878, before a congressional committee inquiring into reorganization of the army. Colonel Gibbon testified, "I think that Joseph and his band are the objects of the greatest possible injustice at the hands of the government, and that, as a result arising from the management of them (and I presume the Indian Department is responsible for that), they were actually forced into rebellion." Though sympathetic to the plight of the Nez Percé, Gibbon promptly obeyed his orders to intercept Joseph's band. The determination with which he pursued his quarry revealed that his personal convictions were overruled when duty called.*

*"The Pursuit of 'Joseph' " appeared in* American Catholic Quarterly Review 4 *(April 1879): 317–344, and "The Battle of the Big Hole" appeared in* Harper's Weekly, *December 21, 1895, pp. 1215–1216, and December 28, 1895, pp. 1235–1236.*

*L*ate in the fall of 1876 a band of the Nez Percé Indians, on their way from their homes west of the mountains to the "Buffalo country," stopped for a day or two at the post of Fort Shaw. The various bands inhabiting the western part of Montana and Eastern Idaho have been accustomed, for many years, to make this trip for procuring supplies of buffalo meat. Coming east in the fall, they remain amongst the buffalo during the winter, and return to the west in the spring. This visit was, therefore, no novelty to the garrison of Fort Shaw, and derived its interest from future events, for the chief of the band was the since celebrated "Looking Glass."

The chiefs called upon the commanding officer, as usual, were kindly received, and supplied with some necessary provisions, which, singular to say, they never *asked* for, but always took. They were invited to give us an exhibition of a *sham* battle. To this they consented, and, at the hour appointed, the whole garrison turned out, when the distant shots and loud yells of the warriors were heard as they approached the post from their camp down the river. Firing their pieces in the air and uttering their peculiar yells, they approached the post in a motley crowd, their horses prancing, their drums beating and their gay, painted feathers fluttering in the breeze. After marching in this fashion entirely around the garrison, to show off their gay trappings and hideously painted faces, they assembled for the fight on the prairie outside the post. Dividing into two parties, they went through the manoeuvres of a supposed conflict, charging and firing at each other, advancing and retreating, tumbling from their horses to simulate the killed and wounded, and now and then dismounting to fight on foot, when they jumped about like so many capering monkeys, all the time uttering the most frightful yells. The whole thing was looked upon by the spectators as a most ridiculous farce, and the remark was frequently heard, "If they do not fight better than that when they go into a real battle, they will not do much harm to the enemy." Many of those looking on, had occasion afterwards to recall the reflection, and an incident of the sham battle, regarded as peculiarly comical at the time, was strongly impressed upon our minds by after events. During a pause in the conflict, the half-breed interpreter approached me and asked for some *rags*. On inquiring as to what he wanted with them, he said "to make a fire." I suggested a handful of hay. This was obtained, and when the battle recommenced, an Indian, crawling up towards the opposition party, deposited his hay, and with a match set it on fire. The wind being favorable, the smoke was carried into the faces of the enemy, and behind it the now victorious party charged forward with loud yells, and drove their enemy from the field in wild confusion, and thus ended the fight. This incident, derisively looked upon as child's play at the time, many of us had occasion afterwards to recall under more serious circumstances.

In the following June, reports began to reach us of hostilities having broken out among the Nez Percés, west of the mountains. The region where the first conflicts between the troops and the Indians took place is not only west of the main divide of the Rocky Mountains, but west of the Bitter Root range, a high, rugged range, running north and south, over which passes, for nearly one hundred miles, a rough, difficult mountain trail, known as the "Lo Lo Trail," entering the Bitter Root valley a few miles above the town of Missoula, Montana Territory. The difficulties of the trail are graphically described in the journal of Lewis and Clark, who passed over it seventy-one years ago, and named the stream issuing from it to the eastward, "Traveller's Rest Creek"; for here their expedition rested one day before encountering the perils of the trail, after their trip down the *Bitter Root,* by them named Clark's River.

Early in June two small companies of infantry had been sent from Fort Shaw, to establish a post near the town of Missoula, and between that place and the mouth of "Traveller's Rest Creek," or Lo Lo Fork. This was the only post in Western Montana, and the nearest one to the scene of hostilities.

To meet any emergency in Montana, the number of troops available was very small, for all the cavalry, comprising one-half the strength in the Territory, had early in the spring been ordered for service down the Yellowstone River. This left for our sole dependence ten companies of infantry, occupying five different posts and scattered for a distance, north and south, of some 250 miles, with the outlying post near Missoula, nearly that distance to the westward.

On the first report that the hostiles were moving eastward, one company was hastily dispatched in wagons from Fort Ellis, and, after a rapid march, reached Missoula, but not until after the Indians had succeeded in passing into the Bitter Root valley. This took away every available soldier from Fort Ellis, and immediately afterwards, on the receipt of positive intelligence that the Nez Percés were moving over the Lo Lo Trail, a concentration of troops at Fort Shaw from the posts of Fort Benton and Camp Baker was ordered. This concentration was effected on the 27th of July, and the following day the little force, consisting of seven officers and seventy-six men, filed out of Fort Shaw, followed by its pack-mules, and took up its march for Missoula, 150 miles distant. As we were to march via Cadotte's Pass and now knew its location, we were able to strike for it in a "bee line," which in a country like this, intersected with hills and valleys, is not quite as straight as the "crow flies." Our mules, unaccustomed to packing, gave a good deal of trouble, and no one knows, except after trial, what trouble an obstinate mule *can* give under the pack or *over* it, when he puts his whole mind to it. In consequence, the first day's march was short. Several of the mules, apparently coming to the conclusion that they preferred a comfortable stable and plenty of grain at Fort Shaw, to a life in the open air and scant grass, after scattering their loads of bacon and hardtack over the prairie, galloped back to the post, and it was past midnight before they were recaptured and taken back to camp.

It was late the next day before we reached the Dearborn River, twenty-five miles distant. Here we nooned for three hours, feasting on delicious fresh trout caught from the bright, clear, cold stream, and then resumed the march towards the mountains, following the trail leading towards Cadotte's Pass. As the shadows of approaching sunset commenced to fall across our path, we bivouacked for the night well up towards the mountains, having dispatched our little party of mounted men across the summit as an advance guard; for it was desirable to get ahead as rapidly as possible. The route up the Big Blackfoot (the Cokalahishkit of Lewis and Clark) from Missoula and through Cadotte's Pass was the shortest and usual route followed by the Indians coming across the mountains, and if these hostiles succeeded in eluding or overpowering the small force near Missoula they would in all probability meet us somewhere on this trail. Our force being so small it was a matter of some importance that we should have early intelligence of their approach, and a choice of position to resist them.

The next morning we resumed the march, gradually rising as the trail entered the mountains, until we reached the foot of the steep hill which led up to the summit, where we encountered the snow-storm six years ago in our trip from the west, and at length, after a steep climb of a mile or more stood again upon the summit of the Rocky Mountains. There had been a slight rain the night before and the day was cold and cloudy, so that we felt but little disposition to stay and enjoy the view which opened out to the eastward. We quickly descended the slope on the other side and halted to rest and lunch at a little clear stream, which trickled from the mountain-side towards its long voyage to the great Columbia. Our route now lies down a pretty but narrow little valley, shut in by dense masses of timber, which cover the hills on every side to their very summits. We noon, shortly after striking the main Blackfoot, which comes out of a deep gorge from the south, and simply out of curiosity, but with no hope of catching anything, I put my rod together and cast a fly upon the glassy surface of a deep pool close by our stopping place. It has scarcely touched the water before, with a rush and a splash, a good-sized trout breaks the surface, seizes it, and is landed after a short struggle, a speckled beauty, on the grass; an ample "string" soon rewards a short walk along the stream. During the day we had started up along the trail numerous coveys of the beautiful blue or mountain grouse, the young of which is now just fit for the table; and, with plenty of these, and fresh trout just from the water, we had no cause to complain either of the quality or quantity of our noonday meal.

We pushed ahead in the afternoon, being anxious to get beyond the junction of our trail with that through Lewis and Clark's Pass lest the Indians, if on the road, should give us the slip by that route. The valley now begins to widen out more, and in search of grouse I wander from the main trail with shot-gun in hand and followed by an orderly carrying a rifle. I have just passed a little grove of green quaking asp, and am thinking of nothing in particular, when casting my eyes to the left they encountered a sight which caused me instantly to check my horse and grasp my gun. There, not fifty yards away, lies a fine young white-tailed buck, his thick velvety horns turned directly towards me and his great eyes staring as if questioning my right to intrude on his solitude. Strange to say, he makes no effort to rise, but lies there in his noonday bed looking at me. Quickly unlocking my breech-loader I slip out the small shot cartridges, and seize a buckshot-wire cartridge, several of which I always carry in my belt; but it is somewhat worn, and in my feverish attempt to force it in it gets jammed and the block refuses to close. I fear some sort of exclamation must have escaped me, for the deer not liking the look of affairs slowly rose to his feet and stalked off, the most beautiful and graceful animal I ever looked upon. Hastily jumping from my horse, and dropping my gun on the ground, I ran back a few paces to the orderly, took my rifle from him, slipped in a cartridge, and hastened back to my former position, just in time to catch sight of the deer slowly moving through the timber, and not yet aware of the fact that he was treading upon dangerous ground. A sharp crack of the rifle echoed through the woods, there was a hurried rush and a plunge, and the magnificent fat buck fell, almost at the feet of my orderly, shot through the heart. That night our bill of fare had broiled venison steaks added to it.

We passed the trail leading into Lewis and Clark's Pass without seeing any sign of Indians, and followed down the now enlarged Blackfoot through a wide open valley, dotted here and there with groves of magnificent pine trees towering a hundred feet above our heads. We bivouacked in one of these late in the afternoon, and in the midst of a heavy rain, which continued during the night, soaking everything thoroughly, and sadly interfering with sleep. The stream is literally filled with fine large trout, and enough were obtained to supply the wants of the whole command.

The next day opened with rain, but it soon cleared off, and the men having now got on their marching legs, moved along at a rapid gait, passing Lincoln Gulch, a mining settlement, and entering the narrow cañon of the Blackfoot below. Here I received a courier from Helena with news from Missoula, that the Nez Percés, finding Captain Rawn's little force entrenched in the cañon of the Lo Lo Fork, had displayed a force in his front, and then with their main body marched around his position over the hills, out of range of his rifles, and entered the valley of the Bitter Root in his rear. There was great excitement in the settlements, and much apprehension of an approaching conflict, but a later dispatch received from Captain Rawn informed me that the citizens who had accompanied him as volunteers to the Lo Lo Pass had returned home, after making an agreement with the Indians that their lives and property should be safe. The Nez Percés had then moved up the Bitter Root valley away from the direction of Missoula.

The important question now with us was, which way were they going? Knowing that their natural route lay along the one we were travelling, I rather anticipated they would move *down* the Bitter Root and up this trail, but I knew also that they would never enter on such a mountain pass encumbered with their women, children, and herds, without thoroughly scouting ahead to see that the coast was clear. When, therefore, the soldier who brought me the dispatch from Captain Rawn stated that he had met on the trail, and travelled with for some miles, nine armed Indians, who told him they were Nez Percés, and were going across the country to join Joseph's band on the Bitter Root, he telling them that he was coming up the trail to meet me, I felt well assured they would not bring their camp by this route, unless, pressed by General Howard from the rear, they should feel themselves compelled to attack my small force to clear the road in front of them. Hence we pushed ahead more rapidly than ever, and after leaving the cañon camped in the open prairie on the borders of a beautiful lake, having marched twenty-seven miles.

The following day, August 1st, we continued the march through a high, rolling, open prairie, filled with little streams and lakes, and dotted all over with little rounded knolls or knobs, and as I rose a prominent hill, a light suddenly dawned upon me. As far as the eye could reach in every direction, and bounded only by the wooded hills which bordered the prairie, the surface was one continued series of *knobs;* and I then recalled the description given by Captain Lewis: "From the multitude of knobs irregularly scattered through this country, Captain Lewis called it the Prairie of the Knobs." There could be no question about it. This was the spot referred to, and in fancying that I had discovered in the expedition six years ago, the place so named by Captain Lewis, I was in error. For hours we travelled through this plain landmark, so aptly named by Captain Clark, and nooned at the mouth of a fine large stream, which he calls the North Fork of the Cokalahishkit, and up which a trail leads to the head of Jocko valley, where is located the agency for the Flathead Indians. Our route now, for some distance, lies over some very steep, thickly wooded hills, where our animals labor a good deal on the steep ascents and amidst the thickly fallen timber. The day's march was very hot and tedious, and it was nearly sundown before we halted for the night, after making only twenty-four miles. Here I received another dispatch from Captain Rawn, dated that morning, and informing me that the Indians were moving very slowly up the Bitter Root valley. They are evidently in no hurry to leave, and I think are quietly waiting to see what the troops are going to do, and they will have ample notice, for their scouts are out in every direction, and they are informed of everything that occurs in the valley, and even what the white people themselves know. Captain Rawn also sends me a dispatch just received from General Howard, and dated July 25th. The general states that he will start in pursuit from Kamisch five days afterwards (the 30th). These are five precious days, and the Indians have already made their escape from the pass before the pursuers have entered it. From what I learned afterwards in the Bitter Root valley, the Indians were fully aware of their danger, and of the necessity for haste to get out of the pass, for a number of them, in their free talks with the settlers, said with an air of triumph, "We have got you scared now; a few days ago you had us scared," alluding to when they were in the pass, with Captain Rawn entrenched before them, and, as they thought, General Howard coming up behind them.

The next day, August 2d, we made an early start, and leaving the infantry to follow, I hastened ahead toward Missoula, reported to be fifty miles distant. The trail now once again left the open country, and entered a gorge of the mountains, the scenery becoming wilder and more grand at every step. For miles we were compelled to climb and descend steep mountain-sides on a trail just wide enough for the passage of a single animal, and rendered in places hazardous from loose stones or fallen timber, which sadly tried the strength of our pack-mules and weary horses. The Blackfoot, now a considerable stream, tumbles along hundreds of feet beneath us, whilst on every side mountain peaks tower above our heads. In many places the slopes are so steep that all are compelled to dismount and lead the horses. We stop for an hour to rest and graze our weary animals, and then push ahead again, and near 12 o'clock, when about to stop for a nooning, meet another courier from Captain Rawn, saying the Indians are still in the valley, moving very slowly southward, and evidently watching the whole valley with their scouts. On the report of the courier, that Missoula was only five miles distant, I concluded to push ahead without stopping. But the trail had become still more rough and difficult; we were obliged to travel slowly, and rejoice when we emerge from the mountains and look down upon a level plateau which marks the junction of the Blackfoot with the Hell Gate River, or according to Lewis and Clark (whose baptismal names should be retained), the forks of the Eastern Fork of Clark's River and the Cokalahishkit. For the first time since leaving Lincoln Gulch, we see a house, and a ride of a mile or two through a valley, dotted with farm-houses and grain-fields, where the harvesters are at work, brings us to the little town of Missoula, pleasantly situated on a bright, clear stream, which empties into the Hell Gate, close to the town. After a short halt to get the news, we pass on to the post, which we reach late in the afternoon, after a hard ride of over fifty miles. Lieutenant Bradley, with his mounted party, got in before sundown, and we only awaited the arrival of the infantry, to take up our line of march up the Bitter Root valley. By sending wagons out to the point where the trail emerges from the mountains, the tired infantrymen reached the post at 4 P.M. of the 3d.

Immediately on my arrival I sent a messenger to Charlo, the chief of a band of Flatheads, living up the valley of the Bitter Root, inviting him to come and see me. He arrived the next morning, and through an interpreter I opened the talk with him, by stating that the whole valley was filled with Nez Percé scouts, who were acting as spies, that he and his people were the only ones who knew these Indians and could distinguish them from friendly Indians, and that I wanted his young warriors to go out, capture these spies, and bring them in to me as prisoners. Charlo is a quiet, pleasant-faced Indian, and had very little to say. What he did say, however, was to the point, and to the effect that he and his people were friends to the whites, but that in the present struggle between them and the Nez Percés he could not take sides, and firmly declined to do what I wished. He left the next morning for his camp near Stevensville, and I was obliged to commence the movement up the valley, fearing that the first step we took would be observed by the Nez Percé scouts and promptly reported to their chief. Hoping, however, that there were more of them in the lower part of the valley, and that I might gain one day on them, the command was not started from the post until one o'clock P.M., when, with every man to be spared from the post, the whole loaded in wagons, we pulled out on the road. Crossing the Bitter Root (Clark's) River on a bridge and moving up the west bank over a good road, we passed the mouth of the Lo Lo Fork, where seventy years ago the Lewis and Clark expedition rested for a day or two on "Travel-ler's Rest Creek," and then separated into two parties, the one under Captain Lewis to follow the route we had just passed over, the other under Captain Clark to pursue that we were about to follow, and to rejoin each other on the great Missouri River below the mouth of the Yellowstone.

The march was continued far into the night, and it was nearly eleven o'clock before the command reached its halting-place near Stevensville, about twenty-seven miles distant. It was long after dark when I reached there considerably ahead of the command, after passing Fort Owens, a stockade, inside of which were huddled a promiscuous crowd of men, women, and children, who in fear and trembling had sought safety there from anticipated hostilities. The arrival of the soldiers was a great relief to these poor people, and at the same time created a great excitement. As we rode into Stevensville the loud barking of the dogs brought out all the inhabitants still remaining in the place. The town is located at the mouth of the "Scattering Creek" of Lewis and Clark, and near it is a Catholic mission, to which one of the citizens offered to guide me in the dark. This man proved to be a discharged soldier from my regiment, and was afterwards of great service in guiding us to the Nez Percé camp. On reaching the mission, surrounded by the tepees of Charlo's band of the Flatheads, I was hospitably received by the priest in charge, and sat in his room till the arrival of the command. The head priest of the mission, Father Rivalli, had been confined for a long time previous to his bed by illness, from which he was not yet recovered. His reputation as a successful *physician* was widespread, and having heard so much of him I was glad to receive an invitation to visit him in his chamber. Following the attending priest through an adjacent room I was introduced into one beyond, barely large enough to contain a small bed, a table, and a chair. Here, propped up in the bed, and *reading medicine* by the light of a dim lamp, was a charming old Frenchman, who with a skull-cap on his head and a pair of glasses on his nose, received me with all the graceful cordiality of a past age, which his thirty-five years' residence in the wilderness had failed to obliterate. I was much attracted to the charms of his conversation, and sat talking to him for some time. He informed me that he had come to this country with the celebrated Father De Smet thirty-five years ago, and whilst wondering in my worldly way whether he had not probably gotten about tired of it he said, evidently with the utmost sincerity, "I thank God I shall in time lay my bones amongst these poor Indians." I did not say so to this good priest, but I could not help reflecting how different, under the present circumstances, my ambition was from his.

He gave me a great deal of information in regard to the Nez Percés, who had remained in this vicinity for some days, frequently visiting the town and freely trading with the inhabitants. In the course of conversation he asked me "how many troops I had." Now my experience with human nature, whether embodied in the form of soldiers or not, teaches me that there is a great indisposition to confess one's *weakness,* even when the confessor is a priest, and so I answered in a general way, "About two hundred." "Ah," said the old man, "you *must* not attack them, you have not enough. They are bad Indians, they are splendid shots, are well armed, have plenty of ammunition, and have at least two hundred and sixty warriors." I wonder what that brave old priest, who had voluntarily submitted to so long a banishment in the wilderness, would have said had I told him that "our duty might require some of us at least to *lay our bones amongst these poor Indians.*" I parted with this charming old gentleman with much regret, and shall probably never see him again, but I can never forget the grace of his manner, which was so strongly contrasted by his surroundings, his solicitude for our welfare and safety, and his urgent invitation to call upon him when I came back.

Our camp that night was a sorry one. Very little wood was to be had, the camp-ground was bare of vegetation and dusty, and we went supperless to bed, our animals not much better off than we were, for although allowed to wander forth at large during the night they found scant means of gratifying their hunger in the bare waste which surrounded us. The night was cold, and the next morning, although the camp was astir early, we did not start till 6:30, and before leaving had free communication with some of the citizens, who came to our camp, and we thus picked up a good many items in regard to the Nez Percés.

We were told that during their presence in the vicinity they freely traded with the whites for provisions of all kinds, offering in exchange good prices in gold coin, dust, and greenbacks, which the whites did not trouble themselves to reflect were stained with the blood of the peaceful settlers of a neighboring territory. One scoundrel who visited our camp, I was told, boastfully claimed to have made a profit of $500, in gold, in his trade with this band of murderers and thieves! They also traded off a number of horses and mules captured from our troops in Idaho and stolen from the settlers there, whilst watches and jewelry of different kinds were sold at fabulously low prices. It was even hinted that metallic ammunition was one of the items traded by the whites for these ill-gotten gains.

Some of the people complained bitterly of the action of a self-constituted committee, which it was said had taken upon itself the powers of a vigilance committee, and adopted a resolution that should any white man be charged with an offense against an Indian, he should be at once turned over to the Indians for punishment! We were also informed that when the Nez Percés first came up the valley, many of the inhabitants flocked with their goods to the enclosure at Fort Owens, where a considerable number still remained huddled together as I have mentioned. On the report, however, that the Indians were disposed to be peaceful, and that a brisk trade had been opened with them, goods were hurriedly loaded into wagons at Fort Owens and pushed forward to the scene of traffic, the owners being anxious not to lose the advantages of this new and unexpected market. Whether or not these reports were all true to the disgraceful extent we heard we had no time to ascertain, but the next day brought us into a moral atmosphere of a more healthy tone.

We resumed our trip up the valley, now well settled up with ranches and farms, though far from being as rich and productive as we had been led to expect. At the little town of Corvallis we stopped to noon and gather further news of the Indians, who generally had up to this time committed very few depredations and spilled no blood. The poor women and children were here found gathered behind the protecting walls of a well-built sod fort, which the hostiles had looked at and commented upon as they passed, evidently pleased at the scare they had created, and comparing it with their own scare when shut in the Lo Lo cañon. Parties of them had visited the town and attempted to trade at the stores, but their reception was in marked contrast to that met with lower down the valley. A Mr. Young, who kept a store in the place, met their advances to trade with a flat refusal, closed his doors and told the Indians plainly that their money was blood-stained and he wanted none of it. They were very saucy, and threatened to burn down his house, but the brave old man stood firm and dared them to do their worst. Although some of the more desperate ones urged extreme measures, they were dissuaded by the more moderate, and the old hero was left master of the field, with the proud satisfaction of knowing his conscience was clear though at the expense of his pocket. After crossing the Bitter Root again, at a ford, we encamped on its bank about sundown, having made about thirty miles. Here we were joined by six citizens, who volunteered to accompany us. Amongst the number was Mr. Joe Blodget, who lived in the immediate neighborhood, was well acquainted with the upper valley, and had been recommended to me as the best guide in the country. He fully came up to his reputation, and proved of inestimable value to the expedition. To his frontier qualities as a good shot and a fine hunter, was added an intimate knowledge of every part of the trail up the valley and across the main divide of the Rocky Mountains into the Big Hole Basin. My first question to him was, "How far can we take our wagons?" to which he replied, "All the way through to Bannock, if you want to." I looked at him in astonishment, for I had been informed positively that beyond a certain point wagons could not go, and had, therefore, brought along our pack-saddles, intending when the time came to cut loose from the wagons and take to our pack-mules. I asked him if he was sure of what he said. When I became better acquainted with Joe Blodget, I never found it necessary to ask him that question in reference to any assertion he made regarding the country we were passing through. He assured me that although the trail was rough and steep in places, he had himself brought lightly loaded wagons all the way over the divide from Bannock. With this assurance we made an early start the next morning, and pushed ahead up the valley, following directly on the trail of the Indians, who on their march up had kept their main camp and herd on the west bank of the river. The trail was plainly marked, and very large, showing the presence of a great number of animals, but no indications of either lodge-poles or the poles of "travois," on which Indians are accustomed to carry their wounded. The camps through which we passed during the day and the two following ones showed that the poles used for the tepees, and left standing in the camps, were collected each day for temporary use, and were not carried along on the march, the Indians being thus able to move much more lightly.

Our road continued good, although we crossed several large tributary streams coming in from the west, and forded the main stream three times, and it was one o'clock before we reached Lockwood's ranche, the last house up the Bitter Root valley. Here we stopped to noon, get dinner, and rest and graze our animals. Mr. Lockwood, the owner of the ranche, was with us, having with his family left his home, and sought safety in one of the forts lower down the valley. On now returning to it he had occasion to recognize the futility of the truce between the Indians and the inhabitants of the Bitter Root valley. His house inside was a perfect wreck. Trunks were broken open and their contents scattered about, whilst furniture, crockery, and everything perishable was broken up and strewn over the place in every direction. The Indians appear to have been kept under very good control whilst in the lower valley, and I presume this mischief was done by some straggling party, or possibly by the rear guard, who may have felt unable to resist the inclination, just as they were leaving, of giving the white man a specimen of their vindictiveness. Blodget tells me that they paid his place a visit and carried off a number of things, including a favorite *coffee-pot,* which he was "bound to get back or its equivalent." Some of the citizens who accompanied us have been scouting ahead, and report that at nine o'clock this morning the Indians were in Ross's Hole, a distance of one day's march ahead of us. Feeling sure that the chiefs were kept fully advised by their scouts of every step we took, my hopes of getting a blow at them were very remote, unless by speedy movements and a surprise; the character of the country ahead being such as would prevent my column from being seen at any great distance. When I found, however, that they were not increasing their speed at all, and seldom marched more than twelve miles a day, the question of overtaking them by marching double that distance was simply one of time, provided we remained undiscovered, and these relative distances remained the same.

The trail of the Indians still continued up the bank of the river, and a short distance above Lockwood's ranche, the smoke of their old camp-fire, probably two nights old, was seen. Just at this point what is known as the southern Nez Percé trail came in from the west, and it was possible that by this trail the Indians may have received some accession to their number from straggling bands coming from the Clearwater country. As the camps in front of us had now passed this trail, it was evident the Indians had no intention, as was at one time feared, of returning by it to Idaho.

This point of the trail is of interest from the fact that here, on the 4th of September, 1806, the Lewis and Clark expedition first struck the valley of the Bitter Root, the river being named after Captain Clark, "he," says the *Journal,* "being the first white man who had ever visited its waters." The *Journal* describes the first meeting with the Indians of this valley, who were undoubtedly Flatheads, and whose descendants still occupy it. Victor, the father of the present chief, Charlo, lived until only a few years ago, and was present at this meeting of Lewis and Clark. From Joe Blodget, who knew him well, I received many interesting reminiscences of the, to the Indians, important event. He says that Victor had often described to him this first meeting with white men, and how from their pale faces they supposed they were *cold,* and covered them with robes. He also told a story which I suspect had a more modern origin, as I do not think friction-matches had at that day been invented. The story goes that one of the white men whilst in the council took a little piece of wood from his pocket and scratching it upon a stone a flame burst forth, much to the amazement of the Indians, who immediately pronounced the white man "great medicine." Apocryphal or not, the incident may serve to illustrate how the ignorance of a primitive man would readily attribute to some supernatural cause a thing so simple to us as the ignition of a friction-match.

In imitation of Captain Clark, we are now, instead of turning into this trail to the west, going to keep on up the Bitter Root, as he did on his way back the next year, and cross the main divide of the Rocky Mountains into the Big Hole Basin, this route being shorter and much better, Captain Clark says, "than that by which we had advanced in the fall," to which I add, the Lord help the *other* route!

We were now compelled to cease following the Indian trail, and take our wagons over a formidable ridge, which rose to the eastward of us, its top crowned with dense forests of pine. Shortly after three o'clock we left the river bottom and commenced to pull up a long steep incline, and the farther we went the longer and steeper it appeared to become. Slowly and laboriously we toiled our way up foot by foot, and at length stood upon the crest of a hill fully a mile long, only to find other hills almost as formidable rising up on the road ahead of us. If you want to know how to try the most amiable of tempers (if you are blessed with such), place yourself in a position where haste is of the utmost importance and where also you find yourself utterly unable to make *any* thing move faster than a sloth. You may possibly be able to fancy how trying is such a position to a temper not the most amiable in the world. However, there was nothing to do but to follow the example of the ant and keep on toiling, which we did, rising hill after hill until we thought it high time that we were approaching the top. But on expressing some such opinion to Joe, he pointed to a *mountain* which rose far above our heads to the right, and said in his quiet way: "The trail goes right over the top of that." We had now passed beyond the timber-line and continued to pull up hill after hill, the trail being in places so obscure that without the assistance of a guide who knew its location it would have been utterly out of the question to follow it even with the speed we did. The sun was now rapidly approaching the snow-clad mountains in the west, and from our guide's description of the road ahead of us it soon became apparent that we would not be able to reach the summit that night, much less descend the slope on the other side as we had hoped. The disappointment, great as it was, did not prevent us from viewing with delight the magnificent scene spread out before us. From the ridge we stood upon, which appeared to be almost on a level with the snow-covered mountains opposite to us on the other side of the valley, the eye could trace down the valley of the Bitter Root the trail upon which we had come, and little clouds of dust at intervals along it showed us where parties of horsemen, volunteers from the valley, were hastening forward to join us. Beyond the valley heavily wooded mountain peaks towered one above the other, culminating in one whose rocky gorges, bare of timber, were filled with immense glaciers, the smooth glassy surfaces of which glistened in the rays of the setting sun, presenting to the eye an Arctic scene in strong contrast with that which immediately surrounded us. On the other side of us, stretching eastward as far as the eye could reach, was one continuous mass of timbered hills, with one isolated bare peak rising above the whole, in the direction of, and near, our guide says, the town of Deer Lodge, sixty or seventy miles away as the crow flies.

Impatient at our slow progress I rode ahead some distance to see what the prospect was, and after winding about through the thick timber and climbing several formidable hills, I reached the foot of one steeper than any we had yet met with, and still not the last one, and giving the thing up in despair reluctantly gave the order to go into camp. Our last wagon got in just at dark, and with no water for drinking or making coffee, and of course none for the animals, we laid down to rest, with many misgivings as to whether the latter, turned loose as most of them had to be, would not desert us during the night in search of water, of which they stood much in need after their hard and constant pull up the mountain. Fortunately we were able, with our sentinels, to keep them in camp, and shortly after four o'clock the next morning we were under way again, of course without breakfast, and pulling up the steep hills in front of us. With all the speed we could make, men assisting with drag-ropes, it was four hours before the last of our wagons reached the summit, the top of the mountain pointed out to us the evening before by Blodget.

And now our work, although still no child's play, became easier, and we rolled along down the steep slope of the mountain, removing the fallen timbers as we went along, until, at 10 o'clock, we halted to cook breakfast in the rolling prairie of Ross's Hole. During the day a number of citizens overtook us, and also two of our officers, who had a long stern chase after us from Fort Benton and Camp Baker. After a good rest and a hearty breakfast we pushed ahead again, and on approaching the Bitter Root River, struck once more the trail of the Indians, and passed through one of their camps.

The last doubt now in regard to their route is removed, and they are evidently going into the Big Hole Basin, over the identical route followed by Captain Clark in 1807, for the trail keeps up the South Fork of the Bitter Root. They do not appear to have increased their speed at all, and we find but one dead horse on the road, shot evidently after he had broken down. Is it possible these Indians do not know we are on their trail, or have they such a contempt for the small force of "Walk-a-heeps"[1] that they want to invite an attack? It is true the thickly wooded country is not favorable to long views, but a small rear guard would serve to give the main camp ample notice, and so far not an Indian has been seen.

Later in the afternoon, having made only thirteen miles, we stop for the night near the head of a little valley and at the foot of the main

[1]Indian name for infantry soldiers.

divide of the Rocky Mountains, on ascending which, Blodget tells us, we will meet with a worse hill than any we have yet seen. Incredible as this appears, our incredulity is fully dispelled the next day.

In the meantime we form our bivouac, and Lieutenant Bradley, in charge of the advanced mounted party, comes to propose a night march for his command and an attempt to run off the Indian herd before daylight. Some twenty-five of the citizens who have joined us volunteer to accompany him, and at dark, with his force increased to about sixty men, all mounted, he leaves us and commences the ascent of the Rocky Mountains. The night proved very cold with a sharp frost. The command was astir early, got off a little after 5 o'clock, and soon commenced to ascend the slopes in front of us. The first ones, obstructed as they were with fallen timber, were bad enough, but we soon came to a part of the road which convinced us that Blodget had not been guilty of exaggeration in his description of it. The hill, almost 45° in inclination, could not be surmounted by winding round it in consequence of the masses of timber, both standing and fallen, and of adjacent precipices, and so had to be ascended direct. In addition to the other difficulties, the roadbed was formed of a mass of loose, shifting, rounded stones, upon which our poor animals could scarcely stand, much less pull. It was a "long road" to the top, and unfortunately had several "turns" in it, and these being very sharp ones, sadly interfered with the working of the long string of mules which we were obliged to attach to each wagon in turn. But the longest road must have an end, and so had this one, for in six hours after leaving camp, we reached the summit and commenced the long, gradual descent on the other side. This was not so difficult; yet it was by no means easy, for the timber, although smaller, stood much thicker on the ground, and a great deal had fallen across the road, which had to be removed before our wagons could pass. The road, too, was very crooked and in places marshy, so that it was a matter of wonder how our advance party could have gotten through at all in the darkness of the night. I received a dispatch from Lieutenant Bradley, before we reached the summit, informing me that the distance he had to pass over was greater than anticipated, and daylight had overtaken him before he had succeeded in reaching the Indian camp, and that he had concealed his party in the hills to await our arrival. Speed was now all the more important, as, should the Indians discover him, they might succeed in overwhelming his little party before we could join him.

Lewis and Clark's *Journal,* under date of July 6th, 1807, says, "On reaching the other side, they came to Glade Creek, down which they proceeded, crossing it frequently into the glade on each side, where the timber was small and in many places destroyed by fire." This was precisely our experience now, except that having wagons instead of pack-mules, we were obliged to cross Glade Creek more frequently. As we proceeded, the crossings became more difficult, obscure and overgrown with brushwood, and here Blodget's services were inestimable to us. Riding ahead, he seemed to follow the obscure wagon-track by instinct, scarcely ever failed to hit at once the right crossing, and where that was washed out, to discover another. In this way we pushed ahead all day, not even stopping to rest or graze the mules, until our wagon-master came to complain that his mules were dropping in their harness, and his teams unable to go much farther. We then halted long enough to water and exchange the most wearied mules for some of the loose ones, and then resumed the march, for we had in the meantime passed another of the Indian camps, which showed us that the Indians had made another short march, and were as yet not alarmed. As our impatience to get forward increased, the difficulties of the route seemed to redouble. Again and again we recrossed the creek into the "glades" on each side, struggling through thick timber and in places swampy flats, in which our wagon-wheels sunk to the hub. Blodget informed us that we had one sharp, short hill to pull up, and after that would have but little trouble. We had just reached the foot of this, and were preparing to double teams, when Bostwick, our Fort Shaw post-guide, rode up, and with a glow of excitement on his face, exclaimed, "We've got them, sir, we've got them!" at the same time handing me two bits of paper. One was from Lieutenant Bradley,[1] the other from Lieutenant Jacobs, who accompanied him, and both of the same import.

The command was hid in the hills, within a short distance of the Indian camp, the herd of which had been seen, and by it the camp had been nearly located. It was thought the Indians had discovered the pres-

---

[1] As the last thing ever written by this officer, who was killed the next morning, this note is appended entire.

Aug. 8th, 1877

BATTALION ADJUTANT,

SIR: I have the honor to report that I have personally seen the indications of an Indian camp situated in Big Hole, about three miles from my position. Lieutenant Jacobs accompanied me, and I have requested him to write a line in reference thereto. We saw horses grazing and mounted Indians, heard a gunshot, and the sound of axes. They evidently design staying all night, and from the anxious manner they have scouted the valley to the east, I judge that they have discovered a force in their front. They have seen my camp, but I do not expect them to attack me. Were the infantry to come up to-night we could attack them at daylight with great advantage, taking them in rear, as we have scouted the country well and found a safe and concealed route over the hills.

Very respectfully,
JAMES H. BRADLEY.

Marked, Received August 8th, 5.10 P.M.

ence of the command, but that the camp might be surprised. Giving orders that the rear company (which happened to be Captain Logan's) should remain with the train, to help it up the hill, and push it along as fast as possible, I brought the remaining five companies to the front, and with the little mountain howitzer, hastened forward. But it was nearly sundown before we reached Lieutenant Bradley's position, near the mouth of the little valley down which we were travelling. Directly opposite the mouth, and projecting out into the open ground of the Big Hole Basin, was a high, bare hill, from the top of which a man could have looked directly up the valley, and have plainly seen every movement in it at the point where we stood, near which Lieutenant Bradley's party had been lying ever since early daylight. I was assured, however, that no Indians had been seen there, that the camp was supposed to be three or four miles distant down the stream to our left (east), and that it was resting in apparent security, Lieutenants Bradley and Jacobs having gone through the timber near enough to see a part of the animals grazing, to hear the sound of axes, and to hear the report of a rifle. It was now so late that it was not deemed best to move at once to the attack, but to wait for darkness to cover our march, and make the assault at daylight. The men were therefore permitted to rest, get something to eat, but without fires. The train was brought up, and just at dark closely parked in the bottom, the tired animals turned out to graze, and guards posted, to prevent them from straying. Additional ammunition was issued, so that each man should have ninety rounds, and all laid down to rest and wait for eleven o'clock, the hour designated for the movement to commence. I found that one of the citizens had preceded the column and been down to the mouth of the valley, from where he has seen some of the tepees, and he informed me of his ability to conduct us to the camp in the darkness.

It appeared to me so incredible that the Indians, knowing, as I supposed they necessarily must, we were on their track, should have no rear guard out or scouts to watch us, that I could not divest my mind of an apprehended "trap," and a fear, that whilst we were moving to surprise them we should ourselves be surprised. As may be imagined, therefore, not much of the time between dark and eleven o'clock was spent by me in sleep. To sleep, one's mind must be at rest, and mine was very far from it. We were obliged to leave a few men with the train, and I would gladly have taken our howitzer with us to add to the strength of the little command, but the trail was known to be rough and obstructed by timber, and the noise of removing this would in all probability betray us to the enemy. It was, therefore, decided to leave it behind, with orders to start to join us at the first break of day, bringing along a pack-mule loaded with two boxes of extra ammunition.

Promptly at eleven o'clock the command commenced its silent movement down the trail, all on foot except myself, Lieutenants Jacobs and Woodruff, and Bostwick, the Fort Shaw guide. Not one of these four horses got out of the battle with us alive. Lieutenant Bradley, with his party of soldiers, increased by thirty-four citizens, was placed in the advance, and arm in arm with the guide he moved off at the head of his party. The rest of us stumbled along after him in the dark, for I found it more satisfactory to walk than to ride. We tripped over the fallen timber, and now and then crossed streams and marshy places where we sunk over shoe-tops in mud. Once or twice a break occurred in the column, and the rear part got lost, so that the front had to halt, and finally to march at a snail's pace to enable the rear to keep up. The night, although bright starlight, was still so dark that objects could not be seen more than a few feet off. At length the trail began to improve, and skirting along the foot hills of an open valley we caught sight of a light glimmering in the distance. Strict silence was now enjoined upon all, and once or twice I moved to the front to counsel with and give instructions to Lieutenant Bradley. Light after light now came in plain sight off in the valley to our right, and still with the apprehension of a trap before me I could scarcely hope we would not be discovered, and every moment expected to hear the crack of a rifle. Still we moved silently forward until, passing through a little belt of pine timber, which afterwards played an important part in our operations, we merged into the open beyond to find ourselves in the presence of a large herd of horses feeding on the hillside. As we approached the horses commenced to neigh, and the cry was taken up along the side-hill in a way which made me feel very uncomfortable. Fortunately, however, they did not become alarmed, and as we moved along the trail those nearest to us simply moved out of the way. The lights had now increased in number and the forms of the tepees could be indistinctly made out in the creek bottom below us. The dogs now commenced to bark, and as we halted abreast of the camp the cries of babies and the tone of conversation between the adults could be distinctly heard. The command now all laid down in the trail to rest and await the break of day, some of the men falling asleep. Those of us who did not do so had time to reflect upon our position, and this is the way it looked. Here we were, directly in the presence of, and undiscovered by, a band of hostile Indians. Their tepees, with their women and children, most of them asleep, were lying almost at our feet, whilst a large part of their herd, though by no means all of it, was on the opposite side of us. As soon as daylight came we would be discovered if we did not discover ourselves before, and then would come the conflict. Impressed with the importance of getting possession of the large herd which seemed to be almost within our grasp, I turned to Bostwick and directed him to take a few of the citizens, get round the herd and drive it back on our trail. He replied at once, "Why, General, there are probably a number of warriors around the herd guarding it." He was an old frontiersman, had lived for years amongst the Indians, and knew their habits well. His remark appeared to me so plausible, that impressed with the importance of not too soon creating an alarm I yielded at once to his suggestion. Almost immediately afterwards he said, "They have discovered us; don't you hear them?" I listened, and certainly there appeared to be more conversation and a stir in the camp; but this seemed to subside almost immediately, and we strained our ears to catch any new sound. "If they have not discovered us," said Bostwick now, "their fires will all die down, and just before daylight you will see the squaws begin to light them up again as it gets cold." A portion of the command, deployed as skirmishers, was now sent down into the bottom, and as a faint light appeared in the eastern horizon, a firebrand was seen to move from one tepee to another in the camp from which now not a sound issued. The whole command except one company was now sent down into the willow-covered flat, and the word passed along to push forward to the village. As the light increased the features of the landscape came into view. At the foot of the bluff (some thirty or forty feet high), upon which we stood, commenced the flat of the creek bottom, covered except in spots with a thick growth of willows, in places almost impassable. This extended some two or three hundred yards across to Ruby Creek, a fine bold stream, in places waist deep. Between the foot of the bluffs and Ruby Creek extended up and down the stream an old bed of the creek, now a stagnant slough filled with water and soft mud. On the opposite side of Ruby Creek was the Indian camp, extended out in a straggling open "V" along the bank of the creek. The line moved slowly forward, men and officers wading the slough and struggling through the brush as best they could. It was now getting so light that the whole outline of the camp could be made out, as well as the forms of our men as they moved forward. The camp was as still as death, and no sign of life was visible except the gradual increase of light in the camp-fires, where the squaws were evidently replenishing them.

Suddenly off on the left of the line a single rifle-shot broke on the still morning air, followed by another, and another, and then the whole line opened, and with a shout swept forward towards the tepees. The startled and completely surprised Indians rushed from the tents only to find themselves cut down by a withering fire from the brush, towards which some of them instinctively ran for shelter, whilst most of them scattered away from the fire out on the open prairie and up and down the creek. The last remaining company was sent in on the right at a run, and reached the upper end of the village, just where the creek, making a bend towards us, afforded by its steeply-cut bank admirable shelter to the Indians, who, huddling together, opened a fire upon our men as they entered the village about its middle at the apex of the "V." These were now taken in the rear, many of them slaughtered, and with loud shouts of triumph the whole command swept through the village. Many of the Indians still remained in the tepees, and some still alive and unwounded fired upon the men when tearing open the tents. One young officer narrowly escaped death at the hands of a squaw, who fired a pistol at him as he opened the door, and the next moment fell dead with a bullet through her brain. Some of the women and boys fought like men, while others sought safety behind the creek-banks, crouching down with the water up to their waists. In crossing the stream near the upper end of the village I saw three of these poor wretches, one with a baby in her arms, seated in the water behind a clump of bushes, and as I passed along one of them made me a salutation with her hand, as if to claim my protection. I tried to explain to her that she was safe, and beckoned her to come out, but none of them moved, and they remained there till we left the village.

Although we had complete possession of the village, and had commenced to set fire to the tepees, the Indians had not by any means given up the fight, and we soon began to feel the effects of their long rifles and their superior marksmanship. But few of them remained in the brush near the village, but these few at every favorable opportunity sent a bullet whistling into our scattered disorganized ranks as the men ran from tepee to tepee setting them on fire, and shots soon came pouring into us from all directions. Depressions on the open prairie, points on the distant hills, and the trees and rocks on the trail we had just left, three and four hundred yards distant, were occupied by these unseen marksmen. The fire was not heavy, that is, was not very rapid and continuous, but at the crack of almost every one of those distant rifles some member of the command fell, and with this kind of fire we could not compete, for (it must be admitted), with very few exceptions, the command did not contain any such marksmen as these Nez Percés, drilled to the use of the rifle from childhood, showed themselves to be.

I noticed that as soon as the rifles commenced to crack, all the different herds of horses ran right up together, bunched up like a flock of frightened sheep, and then moved off. The small herds in the valley were soon under control of the Indians, and immediately after we got possession of the village mounted men could be seen moving at full speed over the hills, some giving orders and others collecting the horses.

It soon became evident that losing men rapidly by the close fire of the Indians and unable to inflict any more harm upon them, it was necessary that we should occupy some position where we would be more on an equality with our foe. Orders were therefore given to leave the village and withdraw towards the bluffs we had started from. This was done, and as soon as the command reached the foot of the bluffs, and was protected from the fire coming from the high ground on that side, and hidden on the other side by the brush of the valley, it was pushed along towards the point of small pine timber which projected into the valley and through which we had passed the night before. This was already occupied by a few Indians, and these being driven out we took possession of the timber and disposed the men behind logs and other obstacles, prepared for a defense, which all knew we should soon be called on to make; nor were we permitted to wait long.

Just as we reached the timber, two shots from our little howitzer, which it will be remembered was to follow us at the first break of day, were heard up the valley, and about a mile from us; of course we knew that this meant the death-knell of the little party with it, and as the Indians were thus shown to be between us and our inadequately protected train, the fear was a very natural one, that that too had, in Western phraseology, "gone up."

We had, however, but little time to speculate upon such subjects, or give much attention to any matters beyond the limits of our contracted horizon, for the Indians had now gathered about us, and from the timber above and the brush below, their rifle-shots began to seek out every exposed spot in our position. At first the men excitedly replied to every rifle-shot with a perfect shower of bullets, so that the Indians drew sometimes fifty bullets for one of their own, and every effort of the officers had to be exerted to restrain the firing, lest we should fall short of ammunition, and thus become an easy prey to a determined dash of the Indians. That they would make at least one such was confidently felt by all, and preparations were made to meet it. The men were distributed according to the needs of each point, and under the sharp fire which now assailed us, logs were placed in position and holes dug in the soft sandy soil with the invaluable Rice bayonet.

In the meantime, and whilst this fight was going on, a wail of grief came up from the Indian village as the extent of the damage we had done there became known, and the shrill cry of the squaws was mingled with the exhortation of the chiefs as they urged on their followers to wreak vengeance on us; one particular voice in the village could be distinctly heard by us haranguing the camp, and it seemed to have its effect upon the Indians who surrounded us, for when that paused an

Indian in the timber above or the brush below would shout out his commands, the others would respond with yells, and a shower of bullets would come whistling through the timber, cutting the limbs from over our heads and now and then striking someone less perfectly protected than the rest. These volleys, which at first caused almost every rifle of ours to go off in reply, were now received more coolly, and the men learned to watch for the smoke, and fire at that more deliberately and of course with greater effect. Finding too that the Indians showed no disposition to expose themselves unnecessarily in the open ground, and stuck to their trees and logs as closely as we did, all became more confident, and now very little ammunition was wasted in replying to these volleys.

The Indians, after loudly lamenting their dead, soon began to take down their tepees, and after packing up their things and collecting their horses the main body moved off over the hills to the southward. The fighting force, however, still remained around us, and as if watching the progress of the fight, small parties of mounted Indians, evidently attending the chiefs, remained on the hills, whilst a large herd of horses made its appearance on a prominent hill to the eastward of us and remained there till late in the afternoon.

The long weary hours of the day wore on with more or less firing all the time, and even when there was a lull the slightest imprudence on the part of anyone in exposing himself was sure to cause a shower of bullets. Our poor wounded were placed in the most sheltered position, and dragged through the long painful hours with such attendance as we were able to bestow upon them, for we were without a doctor, and such few medical supplies as we had were of course with the train.

The Indians, despairing of carrying our position by assault, now resorted to a stratagem, which strongly reminded us of one feature of the sham battle at Fort Shaw, mentioned in the forepart of this article. A strong breeze was blowing from the west, and from the grass which grew upon the hillside in that direction a wreath of smoke was seen to rise. This soon gathered in volume, and the fire commenced to sweep towards us over the hill, driven forward by the breeze. This was a new and dangerous foe, for although the grass about us was sparse and green, much of the timber was dead and dry, and should the fire reach any of the heaps of dead timber and brush near us, we would be smoked out of our position like rats in a hole, and the Indians would doubtless take advantage of our being blinded by the smoke, to make that dash upon us which everyone had been anticipating ever since we reached the position. The progress of the fire was, therefore, contemplated with an anxiety which I suspect no one can feel unless staring grim death directly in the face, and as each new puff of smoke was wafted towards us it seemed to give us a foretaste of what we might have to suffer when, blinded by thick clouds of it, we might be called upon to meet a desperate charge of our foes. Everyone nerved himself anew, and grasped his piece ready to act when the crisis came, and knowing that there was nothing to be done for anyone except to die right there; for to retreat was out of the question. *There was no place to retreat to.* Slowly the fire struggled along through the thin grass, now dying away, now shooting up with fresh vigor as it reached some little pile of dry brush in its path, each fresh progress greeted with exultant yells by the hidden savages, and a sigh of relief escaped more than one of us when the wind slowly died out, and the fire on the side-hill followed its example.

The hostile demonstration now somewhat abated, but the slightest imprudence was sure to bring a reminder in the shape of bullets, to show us the enemy was still on the alert. As night closed in upon us, we came to the conclusion that the Indians would postpone their attack till morning, and after contracting our lines and making what additional dispositions we could to meet it, we prepared as best we could for a night's repose. Of course much rest was out of the question, for in addition to the fact that the Indians kept up their fire at intervals till a late hour, the night was very cold, we could build no fires and had no blankets. Notwithstanding all these drawbacks, and the knowledge of our peril, the officers had to keep constantly on the move amongst the exhausted men to keep them on the alert, and prevent them from going to sleep. The disciplined soldier, accustomed to look for orders from his officer, can, under such circumstances, throw off all responsibility from his mind and sleep soundly in the midst of danger. With the undisciplined it is different, and we soon become aware of this from the feeling developed amongst our civilian allies. During the night, whilst dozing, covered up in pine boughs, I became aware of a conversation going on between one of our officers and a citizen, and my attention was arrested by the officer saying he did not wish the citizen to express such sentiments as he had uttered in the presence of our men. I found on inquiry, that the man had been expressing the conviction that at daylight in the morning the Indians would make a desperate assault on us, and that we were all bound, in his expressive phraseology, "to go up." He was therefore in favor of taking advantage of the darkness to get away. I spoke very sharply to him, told him he was now by his own act under military control, that the command was going to remain where it was, and he must remain with it. Notwithstanding this he and a number of the other citizens stole out of camp under cover of the darkness and made their escape.

Before night closed in I engaged two of the citizens who knew the country, to start during the night and carry through dispatches to Deer Lodge, some ninety miles distant. They got off about midnight, travelled all the way to French's Gulch (forty miles) on foot, there borrowed horses, and took the first news of the battle to Deer Lodge. By them I sent an official dispatch to General Terry and one to Governor Potts, asking for transportation, medical supplies, and doctors for our wounded. I wrote a similar request to be shown to anybody our couriers might meet, setting forth our wants, supposing that our train had been captured, and that we would be entirely dependent upon what the settlers could send us for food, and to get our wounded away from the field. These two dispatches were taken to the telegraph office in Deer Lodge, and *both* dispatched as if directed to Governor Potts. This gave rise to the impression that they were not authentic, though some of the papers, in order to correct what they deemed an error, gave the dispatches different dates, and represented one as written on the eighth day before the battle!

Shivering with cold, it was no difficult matter for us all to be alert at the first appearance of daylight, ready for the anticipated assault; but it did not come, and as the sun cast his warming rays upon us, we began to realize that our perils were probably over. At half-past six a citizen rode into our camp from the direction of the train, announcing himself as a courier from General Howard. He was asked if General Howard was on his way up, and a loud cheer burst from the men around me as he answered in the affirmative. He was then asked in regard to our train, but said he had seen nothing of it, and this confirmed the impression that it had been destroyed. On being cross-questioned, however, he admitted passing in the darkness a number of animals, which he took for Indian ponies, and that he might have passed the train without seeing it, which turned out to be the case. Half an hour afterwards another messenger from General Howard, a sergeant of cavalry, came in, and although his dispatch was previous to the one just received, his arrival relieved our minds in regard to the safety of our train, for he informed me that he had spent the night before at it, being unable to come to us the afternoon before on account of the Indians who were about us.

Scouts were now sent out and communicated with the train, but these encountered Indians, who again made their appearance around us, and a part of our force was sent out to bring the train to us. In the meantime we were without provisions, and now that the mental strain of anxiety was removed, empty stomachs began to assert their rights and cry aloud for food. The only one of our four horses brought out of the fight was wounded, and soon after we reached the timber he was killed by one of the shots fired at us. That night he was butchered, and before our train reached us the next day horse-steaks were voted very palatable.

After we had time to think over the incidents of the day, one was recalled which created a good deal of amusement. The second messenger who came to us, the cavalry sergeant, had a small piece of bread and a smaller piece of ham, which he very generously turned over to me. It is customary whenever men from another command reach a post to "attach" them to a company of the garrison for the purpose of drawing rations. The adjutant *says* that as soon as I got the sergeant's bread and ham I called to him and directed him "to attach the sergeant to a company for rations." He conducted the sergeant to where an unskinned, somewhat repulsive-looking *horse-leg* was lying in the dust, and said: "Sergeant, here is the commissary, help yourself!" The sergeant replied he had been to breakfast and didn't feel hungry just then.

Our train reached us about sundown, and the camp was soon enlivened by brisk fires, around which the men gathered to recite the incidents of the fight, whilst the much-needed provisions were cooking, and for the first time we learned of the particulars of the struggle with the howitzer. In its attempt to join us, the men in charge of it were encountered by Indians, who opened fire upon them when it had reached within about a mile of us. Two of the men cowardly ran at the first fire, whilst the others loaded and fired the piece twice, and then, the horses being killed, used their rifles until, one of them being killed and two of the others wounded, the remainder succeeded in making their way back to the train under the guidance of Blodget, who was with them. They threw away the friction primers, so that the gun could not be fired, and then left it, together with over two thousand rounds of extra rifle ammunition, in possession of the enemy. We recovered the gun afterwards, but the Indians had taken off and carried away the wheels, implements, and shells, portions of which were afterwards found high up on the adjacent hills. That night late, after all but the guard were snugly wrapped in their blankets for a good night's rest, we received a parting volley from a distance, which had the effect of sending us hurriedly to our rifle-pits, but this proved to be the final farewell, and we saw no more of our foes.

Thus terminated the battle of the Big Hole, or as some of the papers got it, Big Hole *Pass*. It was fought on the open prairie, on the banks of Ruby Creek, a tributary of the Big Hole River, the "Wisdom River" of Lewis and Clark. Our total loss was twenty-nine killed, including two officers, Captain Logan and Lieutenant Bradley, and forty wounded, including five officers, one of whom (Lieutenant English) afterwards died. The loss on the part of the Indians was estimated at between eighty and ninety killed, most of those left on the field being buried, when we next visited the site of the village, on the 11th. On the morning of that day a party was sent over the field to bury our dead. All

THE BATTLE OF THE BIG HOLE
This artistic portrayal of the fighting at Big Hole, Montana Territory,
appeared on the front page of *Harper's Weekly* on December 28, 1895.

were recognized and buried where they fell. The number of Indian dead
would have remained a matter of conjecture to us, but for the fact that the
Indian scouts who came with the advance of the Oregon column, which
reached our position that day, went upon the field, and with the triple

purpose of recognition, scalping, and plunder, dug up the bodies. In this way the Indian loss in killed became known with tolerable accuracy.

A visit to the site of the village disclosed some facts of interest. The Indians evidently considered themselves safe from any immediate pursuit. Many of their tepee poles, in place of being dry poles, collected for temporary use, as in all their previous camps, were green, carefully peeled, and bored at the end for permanent use. In addition to this, large quantities of the *Camas* root had been collected, and pits were found where it was being prepared for food. For this process, three days, we are told, are required, so that the Indians intended to occupy that camp at least that length of time. They evidently had not the slightest idea of being disturbed.

Whilst our burial parties were occupied on the field, on the morning of the 11th, General Howard, with a small escort, rode into our camp, and right glad were we to see him, for his arrival assured us of speedy medical assistance for our wounded. Howard had pressed forward, ahead of his troops, with a few Indian scouts and mounted soldiers, supposing he was coming to the relief of a sorely pressed and starving party. He was, therefore, greatly surprised to find us out of all danger and better off for food than he was. His medical officers reached us early the next morning (12th) and thoroughly examined and dressed all our wounded. To my surprise they informed me that among all the wounded, there was but one single case in which a doctor on the spot could have been of any material assistance. That was a man whose cheek had been laid open with a bullet, and had a doctor been present he could have sewed it up, and prevented an ugly scar. General Howard's cavalry got up in the afternoon, and as his supplies and infantry had not yet arrived, I turned over to him all the surplus provisions we had. And with his cavalry reinforced with fifty of my infantry, he the next day (13th) continued the pursuit of the Indians, now some twenty-five miles away, in the direction of Bannock, whilst the remainder of my force, the wounded loaded in wagons, and two of the worst cases on Indian "travois," constructed on the spot, moved out eastward over the rough prairie towards Deer Lodge, some ninety miles away. The horrors of that march for those having wounds can not easily be imagined. With the exception of Lieutenant English and Sergeant Watson, who were the two carried on "travois" constructed in our camp, and both of whom afterwards died in Deer Lodge, all the wounded were carried in common baggage wagons without springs. For some distance there was no road, and our way lay over a rolling prairie, covered with bunch and buffalo grass and sage brush. As our wagons bounced over these, the effect on the wounded may be imagined, but cannot be described.

After we had proceeded about twelve or fifteen miles, our hearts were gladdened by the appearance of a great crowd of ambulances, wagons, buggies, etc., loaded with all sorts of necessities and luxuries, which the good people of Deer Lodge, Butte and Helena had promptly started out to our relief. Our progress now towards the settlements was both more speedy and more comfortable, and our entrance into Deer Lodge, two days afterwards, will not soon be forgotten by any number of the little party. The whole town turned out and gave us a reception, and, best of all, the ladies of the place came forward and took complete charge of all the wounded, feeding and fostering them until the unwounded ones sighed at the absence of wounds, which would have entitled them to such attentions.

# The Battle of the Big Hole

*I*n that vast region which extends from the Missouri River where it runs north towards the great bend at Fort Benton, westward to the Pacific Ocean, the country, until the great plains of the Columbia are reached, is a tangled mass of precipitous, rugged, and difficult mountain ranges, through the lowest gaps of which railroad tracks are now laid. But in 1877 the roads were few and rough, and the trails almost impassable for any animal less nimble-footed than a mule. The main range of the Rocky Mountains (the Divide) comes first, just west of Helena, the capital of Montana, but is by no means the most formidable of these ranges. The range, trending south from Helena, afterwards makes an abrupt turn to the westward, and after meeting the Bitter Root Range turns southward again, and making a great sweep to the south and east, strikes the western edge of the Yellowstone National Park. The space inside this great bend of the mountains is known as Big Hole Basin. On its western edge the Big Hole River (the Wisdom River of Lewis and Clark) takes its rise, and in the northwest corner of the Big Hole Basin occurred the fight with Chief Joseph in 1877, the battle taking its name from its location. The fight took place, in fact, on the banks of Ruby Creek, a tributary of the Big Hole River. Fort Shaw, on Sun River, is some eighty miles nearly north of Helena, whilst Fort Missoula is nearly west of that town and at a greater distance. A person leaving Fort Shaw could travel south, and passing through Helena, reach the Big Hole Basin without crossing any range of mountains, but to reach that basin by way of Fort Missoula he would have to cross the main divide of the Rocky Mountains twice, once east of Fort Missoula, and the second time south of that post.

Directly west of Fort Missoula, located on the Bitter Root River, one of the tributaries of Clark's Fork, the largest branch of the Columbia River, are the Bitter Root Mountains, by far the most rugged and difficult range in that section of the country, and beyond that all the way to the Pacific coast are various ranges not connected with my story.

The Bitter Root runs almost due north for nearly one hundred miles before it empties into Clark's Fork below Fort Missoula. The Lewis and Clark expedition in 1805 first reached the river near its source, and it was named Clark's Fork, Captain Clark being the first known white man to stand upon its banks. The party travelled down the river to within a few miles of where Fort Missoula now stands, and at the mouth of a stream flowing from the west the plucky explorers stopped for a rest and to take their bearings. They named the stream "Travellers' Rest Creek." They then followed up Travellers' Rest Creek, crossed the Bitter Root range, and after incredible labor and hardships reached the Clearwater branch of Snake River, where they built boats and proceeded down to the mouth of the Columbia River. On the Clearwater they met and established friendly relations with a tribe of Indians (Chopunnish) whose cruel fate nearly three-quarters of a century later (1877) was to mark the culminating point of the maltreatment of the Indians in this country. To reach their country the Lewis and Clark expedition, amidst all sorts of hard work and deprivation, were compelled to kill and eat some of their horses. The trail they followed, named by them from Travellers' Rest Creek, afterwards became known as the Lo Lo, and is the identical route followed by Chief Joseph, with his tribe of Nez Percé Indians in 1877, when driven from his country (guaranteed to him by solemn treaty twenty-odd years before), followed by the United States troops from Oregon and Idaho.

In the latter part of July, 1877, I was enjoying myself on a trout-fishing trip across the Missouri River and about twenty miles from Fort Shaw when, on returning to camp in the afternoon, I found a courier from the post bringing me telegraphic information from Chicago that the Indian hostilities in Idaho had resulted in Chief Joseph and his band of Nez Percés starting eastward towards Montana. It became necessary to arrange at once for resisting the anticipated inroad into my district. Orders were issued sending a company of infantry (Browning's, Seventh Infantry) in all haste in wagons from Fort Ellis direct to Fort Missoula to re-enforce that post, occupied by two companies (Rawn's and Logan's, Seventh Infantry). One company (Comba's) was ordered from Camp Baker to Fort Shaw, and another from Fort Benton to the same point. It required some days to effect this concentration, but on the 27th every officer and man available—eight officers and seventy-six men—started for Fort Missoula to cross the Rocky Mountains at what was known as Cadotte's Pass. The distance was 150 miles, and with our provisions and bedding carried on mules, taken from the teams at the post and stowed on the best pack-saddles available, the movements of the little column were at first very slow. The trail in many places was very steep and exceedingly rough, especially on the western part, but on the fifth day (August 1st) we had accomplished one hundred of the one hundred and fifty miles, and at our bivouac that night received our first news of what was transpiring near Fort Missoula. Captain Rawn, in command of that post, learning through scouts that Chief Joseph and his party with a large herd of horses was on his way east over the Lo Lo Trail, moved out with every available man at the post, and, accompanied by a party of citizens, took up a position in a narrow part of the Lo Lo Valley, fortified it, and awaited the approach of the Nez Percés. This was on the 25th of July, two days before we left Fort Shaw. Two days after, the enemy made their appearance, and under a flag of truce Captain Rawn met and talked with Chief Joseph and some of his principal men. The Indians exhibited every disposition to be on friendly terms with the citizens of Montana, with whom they declared they had no quarrel. But Captain Rawn told them they could not enter the Bitter Root Valley without laying down their arms. The negotiations were renewed the next day (28th), but no agreement was reached, and the Indians exhibited a good deal of anxiety and were evidently apprehensive of the approach of the troops from Idaho, which, however, as was afterwards ascertained, did not commence the pursuit until two days later (30th), and did not reach Captain Rawn's position until the 8th of August, the day preceding the battle of the Big Hole.

Chief Joseph, however, could not afford to wait, and finding Rawn determined to resist his exit from the cañon, he very skillfully passed his whole camp, including an immense herd of horses, out of sight around the flank of Rawn's little command, reaching the Bitter Root Valley behind him. Most of Rawn's volunteers, solicitous about their families up the valley, left him, and when he marched back to the mouth of the cañon the Indians had disappeared up the Bitter Root Valley, leaving a strong skirmish line to confront him, which leisurely withdrew as he approached, and he returned with his command to Fort Missoula to await our arrival. The next day I pushed on, and after a ride of fifty miles, most of which was over a rough steep trail, I reached the post, the command arriving the next day.

The whole valley was in a turmoil of excitement; Joseph with his band, their families, and their horses was moving south along the river and through the white settlements, committing no outrages as far as we

CHIEF JOSEPH
John Gibbon was sympathetic to the plight of the Nez Percé tribe, but his duty forced him to attack Joseph's village at Big Hole. Photo courtesy the Library of Congress.

could hear, and were in full communication with both the whites and Indians. These latter were a part of the Flathead tribe, and occupied land in the Bitter Root Valley, their chief, Charlo, being with them. I sent for Charlo and tried to induce him to engage some of his people to act as guides and scouts for us, but he declined very positively to take sides in the contest, and I was very much afraid that some of his people, who probably sympathized with the Nez Percés, would give them news of our arrival in the valley and of our movements. Hence it was a matter of some importance to conceal our movements as much as possible, not a very easy matter in such a country if scouts should be posted on the hills bordering the valley. Sending a dispatch by courier to General Howard, coming over the Lo Lo Trail, urging him to hurry forward, I remained one day at Fort Missoula, and then at one o'clock on the 4th left the post with fifteen officers and one hundred and forty-six men, pretty well concealed in wagons, and travelled far into the night before we made our dismal bivouac, at a distance of twenty-seven miles, near the little town of Stevensville, where a number of Flatheads were clustered around a mission under charge of old Father Rivalli, who had been nearly forty years amongst the Indians. From the old bedridden priest I obtained, the next morning, valuable information in regard to the Nez Percés, their numbers, conditions, and character. The old man showed great anxiety as to the number of men I had, and said, with great emphasis, "They are a dangerous lot—a very dangerous lot." From all I could learn they had a very large herd of horses, and numbered about two hundred and sixty warriors, all well-armed and abundantly supplied with ammunition, an additional amount having been traded for since they reached the valley.

The next day was Sunday, and as we pushed along for thirty miles up the valley, evidences of the fears of the inhabitants were constantly met with, though no reports were received of any kind of depredations on the part of the Indians, except that some of them acted quite boldly and impudently; and this in itself, in an Indian, is sufficient to make people (especially when there are women and children) feel very apprehensive and fearful that the worst is about to happen. We reached old Fort Owens after dark, and it was pitiable to find the place packed with the families from the adjacent country. At Corvallis a little sod fort had been built, the inside of which presented the same sight we found at Fort Owens. The appearance of our little band of "bluecoats" was greeted with every evidence of delight, and the change from a strained condition of apprehension was very marked.

Up to this time our march had been on the east side of the river, the Indians having followed the west bank, only a few having crossed to our side as they moved along; but that night (5th) we crossed the river, and thereafter followed more or less closely the Indian trail. The question now was simply one as to how long it would require to overtake the Indians. The trail showed the passage of an immense herd of animals, and in places where the ground was soft from recent rains the mud was banked up in great ridges where the horses, following each other, had stepped into the tracks of those ahead. If we overtook them before they crossed the Rocky Mountains, our task would be a short one; but if not, we should probably have to abandon our wagons and use pack-mules for carrying our supplies, pack-saddles having been brought along with that view. But on Sunday night six citizens joined us, one of whom, Joe Blodget, had been frequently mentioned to me as a man better acquainted with the country than anyone in the valley. Joe assured me we could take our wagons all the way across the Divide, and that he himself had brought light wagons over from Bannock in the Big Hole Basin. This was very satisfactory news if we were obliged to follow the Indians over the mountains, as everyone will acknowledge who has had any experience in an attempt to turn draught-mules into pack-mules. They resent it as an insult, and the chief sufferers are the owners of the articles packed.

At the extreme head of the Bitter Root Valley is a pocket or little valley entirely surrounded by mountains, which was the place where the Lewis and Clark expedition, in 1805, first looked upon the waters of the Bitter Root, then named "Clark's Fork." This pocket is called Ross's Hole, and is now reached from below by a well-graded road up the cañon lying immediately below it. But in 1877 that way was barred to wheels, and the trail followed by the Indians was a narrow and difficult one. To get to Ross's Hole, therefore, we were obliged to climb a spur of the mountains second only in difficulties to that over the main range, which we were to cross two days later. At the foot of this spur stands Lockwood's ranche, where we found the first and only evidence of depredations seen in the valley. The house was thoroughly gutted, probably by "stragglers"—the pest of all armies, civilized or savage. Broken crockery and furniture, ripped-up bedding and clothing, were strewn all over the place, and the owner (a veteran volunteer of the Civil War), who joined our party, looked with sad and revengeful eyes upon his wrecked home.[1] We reached this point at one o'clock, and whilst we nooned there the scouts reported that the Indians had been in Ross's Hole at nine o'clock that morning. All that afternoon was occupied in climbing the steep mountain and dragging up our wagons behind us. The trail was almost obliterated in places, and but for Joe's knowledge of the features of the country, we must have been lost in the mountains, and all our labor would have gone for naught. As the sun went down and darkness began to gather around us I anxiously inquired of Joe if we were near the summit. Pointing to the *top* of a mountain ahead, he said, "Our trail leads right over that peak." It then became apparent that our chances for reaching Ross's Hole that day were slim indeed, and I reluctantly gave orders to bivouac for the night, and with some difficulty we kept our animals from travelling off in search of water till daylight, when the march was resumed, without breakfast, or even that prime necessity to a campaigner, coffee, for we were without water to make it. We were four hours in pulling up the worst hill I ever saw. At ten we halted at the bottom of the mountain for breakfast, and then continued our way through Ross's Hole to the foot of the main divide, where we bivouacked at sundown, having made only thirteen and a half miles. During the day two of my officers and a number of citizens joined us from the rear, and I

---

[1]He was very severely wounded in the battle which followed.

received a letter from the Secretary of Montana telling me that the pass in the mountains ahead of us was not occupied, as I had hoped it would be, by the territorial militia. Hence our chase was a stern-chase indeed, with no hope that the Indians could be delayed by any body of troops in their front. After we struck the Indian trail we had been passing, each day, two of their camping-grounds, so that if this relative rate was kept up it was only a question of time when we would overtake them; but it was to be feared that they might discover our pursuit, and either hasten their march, or, what was more probable, turn upon us, and with their superior numbers so cripple us as to render any further pursuit out of the question. To *surprise* them, then, was vital to us in either event. As our crossing the formidable divide in front would necessarily be very slow, it was decided on the evening of the 7th to send forward, by a night-march over the mountains, Lieutenant Bradley with his mounted men, re-enforced by twenty-five citizens mounted, with the hope of capturing or cutting off the large herd of horses before daylight the next morning, and thus crippling the camp, and detaining the Indians until the slow-moving infantry could get up. This party left us just before dark. At five the next morning the main body started and commenced to climb the steep ascent. So steep and difficult was it that we did not reach the summit, only about two miles off, until after six hours' hard work, and then only to hear from the advance party that it had not succeeded, the distance being much greater than was supposed, and that the vicinity of the camp had not been reached until after daylight, when any surprise was of course out of the question. The descent on the other slope was very gradual and the road generally good, but the distance was great, and the command was pushed rapidly ahead, the men much of the distance in the wagons; for now it was a matter of the greatest importance to get the command together before the Indians should discover the presence of the small advance-guard. Our steps were hastened by a dispatch from Lieutenant Bradley that he had located the hostile camp within a short distance of where he was concealed in the timber, but that the Indians had not yet discovered his presence.

Leaving the wagons to follow, with a few men to guard them, the rest were pushed rapidly forward on foot, and near sundown we reached the advance party lying concealed in the hills, with the open plains of the Big Hole Basin in plain view in front. Here they had lain since the early morning, but Lieutenant Bradley and Lieutenant Jacobs, who had accompanied him as a volunteer on the night-march, had not been idle. They had, with great nerve, determination, and judgment, proceeded in person to a point in the hills overlooking the location of the camp, and by climbing trees had seen parties of horses and horsemen and heard the chopping and other noises proceeding from the camp itself. This was information of the highest importance, and vital to our successful operations. But any further action for the day was precluded by the close approach of night and the necessity for rest and food for the party. It was therefore decided to corral our wagons when they arrived, get something to eat, and wait until eleven o'clock. This was done as quietly as possible, and of course without any fires; and promptly at eleven, leaving our wagons and all our horses except four, we silently stole from our temporary bivouac, and following the trail along the foot-hills as well as was possible by the light of the stars—there being, fortunately for us, no moon. Stumbling along over rocks and fallen timber and through streams and mud, we at length reached more open ground, where the walking was better, and the country of the great Big Hole opened out before us.

The trail led us along the bluffs overlooking the brush-covered valley of Ruby Creek, and as we moved stealthily forward I could hear a cautious whisper, "There they are—look!" On the opposite side of the little narrow valley lying at our feet a single light appeared, glimmering in the darkness, and then another, and Bostwick whispered, "A couple of straggling tepees." Soon getting abreast of these, we caught sight of numerous lights lower down the valley, and the main camp of our enemies was as plainly in sight as the dim starlight permitted. Our trail now led us through a point of timber composed of small pines, jutting down from the hills, and emerging from that we were startled by moving bodies directly in our path on the sidehill, and realized the fact that we were almost amongst a herd of several hundred horses, many of which as they moved away commenced to neigh and whinny. The startled dogs in camp took the alarm and commenced to bark, and for a few anxious moments it seemed as if discovery was inevitable; but the startled horses moved away up the hill, and we glided along between them and the camp, and halting directly opposite the lights, sat down on the trail to observe and await events. If we had been discovered we should soon learn it, and in the most offensive way. All ears were therefore bent towards the sleeping camp, but no stir was perceptible, the barking of the dogs died down, as did the fires, and every now and then the sleepy cry of a baby could be heard, or the chatter of a few wakeful squaws. During this long anxious wait (for we lay here fully two hours, shivering in the cold), and in the midst of the intense strain, I was startled by seeing, right in my line, a bright light suddenly appear. An impatient soldier, unmindful of the surroundings, and burning for the soothing effects of tobacco, had struck a match with which to light his pipe. Under other circumstances the man might well have been shot on the spot, or knocked over with the butt of a musket. But this would have been worse than the match, and he was quietly told by the nearest officer to put out his pipe, and give no further cause for alarm. Up to this time the most wonderful thing to me was that we had gotten into the very presence of the Indians without discovery. Thinking over our position, it very naturally occurred to me that here we were in precisely the position I desired the mounted advance to take twenty-four hours previous. We were between the Indians and a large part of their herd, and it would be an important matter to run the latter off, and thus partially, at least, set the camp afoot. I therefore told Bostwick to get three or four of the citizens and drive this herd quietly back on our trail. But Bostwick, who had spent all his life amongst the Indians, objected that this course would certainly create alarm, and render a surprise impossible.

This was to be avoided by every means, and his assertion that the Indians would never allow the herd to remain unguarded settled the question. I have often regretted since that I did not insist upon my order being carried out, for the herd had no guard, we should have made an important capture, and Bostwick's life would have been saved.

Everything now died into perfect quietness in the camp, and even the dogs seemed to have been lulled into silence, and Bostwick said, "If we are not discovered, you will see the fires in the tepees start up just before daylight, as the squaws pile on the wood."

As the sky in the east began to brighten, the fires began to blaze all through the camp, and the troops were sent down into the creek bottom and ordered to push quietly forward through the thick brushwood, wading the sloughs, in some places up to the men's waists. The distance to the stream, along the further bank of which the camp was pitched, was several hundred yards from the bluffs, and in some places the brush was so thick and impenetrable that the troops were broken up into squads before they got close to the tents.

Seated on my horse on the bluff and overlooking this movement as well as the dim light permitted, with every sense on the strain for the first sign of alarm, I was startled by a single shot[1] on the extreme left of the line; and as if answering the shot as a signal, the whole line opened, and the men, rushing forward with a shout, plunged into the stream and climbed up the opposite bank, shooting down the startled Indians as they rushed from their tents pell-mell, men, women, and children

---

[1]The left of the line was formed of Lieutenant Bradley's men and the citizen volunteers. As these pushed forward through the brush, an Indian on horseback suddenly made his appearance, following a trail in the brush, going undoubtedly to look after the herd on the hillside behind us. He was at once shot by one of the men, and it was this shot which gave the alarm.

together. Like a flock of startled quail, the first impulse was to seek shelter in the brush behind the abrupt creek bank; but finding themselves rushing directly into the arms of our men, many broke for the bluffs on the opposite side of the valley, some of them dropping into any hole offering protection. Near the upper end of the camp the stream made a sudden turn towards us, with a steep bank next to the camp. To this bank many rushed and crowded behind it. As the troops on the right of the line swept around through an open space, the men found themselves directly behind these, and here the greatest slaughter took place. Within twenty minutes we had complete possession of the camp, and orders were given to commence destroying it. But the Indians, although badly stampeded, were not disposed to give up the fight, and shots began to come on us from all directions—from the brush up and down the stream, and more from the bluffs on the other side of the valley, and finally from the bluffs on our own side; behind us, and in the attempt to rip open the tepees, our men were fired upon by those within who had not had time to escape, some of the shots being from pistols in the hands of squaws and boys. Crossing the bottom from the bluffs on horseback with my acting adjutant, Lieutenant Woodruff, we received a fire from some of the Indians in the brush, and on reaching the camp I discovered a party under the leadership of Captain Browning making a rush for the bluffs some hundred yards away with the idea of driving off the Indians there concealed and firing upon us. Our numbers were entirely too small to run the risk of a division, and the party was hurriedly recalled, but not before First Sergeant Robert L. Edgeworth, of Captain Browning's company, fell—a gallant young soldier of fine record—and several others of the party were killed or wounded, and whilst a part of the command was deployed in two lines of skirmishers to clear the brush, the rest were employed in attempts to destroy the camp. This last we were almost immediately obliged to give up, for the shots now came from all directions, and almost every time one of their rifles went off one of our party was sure to fall. Spurring my horse across the stream and up the steep bank on the other side, I realized the fact that horseback was not the healthiest position to be maintained. Four horses only were taken into the fight, three of them had already been shot—the rider of one being killed, the rider of another wounded. Hastily dismounting and holding my horse's rein, I stood looking at the scene around me, when an officer close by called my attention to the fact that my horse was wounded, and glancing around, I discovered that the poor beast had his foreleg broken near the knee. I had, in a dim way, realized the fact that I had received a shock of some kind, but it took me a second or two to discover that the same bullet which broke my horse's leg had passed through mine; but I was more fortunate in the fact that it had not broken the bone. It is said that frequently the first impulse of a man when shot in battle is to run away. I am not very clear as to whether this was true of me or not. I can only say that what I did was to run or hobble back a few steps and plunge into the cold water of the stream over my boot-tops. If I had any intention of running away farther, the cold water must have recalled me to my senses, and made me realize the fact that my little force was in what is said to have been "the ideal position" for an army entertained by one of the prominent commanders during our Civil War. We had no "line of retreat," nor "base of supplies" to attend to, and "our front" appeared to be in the form of a circle.

One thing had now become very apparent. We were occupying an untenable position, and longer continuance in it could result only in increased losses and inability on our part to retaliate. The men were therefore collected, and orders given to move back towards the bluff we had left in the morning, and in the direction of the point of timber jutting down into the valley, and heretofore mentioned. Everyone knows the demoralizing effect of a retreat in the face of an enemy. We had to pass an open glade in the valley, where the Indian sharp-shooters posted on the high ground had us in plain view, and here several of the party were shot down. As we reached the foot of the bluff and commenced to rise toward the timber, a young corporal cried out, in a loud voice, "To the top of the hill—to the top of the hill, or we're lost!" I have never witnessed a more striking instance of the value of discipline than was now presented. To the top of the hill was the last place *I* wanted to go or *could* go, and I called out to the corporal to remind him that he was not in command of the party. The men about him burst into laughter. Amongst regular soldiers the height of absurdity is reached when a corporal attempts to take command of his colonel, and the incident really had a good effect by calling attention to the fact that the commanding officer was still alive. We lost no time in getting into the timber, which was hurriedly abandoned by the few Indians there ahead of us. Here we dropped behind such shelter as we found at hand or could hastily improvise, and the officers and men were placed in the best position for defense, in anticipation of the storm which all felt must burst upon us very soon. The trees about us were all small pines, generally not to exceed three or four inches in diameter, but it is a wonder how large such a tree looks under the circumstances which surrounded us, or were about to surround us. Fortunately there were a number of logs and stumps lying about, and those lucky enough to get these were millionaires (for the time being) in safety.

Few of us will soon forget the wail of mingled grief, rage, and horror which came from the camp four or five hundred yards from us when the Indians returned to it and recognized their slaughtered warriors, women, and children. Above this wail of horror we could hear the passionate appeal of the leaders urging their followers to fight, and the warwhoops in answer which boded us no good.

Every eye was on the alert watching for signs of an advance, for which we did not have long to wait, and soon caught sight of the Indians creeping forward through the brush towards us, and the more advanced soon got into position and opened fire. I was standing down near the edge of the bluff looking on, with one or two officers near by, when suddenly a shot was heard, and Lieutenant English, standing close by my side, fell backward with a cry. A bullet had gone through his body. The men now began to fire rapidly, and were excitedly throwing away their ammunition. This was soon checked by the officers, and the men cautioned to fire only when they could see distinctly and take deliberate aim.

When leaving camp the night before our twelve-pounder mountain howitzer had of necessity to be left behind, for fear the noise of the wheels would give the alarm, but I gave orders that at early daylight it should start after us with a pack-mule loaded with two thousand rounds of extra rifle ammunition. Soon after we reached the timber two shots from the howitzer were heard back on the trail, and we realized the fact that the Indians in taking position around us had intercepted the only re-enforcements we had any prospect of receiving—our howitzer and supply of ammunition. We afterwards learned that the three non-commissioned officers in charge, Sergeants Daly and Frederick and Corporal Sales, made the best resistance they could, whilst the two privates took to their heels, and were never heard of again till they had put a hundred miles between themselves and the battle-ground. As the Indians closed in around the piece it was fired twice, and then the men used their rifles. The horses were shot down, and brave old John Bennett, the driver, was caught under the one he rode, but succeeded in releasing himself as the horse struggled in his death-throes, and escaped into the brush. Corporal Sales was killed and the two sergeants wounded, but succeeded before making their escape in partially disabling the howitzer and throwing the friction tubes away. This was a matter of considerable importance, for, as was afterwards learned, there were Indians in the party who knew something about artillery, and although it would have been a novelty, it would have been a disagreeable one to have been shelled in our wooded retreat with our own gun. As it was, the Indians, after capturing the piece, completely dismantled it, took off the wheels, concealed the howitzer in the brush, and carried the sponge staff, handspikes, and other implements to the top of a neighboring hill.

In the meantime the Indians had been gathering around us in increased numbers, crawling closer and closer in the brush below and down the timbered gulch behind us. But here their superior marksmanship was not as great as in the open, and the fire of our rifles compelled them to keep well under cover. Aware of our inferiority of numbers, we were constantly on the lookout for them to make a rush upon us, urged on as they were by the loud shouts of their leaders, who were constantly answering each other from the valley below us and the hills above. But the charge never came, although the firing was kept up all day, and was at times very close and deadly, and we lost heavily in killed and wounded, but had the satisfaction of knowing that we inflicted some loss upon the Indians, which warned them against pressing us too closely.

And now a thing happened which carried us back to a scene enacted at Fort Shaw the year before by this very band of Indians. They were in the habit every year of crossing the Rocky Mountains to visit the buffalo herds in the Missouri River country, and during one of these trips stopped a few days at Fort Shaw. The ladies at the post were very anxious to witness a sham-fight, and the Indians agreed to give us an exhibition of one. They came up to the plain just outside the post, mounted and tricked out in all their war-paint and feathers, divided themselves into two parties, and went through the form of firing at each other with blank cartridges. Whilst standing looking at the rather ridiculous scene one of the warriors came up and in broken English asked for some rags. I suggested a handful of hay from the neighboring corral. This was soon obtained, and being lighted with a match, one side charged under the supposed cover of the smoke and drove the other party from the field.

Every lull in the firing was taken advantage of to strengthen stealthily our position by arranging logs and digging dirt, especially for the protection of our wounded, some of whom were lying in a little depression, each with a loaded revolver close at hand, to be used at need in the expected charge, or as a last final guard against torture. We had just commenced to congratulate ourselves on the wholesome dread of our position with which we had inspired the Indians, and to indulge the hope that no attempt at a rush would be made, when the gentle breeze blowing from the west brought to us the smell of *fire,* and a little later a line of burning grass made its appearance on a hill close by, sending its stifling smoke ahead of it. The scene at Fort Shaw came up vividly before us; but this was no sham-fight, and this blaze meant possibly defeat and death, perhaps worse. Slowly the line of fire kept crawling forward, for the grass was thin and not very dry; and we watched it with intense interest, increased by the redoubled yells of the Indians, who evidently thought now that triumph was coming to them at last. The smoke, whilst not very thick as yet, was sufficiently inconvenient, and the close proximity to our lines of some heaps of dry brush sufficed to cause speculation as to the probable result should this fire ever reach them. The danger of a rush being made upon us seemed now more imminent than ever, and everyone was on the alert, expecting it whenever any slight increase of the rifle-shots was noted. But the smoke did not materially increase, and in a short time, to our great relief, the wind gradually died down, and then shifting to the southward, all fear from fire vanished. With the disappearance of apprehension and the smoke hope rose with us, but fell with the Indians, and although they continued to fire upon us more or less all day, and at times up to eleven o'clock at night, we had, at daylight on the 10th, demonstrated our ability to "stand them off," and when at that time they made no attempt to assault us, it became very apparent they had given up the fight—not disappearing entirely, but in a great measure abandoning offensive operations. Soon after they regained possession of their camp they began to strike their tents, and shortly afterwards the whole camp outfit, with its herd of horses, moved off over the hills southward; the fact, however, was observed that they did not go out of sight, but halted on the hills, evidently waiting for the result of the contest with us, and possibly fearful of getting too far away from the fighting force.

The discomforts of that night cannot well be exaggerated. We were all soaked to the waist; we had no covering except pine boughs, and the night was cold enough to freeze the water in the ponds near us. We had nothing to eat, and the *extra* rations furnished by Lieutenant Woodruff's horse were, from the lack of fire, not available till daylight. This horse was the only one of the four taken into the fight which escaped alive, and he was killed inside our lines soon after we took position in the timber. During the night he was skinned and cut up ready for use in the event of the siege being continued the next day, when a part of him was eaten whilst we waited for the arrival of our supply wagons. There was, of course, but little sleep in the party, for a large portion had to be kept awake, anticipating a night attack, which, I afterwards learned from Chief Joseph, was proposed and arranged for, but finally abandoned. During the night I sent two runners to Deer Lodge, ninety miles distant, to report our condition. These, a couple of citizens who knew the country, crawled out through the Indians surrounding us and successfully accomplished their mission.

As daylight broke, every man was on the alert in anticipation of an attack, but it did not come, nor were any signs of the Indians to be *seen*; but this never proves they are not about. If our supply wagons were captured we were in a sad condition indeed, with forty wounded on our hands and no means of moving them to the nearest settlements, fifty or sixty miles away. We were therefore rejoiced and the men cheered when a tall, rough-looking citizen rode into our party at half past six to announce the approach of the troops under General Howard. These would bring us surgeons to care for our wounded, and means of moving them if our wagons *had* been destroyed. Fears for the safety of our train were increased by this man's statement that he had seen nothing of it. But, it appeared, he had passed it in the darkness without seeing it. Couriers were sent out to look for it, but these encountered Indians in small parties, and later twenty-five men under Captain Browning and Lieutenants Wright and Van Orsdale, all of whom volunteered, were sent after it, and by sundown our welcome train arrived, with food and blankets, and soon the cook-fires were burning brightly and all eating the much-needed food. These added much to our comfort, and that night we slept more comfortably, but still on the alert; for about eleven o'clock a parting volley was fired into our camp, after which we saw and heard no more of the Indians. Thus ended the battle of the Big Hole. Parties were sent out the next morning (11th) to bury our dead, all of whom were recognized and decently interred. Eighty-nine dead Indians, men, women, and children, were found upon the field.

The killing of women and children was, under the circumstances, unavoidable. The action commenced before it was fully light, and after daylight, when attempts were made to break open the tepees, squaws and boys from within fired on the men, and were of course fired on in turn; but the poor terrified and inoffensive women and children crouching in the brush were in no way disturbed, and a noted instance occurred under my personal observation when her sex saved the life of a woman. Whilst we were in possession of the camp a figure started to run from one of the tepees to the next. Instantly several rifles were brought to the aim, but amidst the cries "It is a woman, don't shoot," the rifles were raised and she escaped unhurt.

General Howard, with a small escort, reached us at ten o'clock on the morning of the 11th, after the Indians had all disappeared. He had hastened forward, supposing he was coming to the relief of a sorely besieged and desperate party, as reported by some of our runaways he met on the trail, but on accepting our rough hospitality he laughingly remarked that coming forward with the expectation of relieving us, he was gratified to find that we were relieving him. His surgeons came the next day and gave the much needed attention to our forty wounded, and reported the remarkable fact that out of this number there was but one who could have been benefited by the presence of a surgeon with our command, and that was a man who had his cheek laid open by a bullet, which, if it had been sewed up, would have left less of a scar.

The following day (the 13th), leaving three officers and fifty men to continue the pursuit with General Howard's command, the balance of my party with the wounded, started for Deer Lodge, and twelve miles from the battlefield met a large party sent out by the warm-hearted people of Montana to our relief, with every comfort which could be hastily gotten together.

A large granite monument, put up by the government to commemorate the battle, now stands in the point of timber made memorable by our siege.

# Enemies
# Become Friends

*The following unpublished article was written sometime after 1890, apparently as a chapter of John Gibbon's recollections, now incomplete, of his postwar career. The first paragraphs of "Enemies Become Friends" have been edited slightly to provide continuity, while a large section of correspondence has been omitted as distracting from the focus of the article. Likewise, the original title, "Chief Joseph & the Big Hole," has been modified to better reflect the article as it is presented here.*

*In his article the general explained how he did everything in his power to facilitate the transition of the Nez Percé tribe to life on a reservation. Whether arranging for the arrest of the troublemaker Sko-las-kin or the purchase of clothing to protect Joseph's band during winter, Gibbon unselfishly assisted his former foes. These spontaneous offers of assistance won the everlasting friendship of Joseph. Throughout their relationship Gibbon, keenly aware that the chief would be sensitive to inquiries, avoided any mention of the fighting at Big Hole. But when spurious claims surfaced that General O. O. Howard had rescued Gibbon's force from imminent massacre, the general felt compelled to obtain Chief Joseph's recollections of the Big Hole battle.*

*This article is located in the General John Gibbon Collection at The Historical Society of Pennsylvania in Philadelphia.*

*T*he meeting at Lake Chelan in 1889 between myself and Chief Joseph, with whom I had had such a death struggle twelve years before and whom I had seen but once since, was exceedingly cordial. Chief Joseph was dressed in a neat suit of army blue cloth with metal buttons, a broad-brimmed felt hat and moccasins and altogether looked so neat and trim that I felt disposed to be ashamed of my rough hunting suit in which I had been wallowing for so long a time. But his bearing and seeming confidence in me was everything to be desired and, through Chapman the interpreter, we sat and talked for hours about his present and past condition and his prospects for the future. In reply to my inquiries, he gave but a sorry description of his prospects. Ever since he had gone on the reservation with Chief Moses and tried to establish his people there and locate them comfortably on farms and in houses, his efforts had been defeated by a number of discontented Indians who did not desire the presence of any strangers in their country to divide their patrimony and share their game which was already becoming very scarce.

General Gibbon and Chief Joseph
These former antagonists became respected friends in their later years, as evidenced by this photo taken during a lull on a fishing trip. Photo courtesy the Marjorie Battles Collection.

Without openly showing themselves hostile to Joseph and his people, they resorted to every sort of clandestine means to annoy them and set at naught their efforts to locate on farms. The Nez Percés would plant stakes to mark the boundaries of their proposed farms and proceed to cut timber for the rails to build fences. In a day or two the stakes would disappear and the boundary lines between the different claims would have to be run over again. Without resorting to any positive acts of hostility, this adverse element would show in many ways its disapproval of Joseph's scheme to permanently settle his people. The state of the case had been over and over again represented to the Indian Department in Washington, but without producing any useful result, and the Nez Percés were gradually losing all hope of being able to do anything for themselves. As they lost heart, their enemies were emboldened by the failure of the government to interfere and became more pronounced in their hostilities. The cattle issued to the Nez Percés by the government were found ham-strung or shot on the side hills where they grazed. Sometimes a Nez Percé hunting or looking up stock would hear a bullet from some unseen rifle whistle uncomfortably near his head. All this story was told with a grace and dignity which did not fail to excite both our admiration and pity for Chief Joseph and showed very plainly that he had about given up all hope of the cherished wish of his heart to establish himself and his people in permanent abodes and try to live like white men.

He made no charges against anybody and it was with the greatest difficulty and the closest cross-examination, aided by the personal knowledge of Chapman, that I succeeded in ascertaining that the ring-leader in these hostilities was a kind of "medicine man" named Sko-las-kin. No one could listen to Joseph's plain, straightforward story without being convinced of its truth and of his personal sincerity and his case enlisted the sympathy of every individual of our party. I was fortunate in having with me Dr. Miner, a man of plain common sense, admirable judgment and strict integrity. He was a man, too, of very considerable political influence in Washington Territory and I gladly accepted his endorsement and assistance in the plan I concluded to adopt with the hope of putting an end to Joseph's trials. I wrote a note to the Indian agent setting forth the condition of things with the Nez Percés, named the author of the trouble, and suggested that Sko-las-kin be at once arrested and removed from the reservation where he was doing so much mischief. Dr. Miner heartily endorsed the scheme and approved, in writing, the proposal. I was in hopes the arrest might be made at once and offered the services of the troops at Fort Spokane for the purpose. But something like a month elapsed before I heard anything more on the subject, when one day after my return to Vancouver I was much pleased to receive from Washington, where my letter had gone, the necessary authority for Sko-las-kin's arrest.

The commanding officer of Fort Spokane was at once instructed to get Sko-las-kin to the post in some way, make the arrest and ship him off the same day under guard to department headquarters, before the matter could be known to his people, every precaution being taken to prevent his escape. When I saw the miserable character who was brought to me at Vancouver I could not help thinking how superfluous was the caution against his escape. Sko-las-kin was a small, insignificant-looking Indian with one leg so bent with either an old wound or the rheumatism that it was with difficulty he could walk, much less run. He professed to be utterly at a loss to understand the cause of his arrest and, on my telling him, positively denied all knowledge of the hostile acts against Joseph and his people. He was sent off to Alcatraz Island in the Bay of San Francisco and there kept as a prisoner and where I believe he still is. Pains were taken to let that part of the tribe with which he was associated know the cause of his arrest and that, if the hostile acts against the Nez Percés were not discontinued, some of the others would share the same fate. The troubles ceased at once and no more interferences with Joseph or his people occurred. The liberty of one individual was sacrificed, but the welfare of the many was secured for once by the power of the government being shown.

Months afterwards Chief Joseph came to Vancouver at my request to pay me a visit and by his gentle, pleasant manners gained the respect and good will of everybody he came in contact with. He was observant and quick to learn and it was not long before he seemed as perfectly at home as any white man when seated at a table handling knife and fork and napkin. Ladies of the station invited him to their tables to breakfast and dine and were charmed with his gentle manners and gentlemanly bearing, whilst the little children seemed to take to him naturally and confided in him readily. It was during this visit that the artist Warner, then in Portland, induced Joseph to sit for his picture and Warner perpetuated his features in bronze by producing an excellent medallion.

The entire confidence of an Indian is difficult to gain, for his whole experience teaches him to mistrust the white man. The parting between myself and Chief Joseph after this visit was quite touching. He clasped my hand and, placing it upon my heart, said he went away fully convinced I was his friend, that if I died before we met again he should feel he had lost his best friend, and if he died first he should go feeling that I was his friend to the last. This faith was in the course of a year to be put to a severe test.

During that time I had left Vancouver and gone to San Francisco to command the Military Division of the Pacific. Late in the fall I received a message from a wealthy gentleman in Portland, who had heard that Joseph and his people were destitute of the requisite clothing to protect them from the rigors of the coming winter, that if I would ascertain what their actual needs were, he would pay any reasonable bill to provide for them. I jumped at the offer and by means of the telegraph soon had an estimate of what clothing was needed, had it purchased in Portland, boxed up and forwarded to Fort Spokane with directions to the commanding officer to send a courier to Chief Joseph, notify him of the presence of the clothing at the post and request him to come in with a party and get it. It was late in the winter before all this was accomplished. In the meantime the trouble with the Sioux had come on, troops were moving from all directions towards the Sioux country, and the news of the pending war spread not only amongst the whites, but into all the Indian tribes as well. The courier who went from Fort Spokane with the message to Chief Joseph to come in and get the clothing was an Indian and reported (from what source it is difficult to imagine) that this clothing was *military uniforms* and that as soon as Joseph and his people put them on *they would become soldiers* and I was going to send them to fight the Sioux in Dakota! Joseph made no effort to respond to the message to go to Fort Spokane and get the clothing.

In the meantime I had ordered Chapman, the interpreter, to proceed to Fort Spokane to aid in communicating with Joseph and distribute the clothing. Finding Joseph did not come in, Chapman proceeded down the river to his camp and on the way learned of the report the Indian scout had carried out. Chief Joseph met Chapman with his usual cordiality, but on the latter inquiring why Joseph had not gone or sent in for the clothing he looked confused and gave some evasive reply. Then Chapman asked him if he had heard the report about its being military clothing. He admitted he had and seemed very ill at ease. Chapman asked him if he supposed General Gibbon would play such a trick as that upon him? He replied he did not understand it and thought, that if his friend wanted him to go to war, he would have given him some notice of his intention. The confidence of an Indian is hard to gain, but once gained, it is lasting and firm except in the presence of a doubt raised by circumstances not fully understood. Those circumstances being explained, as in this case, and the doubt is supplanted by the old confidence. Chapman explained to Joseph that he had seen the whole of this clothing purchased and packed and that there was no military clothing amongst it. Joseph at once sent for it and it reached his camp in time to secure his people from great suffering during the winter.

An incident occurred during Chief Joseph's visit to me at Vancouver, the results of which were important and of interest to all those who were present at the Battle of the Big Hole. When General Howard, then commanding the Department of the Columbia, took the field against Chief Joseph and followed him across the mountains to Montana, he was accompanied by newspaper correspondents who wrote up the campaign more or less. When the campaign ended and General Howard and his troops went down the Missouri River en route west, certain reports appeared in the Chicago papers based, it was stated, on information received from General Howard. One of these statements was to the effect

that General Howard's arrival upon the field at the Big Hole was opportune and that but for his timely approach my command, surrounded and
hemmed in by Joseph's Indians, would have met with the fate of Custer
and his troops! This statement was challenged when it first appeared as
not only without foundation, but absurd, and General Howard denied
that he was the authority for it.

There the matter would probably have rested but for the fact that a
staff officer, who accompanied General Sherman to the Big Hole battle-
field several years after the battle, in attempting to write a description of
the contest which took place, either through ignorance or some other
cause, repeated the assertion in almost the very words that had appeared
originally in the Chicago paper. This gave the assertion a prominence
and standing it never would otherwise have had. From the circumstances
of the case, it bore the appearance of being *General Sherman's* opinion
after going over the ground that, but for Howard's opportune arrival, my
command would have met with the fate of Custer's. Assertions of this
kind, whilst not usually susceptible of proof, cannot very well be dis-
proved unless one can look into the mind of the *leader* in the case and get
from him what governed his actions at the time.[1]

Whilst Joseph was at Vancouver, an anonymous communication
appeared in one of the Portland papers criticizing the propriety of enter-
taining him in the way I was doing, for the reason that but for the timely
arrival of General Howard's command at the battlefield of the Big Hole a
few years before this, bloodthirsty savages would have wiped out of existence the command of the officer who now so warmly received him!

Here was a renewal of the old claim which had been repeatedly
denied and in the very face of the only one who could disprove its
truth—Chief Joseph. Such an opportunity was not to be lost and I took
advantage of it. During my frequent talks with Joseph I had never once
touched upon the Battle of the Big Hole, being impressed with the idea
that he would feel sensitive upon the subject and very naturally have no
desire to talk about a battle in which many of his people, including some
women and children, had been killed and wounded. I therefore had an
interview with him and without telling him my object asked him if he
had any objection to answering a few questions I desired to put to him
in relation to the Battle of the Big Hole. He answered at once very
frankly that he would willingly answer any questions I might desire to
ask. He completely set at rest a claim originally started apparently by

[1]Gibbon attempted to refute these inaccurate claims in correspondence with General O. O.
Howard and General J. C. Tidball which he inserted at this point. This lengthy correspondence
has been omitted.

some irresponsible correspondent, afterwards insinuated by Howard in his book, *The Pursuit of Joseph,* then endorsed by a staff officer of the Commanding General of the Army, not only without any foundation but in direct opposition to the official records in the case on file in Washington, and finally resurrected anonymously by a newspaper in Portland whilst Chief Joseph was present to refute it. The following is the result of the interview:

General Gibbon: "Chief Joseph, I want to ask you something which may call up sad thoughts to you, but I ask it with an object which I will tell you about later. When we had the fight at Big Hole, at what time did you know that General Howard was coming?"

Chief Joseph: "I did not know he was anywhere near there at all. When we were first attacked, I thought the soldiers were from Missoula. The last we heard of General Howard was when we were at Fort Owens near Stevensville. A courier came from Kamia and caught up with us there. He told us that General Howard was moving and he thought his direction was across the mountains towards us. Then again another man from Lapwai told me that General Howard was on the road five or six days behind. This was after I got past Fort Lemhi. It was about Lemhi, near Medicine Lodge."

General Gibbon: "Did you move the whole of your camp on the day of battle (August 9th)?"

Chief Joseph: "We all left that day. We moved out that day and went over to some low meadow land and camped there. Looking Glass said 'Let us go back and attack the forces again.' We all returned to the battle ground that day. Five of us stayed there where we could see the camp and the wagons, with soldiers about it, going to the camp. The wagon was in between the soldiers. Some of the soldiers were in the front, some behind and some on the sides."

General Gibbon: "How far were you from my camp?"

Chief Joseph: "About as far from here to the middle of the Columbia River (about a mile)."

General Gibbon: "I want you to recollect as well as you can whether that was the day of the battle or the day after the battle?"

Chief Joseph: "I *did* miss a day. The day we had the battle (I do not know what time of day) we all picked up and left the battlefield. We stayed that night where we went into camp with the women and children and wounded. Then we came back towards the evening of the second day to a knoll with some trees on it and from there we could see your camp. The soldiers were going back towards the ravine from which they had come on the morning of the battle. I said we are just a little too late and they are going back. But I was mistaken. They were going back after the wagons. Then when they got out of sight we got up on the mountain and looked down. We could see the wagons, but we did not know which way they were going."

General Gibbon: "Those same five men you already mentioned?"

Chief Joseph: "And a good many more. There were lots of us. We could see the wagons going to the battle ground. Some of our men said, 'Let us attack them.' I said no, hold on, let us see what they are going to do. We crossed above where you were entrenched and then came down and went upon a high point from where we could see the wagons. Then we came to near where you were. Some of our party said a part of you stayed there to take care of the wounded. The rest went to get what you left behind. We all left then except five of us. Looking Glass said, 'They are entrenched there, it is a hard game, let us go.' We stayed there to watch. Then the five crossed the creek and came up on the opposite side and we could hear a bell down in the bottom, like on a bell horse. We got up close enough to hear somebody talking. We had one young fellow who was very brave. He said, 'Hold my horse and I will go and see who are there.' He was away a long time and then reported that the horses and mules were all secured. He said, 'If some of you go along I can steal the bell and go steal the horses.' But they would not go. They said it was no use. I spoke to Looking Glass (he was one of the five). Then we gave it up. I said, 'Let us give up this thing, it is not a fair fight. I do not like this kind of fighting (in the night). In the morning if they catch up with us we will fight to the death.' Looking Glass said, 'Very well, let us go.' Three of the young men said they would try to run off the stock and we heard them firing off their guns to stampede it."

General Gibbon: "Was it dark when you left?"

Chief Joseph: "Just in the evening, it was just about dark."

General Gibbon: "The reason I have asked you this is because it has been claimed that you left because your scout told you General Howard was coming and that if General Howard had not come up my soldiers would have been wiped out."

Chief Joseph: "No, that is not so. I did not know anything about General Howard being anywhere near and we moved off when we got ready and did not go far and went into camp."

# Arms to
# Fight Indians

*The results of the Sioux Campaign of 1876 and the Nez Percé Campaign of 1877 were not lost on Colonel Gibbon. Speaking generally, he offered a view of Indian warfare from the perspective of the frontier Regular, a perspective that varied dramatically from the prevalent civilian belief. He explained, "The idea which prevails to a certain extent in the country, that Army officers are blood-thirsty individuals, delighting in war with the Indians for the sake of what is called glory or reputation, or purely through a love of shedding blood, is, I think, entirely an error. There is no cheap glory, but a great deal of hard work, in fighting Indians, and I do not know of many officers of the Army who would not infinitely prefer a state of profound peace with the Indians to one of war under any form."*

*On the practical side, there were important lessons to be learned from encounters with the Indian tribes. In the following article, "Arms to Fight Indians," Gibbon offered his suggestions for the modification of military arms. Stating bluntly that the average Indian warrior was a far better shot than the typical infantryman of the period, he urged that the infantry rifle be altered to produce a superior firearm. This could be done by simply employing techniques civilians had applied for years in adapting military arms to their own use.*

*"Arms to Fight Indians" appeared in* United Service: A Quarterly Review of Military and Naval Affairs 1 *(April 1879): 237–244.*

The question how best to arm troops to fight Indians is a very important one, simply from the fact, now generally acknowledged, that the Indian of this continent, possessed of firearms, is one of the most formidable foes ever encountered on the field of battle.

To decide the question, it might be well to review the experience of the past in regard to the arming of troops for the general purpose of war. Before the introduction of breech-loading arms, battles were fought by troops in heavy masses, the line of battle being usually a solid double-ranked line, in which a *continuous* fire could be kept up only by virtue of numbers—some portion of the men being always engaged in firing whilst the remainder were occupied in the slow process of charging the muzzle-loader then in use. To overcome the resistance of such a line of fire, which could of course place a very limited number of bullets in the air at the same time, bayonet charges of troops, generally in column, were resorted to, the troops being deployed, and using their own fire as soon as they had succeeded in carrying the position assaulted and silenced the fire, by overwhelming them, of the troops defending it. The defense of such a position was strengthened by posting artillery along it, and, if time permitted, by erecting small breastworks, now popularly known as rifle-pits, to protect the defenders, render their loss as small as possible, and induce them to keep up for a greater length of time a fire on the assaulting forces. Accuracy of fire for troops when thus acting in heavy masses was not deemed very essential, the principal object being to get the greatest number of projectiles possible in the air at one time. Hence the old musket (not rifled) was provided not only with a bullet, but with three buckshot, and sometimes with twelve buckshot in one cartridge, thus supplementing the slowness of fire with an increased number of projectiles. On the introduction of the rifle those "buck and ball" cartridges rapidly disappeared, and the practice of what sportsmen call "firing at the flock" gave way before the more accurate rifle practice. As troops improved in the use of the rifle, and it became manifest how destructive this might be made, special corps were formed wherein accurate firing was made a study; but it is remarkable how long old fogyism clung to good "old brown Bess" as the arm for the mass of troops. The rifle, however, gradually gained ground, and when, by the device of Minie, it was discovered that a self-forcing bullet could be used, and the old slow process of rifling the bullet by patches, hammering, etc., dispensed with, the old armament disappeared and the *rifle* became the small-arm of all troops. Accuracy of fire now became of more importance, but the muzzle-loader was still too slow in action. There was not a sufficient number of missiles in the air at one time, and besides, when firing in masses, accuracy of fire did not play the important part it should. It was all very well as long as men distributed singly, in couples, and in threes, and well protected by breastworks or the natural accidents of the ground, could coolly use their rifles with accuracy, but this advantage disappeared in the presence of an assaulting column, and hence the bayonet still retained its hold on military organizations.

Human ingenuity was now taxed to produce the requisite rapidity of fire, and after an almost innumerable number of trials of all kinds practical breech-loading rifles were produced, with which the number of shots a man could fire in a given time was limited only by the rapidity with which he could manipulate the loading lever and handle his cartridges, and just after the close of our Civil War competent breech-loading rifles and carbines were placed in the hands of our troops. Previous to this, however, many attempts had been made, and some of them very successful ones, to still further increase the rapidity of fire by the invention of *magazine* guns—that is, rifles in which instead of the marksman handling his cartridges, this work was done for him by the mechanism of the piece, it being only necessary for him to work that. The arming of our troops, however, has not yet been pushed so far as to issue to them a magazine gun. They have now simply the breech-loading rifle. This is unquestionably an excellent arm. It is the best one our troops have ever had, but it would be premature to say it is the best that could be given them, and it is safe to say that it may be improved even without making it a magazine gun.

It would be absurd to deny that these improvements in arms have had a marked effect on the tactics of battle. It is safe to assert that a body of good, well-disciplined troops in position, and armed with the modern breech-loader, can successfully resist, as long as their ammunition holds out, the assault of any body of troops which can be brought against them in front, even were that body a swift-moving cavalry force; for the rapidity of fire is so great, and the storm of bullets so heavy and destructive, that the head of *any* column of assault would be *wiped out* of existence before it could make itself felt, and the assaulted line still be in just as good a condition as at first for destructive purposes. Cavalry could not reach the line with its sabres, nor infantry with its bayonets. It is not contended that there will not occur some few instances in war where, from a fortunate combination of circumstances, a charge with the sabre or bayonet may result beneficially, but the occasions are so rare, that practically *the sabre* and *the bayonet* are *ruled out of modern military organizations.*

Now, when the wild Indians of this continent were armed with the lance and the bow and arrow, which last, at a distance of forty or fifty yards, was almost as deadly as the revolver, it was an easy matter for our troops, armed with the old buck-and-ball musket, to contend successfully with the red men, even though outnumbered ten to one. But the armament of the Indian has not stood still any more than ours has. The musket, which seventy-five years ago he looked upon with a feeling of horror and dread, we have placed in his hands. He soon discovered it was more reliable, accurate, and safe than his bow and arrow; that it brought down his game and enemy at longer distances, and with ordinary precaution was not affected by wet weather. Still, he had to become skilled in its use, for he discovered that he who was the most skilled killed the most enemies and got the most game, and at the longest and, for himself, the safest distances. As improvements went on in our arms we kindly transferred them to him; and as the arms improved so did his marksmanship, for his livelihood and safety depended upon it. When he got possession of the rifle it became a matter of lifetime study from his earliest boyhood to render himself a competent marksman, and as prowess in war and success in hunting are the very highest tests of manhood in a warrior, we can readily imagine what competition there is to attain perfection in the use of the rifle. When we recall too, how, in days past, a little Indian boy could rapidly gather a crowd of white spectators to look with wonder upon his feat of hitting with an arrow a dime tossed in the air, we cannot but be impressed with the almost unlimited capacity for marksmanship the Indian possesses.

This process of instruction in the use of firearms has been going on from father to son for nearly three-quarters of a century, the arms improving with the marksman and the marksman with the arms, until at the present day an Indian who cannot hit an object the size of a man at the distance of four or five hundred yards would be ridiculed by his comrades and laughed at as a squaw, who would be knocked on the head with a "coup-stick" in war and starve to death when surrounded by game. The day, then, for our troops to meet these warriors when outnumbered ten to one is past. Nay, more than that, they cannot contend against them successfully man for man, except under the most favorable circumstances, and then only by adopting the improved tactics of the Indians themselves.

This brings us naturally to the discussion of the Indian tactics, which are as different from those employed in civilized warfare in Napoleon's time and transmitted to us as one thing can possibly be different from another. Indians never act in masses except under the most desperate circumstances. We frequently hear accounts of the most desperate acts of bravery by individual Indians, but these are usually isolated cases of bravado, and generally performed at a safe distance. An Indian who would *unnecessarily* expose his life with no prospect of benefiting his comrades would be looked upon as a fool. The absurd spectacle, so often laughed over, of the two idiots who (was it at the battle of Crecy?) stepped in front of their commands, and with bows and salutes begged that each might first open fire, has no place whatever in Indian warfare. The Indian's delight is to take every advantage possible of his enemy;

surprise him if within his power, and do him all the harm he can, without suffering any himself. He is all the more pleased with himself if he can slaughter a whole party, the larger the better, without receiving a shot in return. He especially delights to take advantage of the white man, principally, it is thought, because it is pleasing to his vanity to demonstrate his superiority, in at least one thing, to the boastful pale-face; this of course independent of the material advantages which he derives from a surprise. He will crawl and wriggle like a snake, or lie as still as a statue for hours and hours, that he may gain certain information or an advantageous position. In action he takes advantage of every possible inequality of the ground, a stump, a stone, a buffalo wallow, anything to conceal himself from your sight whilst you are exposed to his. They fight as *individuals,* and still appear to be under control of their chiefs. A single warrior will ensconce himself behind a rock, or up a tree, and there for hours pick off man after man with his unerring rifle, seemingly unmindful of the chance that by the changes of the fight he may be surrounded by overwhelming numbers and cut off from all help from his comrades. As he takes no quarter he expects none, and will fight to the last gasp like a grizzly bear, or any other wild animal brought to bay. *Herein* lies his great advantage over any enemy drilled to fight in a body. The peculiar drill of men in masses, and the "elbow touch" of the regular soldier, admirable as they are in ordinary warfare, are utterly thrown away in contests with the Indian. We must drill our men to rely less on each other and more on their rifles, and impress upon them how formidable even a single rifleman is when, protected himself, he knows enough about his weapon to pick off men at four and five hundred yards. Hence in fighting Indians good marksmanship is the first requisite, for we have to contend against the *best marksmen in the world;* with these, who have been marksmen from childhood, we cannot expect to compete by the employment of men, many of whom never looked through the sights of a rifle six months before they are called on to shoot Indians! Hence *practice, constant practice,* must be had in order to perfect our men in the use of the rifle; but before the practice comes we must have, as nearly as practicable, a *perfect* rifle, because to practice with an imperfect one is to throw away our time.

To define what is at the present day a perfect rifle we must go to the "Creedmoors" of the country, and to the extreme frontier, where not only men's livelihoods but their lives depend upon the skillful use of the rifle. For the first time in our army history the arms used by the troops are sought after by the frontiersman, who will make use of almost any means to get possession of what he calls a "needle-gun." But after he gets possession of it, it usually undergoes a transformation if gunsmiths are accessible. The first thing to be done is to *ease* the trigger. No man can shoot accurately a rifle which requires a 7-pound weight to be brought to bear upon the trigger. This is sometimes *eased* by forcing in a small wedge of wood or leather in the space in front of the trigger; but the owner usually takes advantage of his first trip to the settlements to have a hair-trigger placed on his rifle. The next thing is to file down the front sight to a smaller size, and as soon as he can do it replace the rear sight by what is known as a "buck-horn" sight, discarding the elevating sight or "hausse" altogether. This, in our service, is graduated up to one thousand yards, and placed in the hands of men the vast majority of whom cannot hit the side of a barn-door at the distance of a hundred. His sights being now such as to enable him to draw what marksmen call a *fine* sight, and the trigger arranged so that the slightest touch of the finger fires the rifle, the frontiersman considers himself suitably equipped for war or hunting by the addition of a supply of metallic ammunition carried in a "hunter's" belt, called by the Ordnance Department a "prairie" belt, probably because it came from the *mountains.* It is true he has no elevating sight, but he knows that by drawing a *fine* sight his bullet goes right to the mark when this is within a certain range, and he soon learns how much of the front sight should be seen between the "horns" of his rear sight in order to reach certain other distances beyond point-blank, and having learned that, he is, for all practical purposes, a perfect marksman without bothering his head as to how many hundred yards are included in these distances.

A great deal has been said of late about the *superior* arms possessed by the Indians, and efforts are being made by the Ordnance Department to obtain specimens of these superior arms. It is possible that a very few may be obtained; but it may be safely predicted that their superiority will be found to consist chiefly in their being more accurately *sighted* and more suitably *triggered* than our rifles, and that the principal superiority in using them will be found to reside in the character and skillful attainments of the men who handle them.

From the foregoing it will be perceived that the rifle now in the hands of the infantry arm of the service, if resighted and retriggered, cannot be improved upon, at least so far as human insight can venture to predict the limit of improvement; but these two things, and the discarding of the bayonet, are *absolutely* necessary to render the arm what it should be to fight Indians with. That old fogyism and the ruts of the Ordnance Department will still continue to resist these modifications is to be expected; but they will come in time, just as the rifle reached the hands of the troops in spite of the routine affection for "old brown Bess." The day for wet-nursing soldiers is past, and those who have to use these rifles in battle will no longer hear with patience the reasons urged by those who serve at what Shunk used to call "the frontier" (U. S. arsenals) against giving the soldiers as good an arm as they are obliged to face in battle. I know nothing of the reasons urged against sighting the rifles properly, and the only one I have ever heard against the proposition to place suitable triggers upon them is the fear lest *somebody should be hurt*. Now *that* is just what we want, and if in preparing ourselves to hurt somebody we kill or maim a few of our own men by premature discharges, we can console ourselves with the reflection that *in the aggregate* we have saved life. But the fact is that this is no longer an objection against placing a *rifle* trigger upon a rifled gun, for the breech-loader is very seldom charged except just before using, and those who refuse or fail to give us an efficient rifle must be placed in the same category with the old woman who would not let her boy go near the water till he learned how to swim.

The question as to the propriety of arming the infantry with a magazine gun is an open one. I am disposed to think it not advisable, unless some simple and convenient magazine can be adapted to our present rifle, by which, on special occasions, eight or ten cartridges could be fired in rapid succession. It would be better to allow plenty of ammunition for practice, for without skillful marksmanship a magazine gun would only increase the waste of ammunition without a corresponding increase in its effect. We had better follow the example set us by our enemies, the Indians, who very seldom fire with great rapidity, and who make up for their smaller number of bullets by their increased accuracy of fire.

When we come to discuss as to how best to arm our cavalry against Indians, the question is a more formidable one. For if the Indian is a formidable foe to the infantry, he is doubly or trebly so to the cavalry. In the first place, he is a better rider than the ordinary cavalryman, and no wonder. There is no rider, can be none, so perfectly at home on horseback as he who has been a rider from his birth. This is literally the case with the Indian. Some of them are almost literally *born* on horseback. They are as much at home in the use of firearms on horseback as they are on foot, although of course not so accurate in their fire. Any Indian from twelve years of age and upwards can ride, *without saddle or bridle,* or at most with nothing more than a rope tied around the lower jaw of his horse, at *full speed* alongside of a buffalo, and, generally at the first shot, from revolver or carbine, kill or mortally wound his game, picked out at pleasure from the running herd. The men in any one of our cavalry regiments who can do this can be counted on the fingers of one hand, and with the average white hunter it is ludicrous to look on and witness his frantic efforts to reload his firearm when once emptied. In *running away* from an Indian on horseback, the average horseman of the service is almost as much at the mercy of his pursuer as is the buffalo, and hence the aptness of the assertion of an old Indian fighter of the army, "When I *once* dismount my men to fight Indians, I *never* remount except to pursue them." In the pursuit of Indians on horseback the soldier is following a buffalo which has the advantage of shooting back. The Indian, moreover, has the advantage of riding an animal from which he can dismount at will, and when he desires to remount finds his well-trained pony standing quietly waiting for him. Hence our cavalryman needs an arm easily managed on horseback, from which he can fire a number of shots without reloading, and, in case he dismounts, one which will compete with the Indian's arm at long range. The cavalry carbine, it is said, does not combine these requisites. The cavalryman should, therefore, be armed with the revolver for close quarters, and be provided with a rifle with longer range and more accurate fire than the regulation carbine, and in addition be capable of firing a number of shots without reloading—a rifle, that is, which can be efficiently used both on horseback and on foot. The infantry rifle does not meet these requirements. It is long and unwieldy on horseback, and besides is not a repeater. I believe that the Winchester, or some other rifle similar in character, having a good range, and capable on occasions of firing rapidly a number of shots without reloading, would be the most suitable arm to place in the hands of our cavalry. But here the question of *practice* comes in again with even greater force than before. For no matter how good the quality of the arm, it cannot be made to compete successfully with the same arm in the hands of the Indian unless those using it are skillful marksmen. Hence *practice, constant practice,* is absolutely essential, both on horseback and on foot, to render a cavalry company as formidable as it should be before it is hurled into a wilderness, where it is liable to meet a force three or four times its number. An Indian is equipped for war when he has a good firearm, with a reasonable supply of ammunition, one or two good horses, and a piece of buffalo meat, which for a part of the time he probably uses as a *saddle blanket.* The extra horses he leads or drives, and mounts a new one when the one he is on breaks down. To him the deepest and most rapid river is no obstacle to speak of on occasions arising for him to cross it. His horse is trained to swim it and draw him over it. Hence our cavalry to succeed more frequently than they do against this formidable warrior, must not only be well skilled in the use of a good rifle, but in general equipment must approach in lightness as near as possible to his, and must besides ride trained horses which can be made to cross rivers as he does. There is but one way to reach this proficiency of equipment, and that is by inaugurating a system of schools of instruction where both officers and men can be thoroughly drilled in all these things. Unfortunately, the number of our troops is not great enough to enable the authorities to withdraw even a small part from active service in the field long enough to give this instruction, and we shall probably continue to fight the Indian with inadequate means as often as the encroachment of the white settler and the impositions practiced upon him by agents of the government force him into rebellion.

Officers who serve on the frontier are frequently met with the inquiry, made with an air of astonishment, "How do the Indians manage to get these good arms and their supplies of ammunition?" There is but one reply to be made to this question, which is, that the government is represented on the frontier by a colossus. In one hand it holds a scourge, from the other is dispensed to the Indian the best improved means of resisting this scourge. Every trader at an Indian agency, every little frontier town, or country store, is an arsenal where Indians *or* white men can purchase the most improved firearms and any quantity of metallic ammunition that they can pay for. But is it possible, some will say, that the government permits this suicidal policy to be pursued? Well, no; it does not permit it now to the same extent it did, but it is a case of partially shutting the door after the steed is stolen, for only two years ago, when the whole Sioux Nation was arrayed in arms against our little force in the field, *boat-loads* of arms and ammunition were carried up the Missouri River, which were certainly not intended for the government troops.

# Our Indian Question

*Ever since his service in Florida, John Gibbon had publicly expressed his sympathy for the plight of the American Indian. On one occasion he bluntly told a panel of congressmen: "There is no question in my mind that the Indians on this continent are the worst-abused people on the face of the globe. Under our present system they are cheated, defrauded, and encroached upon in such a way that, sooner or later (and it is only a question of time), every peaceful tribe upon this continent will turn hostile; and I would have no opinion of their manhood if they did not turn hostile."*

*In "Our Indian Question" Colonel Gibbon traced the conflict between the "civilization" of the white man and the "barbarism" of the red man. After conceding that the "Red Man is bound to disappear from this continent," he declared that it was the duty of the conquering race to provide for the subsistence and clothing of the vanquished enemy. In order to create a responsible system for meeting the needs of Indians, Gibbon recommended that the Indian Department be transferred from the Department of the Interior to the Department of the Army. Gibbon's article was judged the prize-winning essay for 1880 by the editors of the* Journal of the Military Service Institution of the United States, *who presented him with a gold medal in recognition of his views.*

*"Our Indian Question" appeared in* Journal of the Military Service Institution of the United States 2 (1881): 101–120.

ook around you, see what has been going on for the last three centuries on this continent, draw your own inferences and then say what *must* be the conclusions on "Our Indian Question." When those conclusions are reached see if the American people can be induced to adopt them and act on them.

Something over three hundred years ago all the territory now included within the limits of the United States was in the undisputed possession of the Red Man and *Game.*

The white man landed on the Eastern shore. He was received kindly and hospitably, and hailed as a superior being. So he was superior in many respects. He was more civilized as we understand the term, but he was also bigoted and insatiable of greed. He looked upon the savage as a Philistine to be spoiled, and he was loose enough in principle to hesitate at nothing in getting advantage of him. Under these circumstances it was not long before the irrepressible conflict between civilization and barbarism commenced, and from that day to this it has gone on almost without check or hindrance. Civilization (or rather its representatives), has always proved too sharp for the simple savage. The savage was honest and unsophisticated; the white man unscrupulous and keen at a trade. From the time of the first white settlements on the Eastern coast down through the purchase by Penn of his principalities in exchange for cheap calico, gewgaws, and wampum belts made of shells, not worth the price of collecting on the sea-shore, to the present day when treaties are made only to be broken by the whites, the history of the two races has been one continuous series of frauds and impositions. Under the operation of these the Red Man has been gradually but surely pushed back by the advancing wave of civilization. This has been so steady and persistent that now the best informed amongst the Indians themselves do not fail to recognize the fact that the doom of their race is sealed, and has been from the start.

To the greed and demoralizing principles of the white man the Indian had nothing to oppose except his skill as a hunter and his bravery as a warrior; but he soon learned treachery from his white brother, with the very worst and most demoralized class of whom he was, and is to-day in contact.

The characters drawn by Cooper, so often spoken of at the present day as purely fictitious, are by no means ideal, but people do not recollect the fact that the Indian is a *wild animal* whose untamed nature, adopting the arms and tactics of civilized man, pushes to extreme logical conclusions the results of a state of war. All wars, even amongst the most civilized nations, are savage and barbarous, and even civilized nations will at times adopt measures to succeed from which an Indian would turn in horror. The Indian makes war to win, and his wild nature does not stop at the means any more than a grizzly bear would hesitate to tear and maim the enemy who is striving to kill him or capture his cub. He kills his enemy outright because it is one enemy out of his way forever, but he takes the greatest care of his own wounded and never permits one to fall into the hands of the enemy if he can possibly help it. The blind rage with which he mutilates the dead body of a fallen foe, or inflicts torture upon a live one is only another form of the same feeling exhibited every day in a modified way in every so-called *civilized* war. Whilst he kills his wounded enemy he never seems to anticipate the possibility of his being captured wounded himself, and like any other wounded wild animal resists as long as there is any strength left in him to resist with.

This conflict between the Red Man and the white, when it commenced was not one between pure barbarism and pure civilization, for the first encounter of civilization was with a barbaric civilization calculated to put our civilization of that day to blush.

One cannot read the history of the advances made by the Six Nations without open-eyed wonder at the marvellous organization which was even then threatening to overrun this continent with a consolidated nation not dissimilar in many respects to the white one which now holds sway here. One is amazed to read of a people deemed savage, who, at that day had regular parliamentary meetings looking to the enactment of laws for the government of the whole nation. This Congress, composed of representatives from each tribe duly designated, assembled, at stated periods, in grand council to consider the state of the nation and provide for its welfare. It assembled at a capital where a "Long House" with door-keepers and all the paraphernalia of a civilized congress existed for its deliberations. Besides this *National Congress* each separate tribe had its legislature and legislative hall where all questions especially relating to that particular tribe were discussed and decided. A remarkable feature of these barbaric Congresses was the fact that no law was ever enacted unless it met with the *unanimous* approval of the representatives. Hence no measure could ever become a law until it had been thoroughly discussed and the fact demonstrated beyond question that its passage was of vital importance to the welfare of the nation or tribe. Of course, under these circumstances, the laws were few and simple, and the Six Nations could have required but few lawyers to expound their legal system. Might not more civilized nations take a hint in the matter of law-making from this so-called savage one?

Another remarkable feature of their institutions which tended to consolidate the Nations and prevent any particular tribe from attaining undue influence was that which governed the institution of matrimony. Each nation was divided into *Tribes* bearing the names of animals and birds, such as "Bear," "Eagle," "Fox," etc. No man could take a wife from his own tribe, a Bear must marry an Eagle woman, or a Fox; a Fox must marry a Bear or an Eagle, etc., and the children instead of inheriting from the father as with us, inherited from the *mother,* thus a Bear became the father of an Eagle Sachem and an Eagle Sachem transmitted the powers of his office to a Bear son.

But for the appearance of the white man it is more than probable that this powerful organization of the Six Nations would, in the near future, have extended its sway over the whole of the territory now within the limits of our country. They had already extended their power to the banks of the Mississippi and were preparing for further conquest amongst what are now called the Plains Indians. These, occupying the vast plains of the West, were dependent for food almost wholly upon the vast herds of wild animals, especially the buffalo, which roamed at will over this vast region and literally blackened the prairies in countless numbers from the Ohio River to the main divide of the continent. In most of these tribes nothing like the advance observable in the Six Nations had been made. They were essentially nomadic in their habits, lived in skin tents, or tepees, possessed numerous horses, an inheritance from De Soto's expedition, and moved from place to place as whim, war, or the presence of game dictated.

But the white man came, and the Six Nations were forced to change their offensive operations in the west to defensive ones in the east. Gradually, but surely the line of white settlements moved westward. The Alleghenies were crossed, then the Ohio, and then the Mississippi. All this time the inevitable struggle was going on. Now and then a temporary check, as in more modern times was felt, in the defeat of some expeditionary force, or in some horrible massacre which desolated for a time some thriving settlement. But these served only as checks, and the irresistible wave of civilization swept on with all the more force after encountering such resistance as it experienced in Braddock's field and in the beautiful valley of Wyoming. In this grand march a remnant of the once powerful Six Nations was left behind, surrounded and disarmed in the interior of New York. The great nations of the South, the Cherokees, Choctaws, and Chickasaws were, after a struggle, swept over the Mississippi, leaving their remnant on the peninsula of Florida in the renegade Seminoles, some few of whom are found there to-day.

All this movement of civilization against barbarism, although but too rapid for the poor savage was slow, toilsome, and gradual for the white man. Since the introduction of railroads and telegraphs, it has been accelerated, and in our day the wonderful spectacle has been presented of a single line of track across the continent, literally wiping the savages from its path in a few short years. Had our ancestors of two hundred years ago, been possessed of railroads, the disappearance of the Indians would have been more rapid than it has been.

The conquest of California and the discovery of gold there gave an immense impetus to the struggle between the white and red races, for in addition to the great emigration which flowed across the continent, opening up new fields of exploration and enterprise to the insatiable white man, a line of settlements began to stretch its long arms out from the *western* coast, so that the red man was now pressed from two directions in place of one.

Look at a map of the United States. Observe how in the vast region extending from the 67th to the 95th meridians of longitude scarcely a wild Indian now exists to tell the tale of his race. See how the little green spots designating Indian reservations are diminishing in size and number, and how they are surrounded by a net-work of railroads and settlements. Look at the way in which Kansas and Texas are stretching out their arms to embrace the so-called *Indian* Territory where even now United States troops have to be employed to protect the Indian in a territory guaranteed to him by solemn treaty. Turn your eyes westward and observe how the settlements from there, too, are stretching out into the wilderness from the Pacific Coast. Mark how the little green spots become smaller and smaller as you near the coast, and how they are large only in the centre of the continent where the interest of the white man has not carried him in sufficient numbers to cause their reduction. But that reduction is still going on, for if you will observe the large green patch between the 99th and 104th meridian you will see down in the left hand corner a darkly shaded territory of considerable extent now tinctured green with the rest, but it ought to be black, for that is the Black Hills region now filled with noisy mills and enterprising miners extracting the precious metals from a soil which only twelve years ago was solemnly guaranteed to the great Sioux Nation *forever.* Looking at this map and reflecting on these facts how can you fail to draw this conclusion as an absolute fact: *The Red Man is bound to disappear from this continent.* Philanthropists and visionary speculators may theorize as they please about protecting the Indian against the encroachments of the white man and preserving him as a race. *It cannot be done.* Whenever the two come in contact, (and they are now in close contact throughout the whole vast Western region), the weaker *must* give way, and disappear. To deny this is to deny the evidences of our own senses, and to shut our eyes to the facts of history.

The statement has been recently made by a distinguished army officer that the Indians have not decreased in numbers in the last century. To my mind this statement appears incredible, but there can be no satisfactory proof of either its truth or falsity, for the reason that nothing like an accurate census has ever been taken of the Indians on this continent. Therefore it is impossible to say with confidence whether they have decreased or not. But the probabilities are so strongly in favor of reduction that I look upon it as certain as that the buffalo has decreased in numbers.

This animal which has been for years almost the only food of the Plains Indians, (more especially of late years since the diminution of what they call *small* game, deer, antelope, etc. in contradistinction to the buffalo which is *large* game), has receded before civilization just as the Indian has, until now the vast *single* herd which formerly covered the whole Western country is divided by the Union Pacific Railroad into *two* comparatively small herds, entirely distinct from each other.

The buffalo herd has been called the natural commissariat of the Plains Indians, and as it has become reduced it roams about the region it inhabits in search of food followed by the Indians who cannot be subsisted without it. Wherever this herd is found Indians will be found upon its outskirts slaughtering the animals for food and clothing. Wherever the herd goes the Indians are bound to follow. So inexorable is this law that grave international questions are liable to turn upon the *movement of a buffalo herd.* That the number of buffalo has decreased I think there can be no question, and the reduction of the Indian is a corollary of this and of some others to which I will allude.

War, I think, does not reduce the Indian race to any very great extent, for in the first place the actual loss is comparatively small and in conflicts amongst themselves or with the whites the number slain is not large, whilst the wounded, always carefully protected and carried off, rapidly recover from even the most dangerous wounds, thanks to a strong constitution, life in the open air and a simple diet. But civilization has introduced amongst them various causes tending to check the reproduction and decrease their numbers. The smallpox and other diseases incident to their contact with civilization carry off many, so many at times as almost to destroy tribes. But in the absence of any proper census the most conclusive argument of a decrease rests I think upon this consideration which is equally applicable to the buffalo. The Indian from his nature and habits requires a very much larger area of territory to live upon than the white man. Now when we consider that this vast country of ours was at one time occupied exclusively by Indians and how very small a portion is now occupied by them it seems to me conclusive either that the portion they do occupy must be very much more densely populated than formerly or else they have decreased in numbers, for certainly no great number of them have left our country. In the absence of any specific data to go upon we can depend only upon the observation of travellers and explorers. In the beginning of this century Captains

Lewis and Clark in their expedition across the continent found many large and powerful tribes scattered along the Missouri and Columbia Rivers which we know are to-day very much reduced in numbers, and certainly no one who has passed through these regions of late years would be impressed with the idea that they were at all densely populated. I think, then that we must conclude the Indians have decreased and decreased very rapidly in the course of this century.

If these conclusions are correct what is the question we have to meet? A great race possessed of many noble qualities is rapidly disappearing from the face of the earth before the advancing tide of civilization and white settlements. That they do possess many noble qualities is freely admitted by all fair-minded men who have had opportunities of observing them. That they also possess many low and degrading qualities it would be absurd to deny. But in judging of the acts of others it is a useful experiment to follow the principle of "putting yourself in his place." Let us see how that would work. How would *we* feel, how would *we* act if our country were over-run and wrested from us by another race? If our lands were bought with promises to pay which were never fulfilled? If certain other portions of land were guaranteed to us by solemn treaty and these treaties recklessly violated as soon as precious metals were found upon the land or for any other reason the other race wanted it? If having been deprived of the food which before was ours for the taking, we had been solemnly assured that in its place we should be supplied by good and wholesome food of other kinds and then our wives and children be left to starve, whether because greedy contractors furnished improper food or none at all perhaps for months, perhaps for years? If our men were debauched, say with opium, our women degraded and our children starved if they did not consent to go to school, and learn, say the Greek Alphabet, and recite verses from the testament of an unknown religion?

All these things has the Red Man suffered.

Now I make no complaint that he is being driven from this continent. *That is inevitable: He must go,* and we might as well complain of the steam engine for running over a bull imprudent enough to venture on the railroad track. We need not however be surprised at his offering resistance, nor, considering his wild nature and the wild nature of his treatment, at the character of that resistance. I know an officer of the army who hates two things thoroughly, an Indian and a rattlesnake. The latter he kills always on sight; the former he would treat in the same way if he dared. He says, "If I were an Indian, treated as he is, I would fight till the last gasp, and kill on sight any man, woman, or child of the oppressing race who came within range of my rifle." Thus would the *savage* in us come to the surface under the oppression which we know the Indian suffers, and a distinguished bishop has asserted that we all have a *little savage* in us which comes out at times.

As then the Red Man's destiny is to disappear, the question of all others which meets us in this *Indian Question* of ours is what is our *duty* as a humane civilized people towards this doomed race? We have taken from him his land, his game, and in fact everything which he had and prized before we came here, and taken these at times by means not justified by any recognized system of morals. What does humanity demand shall be paid him? Surely *a subsistence and the means of clothing himself and his children.* These he does not get; sometimes not at all, sometimes in insufficient quantity, although it is confidently asserted that the means *appropriated* by Congress are ample for these purposes. If it were proper to appeal to self interest in favor of a just course it might be stated that the Indian, if well-fed and even passably well-clothed, would never, save in a very few exceptional cases, go to war, and it would be far cheaper in the end to feed and clothe him well than to fight him.

The next question which meets us is how is this feeding and clothing to be accomplished in a satisfactory manner, and this opens a wide field for discussion on which there is a very wide diversity of opinion.

The location and surroundings of our Indian tribes are so nearly identical with those of our frontier garrisons that the most natural suggestion is they should be supplied under essentially the same system.

Our troops, no matter how remote or how isolated their station, are always supplied in a satisfactory manner with good wholesome food, and it is only when unexpected moves take place or new posts are established that any difficulty arises, and it is then only temporary. The army system of supply and distribution is so well understood by the members of this *Institution* that it is needless to dwell upon it any farther than to remark on the perfect system of responsibility enforced. Under this *some* commissioned officer is always held to account for every ounce of supplies received for the use of the troops, and troops need never be badly supplied if the commanding officer attends to his duty; and not even then unless *all other officers* at the post neglect theirs.

I risk nothing in the assertion that no such system of responsibility exists in the Indian Department. Without reference to individual commissioners I am satisfied from personal observation that not only have they no such system in the Indian Department but so far as I have been able to discover they do not in that Department *understand* the practical working, or value, of such a system. In the total absence of any such system how is it possible for the Indians to receive, either in kind or quantity, the articles for which Congress appropriates the funds? Any business man can answer this question without the least hesitation, and yet in the Indian Department they do not seem to appreciate it or, if they do, they utterly fail to act upon it.

I will illustrate what I mean by relating a story I have heard in the West. It makes but little difference whether the story be true or not. It *might* very readily be true under the lack of system in the Indian Department, and it will serve to illustrate many similar transactions coming under my personal observation.

A herd of cows and calves to be used for domestic and breeding purposes started for a distant agency. When it reached there it was composed of all the broken-down oxen and yearlings that could be picked up along the road. All the good cows and calves had been traded off on the way; but remarkable to relate the *number* of head was exactly right, and as long as the *number* was right the receiving agent made no objection, or if he did he was in Western phraseology, *"made all right too."* Now under the army system any such transaction would be impossible, and any second lieutenant can tell you why it would be impossible. *Let us then have in the Indian Department a system of responsibility as near as possible to that followed in the army.*

Attempts have been made at various times to make use of army officers to check such loose transactions as I have referred to, but the result has simply been either that the check was ineffectual, or where frauds were detected and the guilty parties discharged, others were appointed to the vacant positions, and the same old loose system commenced again. In some instances the inspection of supplies by the army officer was carelessly performed, in others he was called upon or not to inspect at the pleasure of the agent and the lack of inspection never seemed to make any difference in the settlement of the agent's accounts. Then, of course, the inspection as a whole can be no check. In one notorious instance a most shame-faced attempt was made to bribe the inspecting officer to pass a worthless lot of stores. There is no means of knowing how often such attempts have succeeded. But the result has been that the Indian Department and the army have become antagonistic. The former seems to consider itself placed on the defensive on all subjects and is but too apt to regard with suspicion and distrust any suggestions coming from army officers. The Interior Department having charge of Indian affairs, its Head must necessarily have the chief decision of questions arising in regard to Indian matters, and it not infrequently happens that important *military* questions affecting the protection of our frontier settlements are sometimes decided by the Secretary of the *Interior* in Washington. A noted instance has recently occurred at an important post on the Missouri River where the antagonism referred to reached such a point that at the request of the Interior Department the post, in the midst of a large tribe was ordered to be abandoned, the Indian agent having expressed an *opinion* that he could control the Indians without the help of the military. Something of the facts leading to this order may be inferred from what occurred just before the receipt of the order at the post. An officer of the post whilst witnessing the delivery of a quantity of beef cattle to the agent had his suspicions excited by observing that the weight of the cattle was excessive. He noticed the smell of blacking and also that the hands of the employee who did the weighing were blackened by handling the weights. An examination of these disclosed the fact that holes had been drilled into all the *iron* weights except one, filled in with *cork* and blackened over. The inspecting officer refused to certify to the receipt of the cattle, kept some of the weights against the protest of the agent, and reported the fact to his commanding officer. The weights were kept locked up, the keys being kept by the agent. An estimate was made as to the amount of loss to the Government and the Indians by these fraudulent weights and it was found to be about 12 per cent.

Once the army system is instituted and the certain and adequate supply of the Indians assured, we are in a position to consider understandingly the question:

*What is the best way to advance the welfare of the Indian and insure his progress toward civilization?*

In considering this very important question we must recollect that all the processes of nature are slow and gradual and that we can hope for no permanent beneficial results, by attempting to force upon a reluctant people a complete revolution in their habits and mode of life. To expect an old savage who, from his earliest youth has been glorying in a wandering life, the pleasures of the chase, and the turmoils of excitements of war and war-dances to suddenly change his whole nature and settle down steadily to the plow-handle is expecting too much of human nature. You might as well take a Broadway dandy, dress him up in buck-skin and feathers, put a bow and arrows in his hand, set him down on the open prairie and expect him to gain a livelihood. *That man's son,* if sent early to the prairies might in time make a very respectable hunter.

I believe then in commencing at the bottom of the structure for improvement and not at the top. The plan then to educate Indian youths of both sexes now in successful progress meets with my hearty approval, and I fully believe will in time result in great benefit to the race.

Can then nothing be done toward the civilization and Christianization of the mass of the Indians, and are we forced to wait until the young ones grow up before any beneficial results are to be looked for? Undoubtedly a great deal can be done to prepare a better field for these young proselytes to work in when they once more return to their tribes. *How* this can be done will now be considered.

One of the earliest forms of society is the *pastoral.* Men were shepherds before they became tillers of the soil, and there is no record in history where a community has been *suddenly* transformed, from a pastoral into an agricultural people, though gradual changes in the course of nature are numerous. It will not do to accept as proof of the opposite principle the few isolated cases which may be cited in this country. I have seen warriors with the *war paint* on their faces following the plow in the corn fields along the Missouri River. But the paint and skin tepee which now and then reared its conical top near the log cabin showed how strongly was the clinging to the old life. Let a whiskey seller, a herd of buffalo or a small war party of hostiles appear in the vicinity and the Indian becomes once more an Indian, more quickly than Cincinnatus became the soldier. Following the plow no more makes him a practical agriculturalist than singing psalms and attending church service makes him a practical Christian.

Thanks to the introduction of horses on this continent the great mass of our Indians are, in their natures, *pastoral.* The horse has become a circulating medium amongst them. A warrior's riches consist mostly of his large herds of horses. The price of wives and other valuables are generally determined by the number of ponies they will bring. The Indian boy, (and girl too for that matter) is from the earliest age a natural shepherd. He is accustomed every day and night to herd his horses, and in time of danger to corral them, with a fence of brush or poles. When they wander from the camp he follows on foot or on horseback the trail with the sagacity of a blood-hound and brings them back. It is a curious sight to see on the hill-sides in the vicinity of a camp the ponies grazing together in groups, as distinct and separate as the families to which they belong. From what has been said it will appear how natural a step toward the future welfare and civilization of the Indian it is to take advantage of his pastoral tastes and habits, give him other domestic animals to herd and in time to replace the mass of his horses with these. The first step should be therefore *to supply each tribe with a goodly number of cows for breeding purposes.*

Kine thrive magnificently and reproduce rapidly in all that vast region extending from the Mississippi River westward. Up to the 49th parallel and probably beyond they live out in the open air and subsist themselves, with no other shelter than the timber found in the river bottoms and gulches, and this sometimes in a temperature low enough *to melt down* their horns which are frequently seen drooping alongside their

faces. This country has in times past supported numerous herds of buffalo. It can still support a like number of the buffalo's kindred, the
domestic cow. The latter wander some, but nothing like the distance the
buffalo does. A herd once occupying a certain range remains there forever. Hence the tribe possessed of a herd need never be obliged to
wander in search of animal food. This at once gives the tribe a fixity in
position which under the buffalo regime is an impossibility. The interests of the Indian now become *localized.* It is the first step toward the
establishment of a fixed abode. A log house, a garden-patch, and a field
of corn follow in logical sequence. When these points are attained the
Indian is on the high-road to a civilized, Christian man. The rapid
increase of his herd not only renders him independent of the buffalo, but
it also assures him a competence in the future. *His future is provided for.* It
has always been a matter of wonder to me that the government should
never have adopted so plain and obvious a step toward the civilization of
our wild Indians whose habits and surroundings accord so completely
with this scheme. As an instance take the Crows. They have a magnificent grazing region for a reservation, upon the eastern portion of which
as late as 1876, the buffalo were accustomed to feed in immense numbers. These will probably now never return there and the Crows have
always to leave their reservation to get an adequate supply of animal
food. If a few years ago a comparatively small sum had been invested in
domestic cattle the Crows would to-day have been independently rich
with plenty of food directly at their doors.

For many years I have advocated this plan the merits of which have
been confirmed in my mind from witnessing the thriving condition of
and rapid increase in the domestic cattle in the Northwest. That it is
eminently practical has already been sufficiently demonstrated in experi-
ments on a small scale under the supervision of the military authorities
on the Missouri River and at Fort Keogh on the Yellowstone. Captured
Indian ponies have been sold and the cash converted into breeding cattle.
The immediate inauguration of this cattle plan is all the more important
for the reason that many of the tribes still occupy sparsely settled districts where for a few years yet the whites will probably not encroach
upon them to any alarming extent, and if the Indians are furnished with
cattle now when that encroachment does come, (as come it must) they
will be in a comparatively independent position, with plenty of food,
and fixed abodes.

Great stress has been laid in this paper upon the absolute necessity
of a sound system of responsibility in the Indian Department and it may
not be out of place in this connection to touch upon a question which
has been very fully discussed for some years both in Congress and the

country at large. This is the question as to the advisability of transferring the control of the Indians from the Interior to the War Department. A very popular idea exists, I think in this country, and perhaps in all others, that the moment a man becomes *a soldier* his sole motive and business in life is to *fight,* that all his aims in life are to fight and destroy, and that he is fit for nothing else. I am disposed to dispute this even as a general proposition, and appeal with confidence to the large numbers of great soldiers not only in this country but in the history of the world who are as much renowned as peace-makers as they are as warriors. The highest type of the soldier is he who fights only when he must. He above all others knows and appreciates the horrors of war and therefore more than any other deprecates a resort to arms. This of course is more apt to be the case in a free and enlightened country than in other and more despotic ones where *the army* as one of the most important institutions is fostered and provided for, even in peaceful times, with the greatest care and attention. It is especially so in this country, where, the army being small, the defense of the country in case of war is so largely dependent upon the force which has to be drawn from the civil walks of life to the great detriment of every civil pursuit. It is above all so in regard to the peculiar kind of Indian warfare in our country. For in this, very few of the recognized rules of warfare are applicable, and the struggle degenerates into a series of operations in small detached parties in which exceedingly hard work and occasionally desperate encounters are the characteristics. In all of these the enemy has as a rule an immense advantage. He is operating in a country every foot of which is well-known to him. He is a better shot, better rider, more easily subsisted, and more inured to fatigue than the mass of our men can by any possibility ever be. Generally he is encumbered by *nothing,* when he has any encumbrance at all it consists of his families in movable camps which can shift their position much more rapidly than our wagon or pack-trains and over a rougher country, and if we concentrate to attack these he concentrates faster than we can and generally places us at a disadvantage. When satisfied that we are too strong for him to resist he scatters, becomes the best partisan cavalry in the world and does the whites more harm than we can possibly retaliate. The campaign of 1876 against the Sioux fully exemplifies all these points. In this kind of campaigning there is plenty of exceedingly hard work, no glory and very little reputation to be gained by anybody, and I risk nothing in the assertion that nine out of every ten in the military service prefer a state of peace to a state of war with the Indians. In the few isolated cases where Indians have surrendered to the military, they have been kindly treated, and well cared for and have become the devoted friends of their captors. More progress has been made toward civilization with these captured Indians under military charge than in any other cases. Indians have been known to say, "Henceforth I am a soldier. *He* does what he promises and I don't want to go back to be under the control of the agent."

The army is directly in contact with the Indian. He is encouraged to come to the military posts which are usually established in his vicinity. There he is kindly treated and, in cases of necessity, fed. If he violates the law or commits any depredations he knows that from there emanates the force to punish him. The agent now has no power to punish except with "Vatican thunders," but too apt to be supplemented with threats of the military which is not unfrequently called in to settle the petty squabbles of the civil agent which would never amount to any importance were the power to punish in the same hand as the one which controlled the reward.

Another important consideration in the case is this. The army officer is obliged to be on the frontier in any case. There he necessarily becomes more or less acquainted with the habits and disposition of the Indian, a knowledge which in the vast majority of cases is lacking in the civil agent who is generally a stranger from a distance totally unacquainted not only with the Indians but with Indian nature. That in some few instances these have proved honest, zealous and successful agents does not militate against the rule that as a general thing they are not successful.

Life on the frontier is at best a hard, laborious and trying one and that at a remote agency a perfect banishment from all the ties of civilization. Those who accept positions there find themselves surrounded by novel circumstances amongst the most prominent of which is a total absence of anything like moral responsibility. They are free to do as they please unrestrained by any fear of detection, should they be pleased to do wrong. With such surroundings a bad man becomes worse, a good one is liable to fall into error skillfully projected by designing knaves. The few bright examples who staunchly stand up for honor and principle excite our admiration, but the many, aided by the utter lack of responsibility in the Indian Department to which I have referred, simply add to the scandals which have disgraced that Department for years. Very strong efforts have occasionally been made by Commissioners and Secretaries of the Interior to bring about a change and work improvements in the Indian Department, but in every instance the system (or rather lack of system) has proved too strong for these individual efforts which have resulted simply in demonstrating more thoroughly than ever to thoughtful men the absolute necessity for a complete change in the *system* itself. Before these attempts at reform, Indian Commissioners,

Agents, Inspectors, even members of the Board of Indian Commissioners themselves have gone down only to give place to others who have repeated the sad scandals, which, whilst they bring discredit to the Government, work cruel wrong and injustice to the Indian.

That some speedy remedy should be found for these great evils impresses itself upon every thoughtful mind, not only because they are evils in themselves and therefore should be remedied, but because their longer continuance works evil to the Indian and prevents us from doing what little we should do to smooth the downward road of this doomed race, once so numerous and powerful on this continent, and from which we have, in accordance with an inexorable law, wrested everything deemed valuable by the Red Man and converted it into a principality for ourselves.

---

Alan and Maureen Gaff are authors of *Brave Men's Tears: The Iron Brigade at the Battle of Brawner's Farm* and *If This Is War: A History of the Campaign of Bull's Run by the Wisconsin Regiment Thereafter Known as the Ragged Ass Second.*

# Index